SEX *for* SALE

PROSTITUTION, PORNOGRAPHY, AND THE SEX INDUSTRY

EDITED BY
RONALD WEITZER

Routledge
New York   London

Published in 2000 by
Routledge
29 West 35th Street
New York, NY 10001

Published in Great Britain by
Routledge
11 New Fetter Lane
London EC4P 4EE

Copyright © 2000 by Routledge
Printed in the United States of America on acid-free paper.

10 9 8 7 6 5 4 3 2 1

Library of Congress Cataloging-in-Publication Data

Sex for sale: prostitution, pornography, and the sex industry / edited by
    Ronald Weitzer.
        p. cm.
    Includes bibliographical references.
    ISBN 0-415-92294-1 (hc.). 0-415-92295-X (pb.)
    1. Prostitution. 2. Pornography. 3. Sex-oriented business.
    I. Weitzer, Ronald John, 1952–.
HQ115.S49 1999   99-28359
306.74—dc21   CIP

CONTENTS

PART III: POLITICS, POLICING, AND THE SEX INDUSTRY

ACKNOWLEDGMENTS

This book would not have materialized without the enthusiastic support of my wonderful editor at Routledge, Ilene Kalish. At the earliest stage when the idea for the book was still fresh in my mind, I benefited from her suggestions regarding themes and chapter topics, and her advice and encouragement throughout the project have been vital and are deeply appreciated. The contributors to the book also deserve thanks for tolerating the impossible deadlines I imposed on them and for producing fascinating and cutting-edge works of scholarship. I am also grateful to Shannon Wyss for her assistance in putting the book together.

LIST OF TABLES

WHY WE NEED MORE RESEARCH ON SEX WORK

Ronald Weitzer

The sex industry has grown dramatically in the past several years. In 1996 alone, Americans spent more than $8 billion on X-rated video sales and rentals, live sex shows, adult cable shows, computer pornography, and adult magazines, and another $1 billion on commercial telephone sex.[1] Rentals of hard-core videos increased from 75 million in 1985 to 686 million in 1998, and about 25,000 stores now rent such videos.[2] Most of the world's pornography is produced in the United States, but there is no shortage of consumers in other countries. In Britain, for example, the industry reaps huge profits.[3]

There has been a steady trend toward the privatization of commercial sexual services and products: Porn has migrated from the movie house to the privacy of the viewer's own house. Video, computer, and cable-TV pornography have exploded in popularity, almost totally replacing the adult theaters of decades past. The advent of the telephone sex industry and escort services also has contributed to the privatization of commercial sex.

Large numbers of people buy sexual services and products. In 1996, 26 percent of Americans (35 percent of men, 19 percent of women) reported that they had seen an X-rated video in the past year.[4] Far more people, of course, have seen such a video or film during their lifetime. In 1991, 11 percent of the population said they had seen a stripper in a club in the past year, and about 0.5 percent had called a 900 phone sex number in the past year.[5] An earlier poll found that 31 percent had attended a topless nightclub at some time in their life, 11 percent in the past year.[6] (There are 2,500 strip clubs in America,[7] though many cities have tried to ban them in recent years.) By early 1999, the percentage of the population that had visited an adult site on the Internet was 17 percent.[8] And a significant percentage of American men have bought sex from a prostitute. A 1994 national poll found that 18 percent of men (and 2 percent of women) said that they had "ever [since age 18] had sex with a person you paid or who paid you for sex."[9] Another major survey found that 16 percent of American men ages 18–59 reported that they had paid for sex at some time.[10] In Britain, one-tenth of men under the age of thirty-five said they had bought sex from a prostitute,[11] and in Canada 7 percent of men reported that they had paid for sex.[12]

Despite its size, growth, and numerous customers, the sex industry is regarded by many citizens as *deviant*: as run by shady people and celebrating and promoting immoral and perverted behavior. Polls show that 72 percent of the American public believes that pornography "degrades women" by portraying them as "sex objects";[13] 62 percent believes that pornographic materials lead to a "breakdown of morals";[14] and, of those Americans who believe in the existence of the devil, more than half say that pornography is "the work of the devil."[15] Most Americans also favor either more controls or a total ban on various types of commercial sex. More than three-quarters (77 percent) of the public thinks that we need "stricter laws" to control pornography in books and movies,[16] and half of the public believes that pornography is "out of control and should be further restricted."[17] When asked about the idea of "men spending an evening with a prostitute," 61 percent of Americans label this morally wrong,[18] and 70 percent says prostitution should remain illegal.[19] Stripping and telephone sex work also carry substantial stigma. In 1991, 46 percent thought female strippers and 45 percent thought male strippers should be illegal at bars or clubs, while an even higher number (76 percent) thought telephone numbers offering sex talk should be illegal for adults.[20] Another poll found that 70 percent of the public favored passing laws that would close all massage parlors and porn shops that "might be centers for casual sex."[21]

What we have, therefore, is a paradox: a lucrative industry that employs a significant number of workers and attracts many customers but is regarded by many people as a deviant enterprise that should be more strictly controlled, if not totally suppressed. Over the past twenty-five years the most vociferous prohibitionists have been locked in battle with opponents who have clashing views on the nature and effects of prostitution, pornography, and other sex work, and over proper government policies in this sphere. The right, and particularly fundamentalist Christians, are disturbed by the danger sex work poses to the family and moral fabric of society. Feminist prohibitionists denounce all sex work as the ultimate expression of gender oppression or "sexual slavery." The other, liberal side insists that commercial sex services are legitimate and valuable occupations.[22] These are fundamentally different paradigms, turning on different images of the workers involved: *sex objects* vs. *sex workers,* quintessential *victims* of male domination vs. *agents* who actively construct their work lives.

I maintain that this ongoing "sex war" has generated more heat than light, and the two sides are so far apart that further lofty debate seems fruitless. But it is not just a problem of too much heat; it also involves gross distortion of the subject matter. Essentialist claims about the "intrinsic" nature of sex work (whether oppressive or liberating) clash with the reality of *variation* in sex work. It is naive to assume that all sex work is essentially the same. There are *different kinds* of worker experiences and *varying degrees* of victimization, exploitation, agency, and choice. As indicated below, there are a number of differences between and among street prostitutes, off-street prostitutes, telephone sex workers, strippers, and porn actors—even though they all sell sex in some fashion.

The purpose of this volume is to provide a fuller understanding of sex work and the sex industry. We need a more careful examination of the ways in which sex workers themselves experience and describe their work (negatively, positively, or indifferently), the operations of specific sectors within the industry, and the politics and control of sex work. This information is necessary to help us make informed decisions about legal and social policies. This volume, which features original chapters on these topics, seeks to avoid some of the common pitfalls that plague much of the commentary on sex work. The most egregious pitfalls are discussed below, along with some suggestions on how to avoid making them in the first place.

AVOIDING SWEEPING GENERALIZATIONS

"Sex work" is a generic term for commercial sexual services, performances, or products given in exchange for material compensation. Examples include prostitution, pornography, stripping, lap dancing, and telephone sex. The "sex industry" refers to the organizations, owners, managers, and workers involved in commercial sex enterprises. All too often, however, the terms "sex work," "sex industry," "prostitution," and "pornography" are used in a sweeping fashion, ignoring important differences within each category. Overgeneralization is especially evident in analytical writings, but it can also be found in many empirical studies. Scholars often fail to specify the subgroup on which their research is based, and instead refer to "prostitutes" or "sex workers" when their research is restricted to, say, a sample of streetwalkers in one city. When it comes to prostitution, the most serious blunder is that of equating all prostitution with street prostitution, ignoring entirely the indoor side of the trade. In nations like the United States and Britain, only a minority of prostitutes work the streets, yet they have received the lion's share of attention from analysts.[23] Street prostitution and indoor prostitution differ in important respects:

1. *Social Status:* There is a status hierarchy in prostitution: Street prostitutes have the lowest status and receive the strongest dose of stigma; upscale workers are somewhat less stigmatized.[24] There is also a hierarchy *within* each level: Street prostitution is stratified by race, age, appearance, and locale—all of which affect the workers' earning potential (race and locale are examined by Judith Porter and Louis Bonilla in Chapter 7). Among indoor workers, status increases from massage parlors to brothels to escorts to call girls.[25] Workers themselves often draw distinctions between their work and that of others in the industry, distinctions that usually reveal some disparagement of other types of workers;

2. *Control over Working Conditions:* Workers vary in their freedom to choose or refuse clients, their access to resources for safety and protection, their independence of or dependence on managers or pimps, and their ability to leave sex work (Wendy Chapkis highlights these differences in Chapter 11);[26]

3. *Experiences at Work:* Workers differ in whether and how often they experience exploitation and victimization in the course of their work: Assault and rape are occupational hazards for streetwalkers,[27] but relatively rare among indoor workers.[28] Risk of exposure to sexually transmitted diseases varies between street and offstreet workers.[29] Prostitutes also differ in whether they find the work even minimally rewarding, other than financially, and in the nature of the sexual encounter itself—ranging from fleeting outdoor transactions to indoor activities that sometimes resemble dating experiences (with conversation, flirtation, and gifts) and that may even include workers *receiving* sexual "services" from clients, as shown in Janet Lever and Deanne Dolnick's unique study of call girls (Chapter 6);

4. *Adjustment to Their Work:* Prostitution does not have a uniform effect on workers' psyches and self-images. One study found that streetwalkers exhibited significant psychological problems, while call girls, brothel workers, and massage parlor workers were "capable of handling themselves well, manifesting good emotional controls, being well aware of conventionality, and doing well in the occupation of their choice."[30] Other studies of masseuses and escorts have found that they took pride in their work,

felt the job had a positive effect on their lives, and believed that they were providing a valuable service.[31] Streetwalkers seldom make these claims, except to sometimes assert that they provide a needed service;

5. *Impact on the Community:* Indoor and street prostitution have very different effects on local communities; street prostitution is more visible and disruptive of the peace, whereas indoor prostitution has little, if any, negative impact on the locale, and, if discreet, there is typically little public awareness or opposition to it (this is discussed further in Chapter 10).

Although we have less information on other kinds of sex work, what we do know points to similar nuances in how the work is structured and experienced. Grant Rich and Kathleen Guidroz (Chapter 3) show that telephone sex workers have some positive (as well as negative) impressions of their work, including the belief that they help to control or reeducate male callers, especially those with perverse or violent tastes; the workers see this as providing a "community service." Exotic dancers make similar claims about stripping's "therapeutic" and "educational" effects on the audience.[32] Sharon Abbott's study of actors in the porn industry (Chapter 2) and Jacqueline Lewis' work on lap dancers in strip clubs (Chapter 12) also document both positive and negative aspects of the work experiences.

Disaggregating sex work into its various types does not mean that we gloss over similarities among the different types—the obvious one being that all sex workers are selling sex, whether "hands on" or from a distance—but disaggregation helps to underscore the need to examine both similarities *and* differences and to investigate *all* varieties of sex work. We know very little about the various types of indoor sex work; most studies examine street prostitution.[33] Likewise, research on pornography is almost exclusively focused on its content or its effects on consumers,[34] not on actors, producers, or the larger industry. This is why Sharon Abbott's chapter on pornography actors is such a unique contribution. Homosexual pornography has also been neglected; Joe Thomas helps to bridge that gap with his analysis of gay video porn (Chapter 4).

Refraining from unwarranted generalizations also means avoiding a priori, essentialist evaluations of sex work. It is always a challenge for observers to suspend value judgments with regard to highly charged topics like sex work, but I would argue that in order to shed light, rather than more heat, on the subject, it is crucial that it be approached as objectively as possible. It is not only activists and pundits who hold strong prejudices about sex work. Some academic research is also colored by the authors' blatant biases. One form of bias is that of absolute *condemnation.* An example is Cecilie Hoigard and Liv Finstad's major book on street prostitution in Norway, in which they insist that prostitution is an "abomination" and a form of "brutal oppression."[35] This is gratuitous moralizing based more on the authors' personal opinions than their findings, and it detracts from their otherwise important research results. Similarly, a recent book on pornography by Gail Dines, Robert Jensen, and Ann Russo is saturated with wild, categorical claims about the evils of pornography, and particularly its presumed role in subordinating women and brutalizing male viewers. Even though the authors (all professors) try to spin the book as a scholarly treatise, they expressly dismiss empirical research ("instead of being paralyzed by the limitations of social science") and rely instead on their own convictions as well as some anecdotal testimonials about the alleged harms of porn.[36]

The obverse form of bias is *romanticization* or celebration of sex work, but this appears infrequently in research studies, because sex work is fairly hard for researchers to glorify, and is much easier to condemn. Shannon Bell describes her book, *Whore Carnival,* as "a recognition and commendation of the sexual and political power and knowledge of prostitutes," which sounds rather celebratory.[37] Others offer glowing assessments, if not outright romanticization. Wendy McElroy tells us, "Pornography benefits women, both personally and politically," a claim that receives only limited support in her book.[38] Similarly, Nadine Strossen observes that "pornography provides information about women's bodies and techniques for facilitating female sexual pleasure, which is otherwise sadly lacking in our society."[39] This may be a factual statement, but it needs qualification in light of the fact that most pornography caters to *male* sexual pleasure, with enlightenment about women's sexuality secondary at best. Other sympathetic spins on pornography are offered by some leading cultural analysts such as Laura Kipnis, Alan Soble, and Linda Williams.[40]

Perhaps a third approach is that of *normalization*—that is, presenting sex work as no different from any other work, and humanizing the individuals involved. This is laudable—up to a point. It may indeed be the case that most porn actors are "like all the rest of us" in their everyday lives, as Wendy McElroy suggests,[41] and that many or most prostitutes are "ordinary women" as Roberta Perkins says,[42] or even "ordinary and likable people" as Arlene Carmen and Howard Moody claim.[43] But this is *not* how they are generally perceived by the public. At the societal level, sex work is still regarded as highly *stigmatized* work, and most of those involved in the buying and selling of sex feel compelled to remain in the closet. It is work, but *not* just like any other kind of work.

The studies presented in this book neither demonize nor glorify sex work: Evaluations are based on concrete evidence, not the analyst's preconceptions.

Sex work may be experienced as both somewhat "exploitative" and "empowering,"[44] distasteful in some respects but rewarding in others. Roberta Perkins writes that "for prostitutes, sex work is a mixture of pleasant and unpleasant experiences."[45] Victimization cannot be ignored; it is utterly real, especially among street prostitutes, who need more police protection and assistance from service and outreach agencies—amply demonstrated in the chapters by Nanette Davis, Maggie O'Neill and Rosemary Barberet, and Catherine Benson and Roger Matthews. But other sex workers are less vulnerable to exploitation and violence, exercise more control over their work, and derive some psychological or physical rewards from what they do—evidenced in the chapters by Janet Lever and Deanne Dolnick, Wendy Chapkis, Sharon Abbott, Grant Rich and Kathleen Guidroz, and Joe Thomas.

WHERE ARE THE MEN?

Male sexual behavior is less subject to social strictures than female sexual activity. Women are categorized as "good girls" or "bad girls," whereas males are subject to less dichotomized evaluation; promiscuous females are defined as "sluts," whereas male promiscuity is a badge of honor. The same double standard pervades our images of the actors involved in commercial sex transactions. Gender bias is evident in public attitudes and cultural definitions of sex workers. When we think of pornography, prostitution, and other sex work, we tend to think of female actors, despite the fact that sex work involves at least two parties (at least one of whom is usually male), and despite the fact that customers are much more numerous than the sex workers who service them.

In popular discourse, female sex workers are quintessential *deviant women,* whereas the customers are seen as essentially *normal men.* There is, of course, some stigma in being a customer, in that it suggests some personal deficiency in men who "have to pay for it." But this stigma is much less than what the prostitute experiences. The very terminology used—whore, hooker, harlot, slut—is heavily laden with opprobrium. By contrast, customers are referred to as johns, tricks, clients, and patrons—fairly tame labels. You may be a bit surprised to learn that a male friend has visited a prostitute, but shocked to learn that a female friend *is* a prostitute.

A gender disparity is also evident in the research literature, which is predominantly concerned with female sex workers rather than male workers, managers, or customers. Very little research has been done on customers, who are extremely difficult to access. Martin Monto's study (Chapter 5) is unique in its evaluation of a large number of arrested customers of street prostitutes. The men were a "captive audience" who opted for a day's attendance at a "johns school" (in lieu of an arrest record) where they completed a lengthy questionnaire on their sexual attitudes and behavior.

The only arena where men have been studied routinely is in experimental research on viewers of pornography. These studies examine the apparent effects of violent and nonviolent porn on male viewers' attitudes toward women and their willingness to display aggression. Overall, findings suggest that viewing violent material (both pornographic and nonpornographic) has an adverse effect on men's attitudes, but it is the *violent* content, not the pornographic dimension per se, that appears to be key.[46] Moreover, these studies are all vulnerable to the test of external validity—that is, whether the findings in a lab experiment can be extrapolated to the real world. The researchers who do this work caution against making such generalizations.

Studies of male sex workers (such as prostitutes and strippers) comprise only a fraction of the literature.[47] These studies point to some important differences in the ways male and female sex workers experience their work, but much more research is needed to corroborate these differences. Similarly, in the voluminous body of research on pornography almost nothing has been written on gay pornography.[48] The chapter by Joe Thomas draws contrasts between gay male and straight pornography, specifically the radically different meanings of pornography in gay and straight cultures. Porn holds a fair amount of *esteem* within the gay community, but carries substantial *stigma* in the straight world, as evidenced by the opinion poll data presented above.[49]

Pimps are largely invisible. They are almost never studied directly; the little we know about them comes from prostitutes, not from the pimps themselves.[50] This scarcity of research applies both to street-level pimps and to managers and owners of indoor commercial sex establishments, who profit from the labors of their workers. Recently, some researchers have argued that fewer street prostitutes have pimps today, but many still do. Police face major obstacles in arresting pimps, since prostitutes rarely come forward and testify against them.

Law enforcement has mirrored the larger cultural bias favoring men. Traditionally, the act of patronizing a prostitute was not a crime in the United States and most other countries. This was largely due to the tremendous status disparity between male clients and "women of ill repute." Prostitutes were outcasts, but patrons were seen as valuable members of society, even if they occasionally dabbled in deviant sexual liaisons. Among the standard arguments for the law's exclusive focus on prostitutes: They are repeat offenders, profit from the transaction, and present a public nuisance. These claims ignore the fact that johns can also create a public nuisance, also benefit from the purchase of sexual services, and also repeat the offense (albeit much less frequently). In public opinion, the double standard is just beginning to erode. A sizable proportion of the American public now favors public shaming of johns, as shown in Chapter 10.

The renowned Model Penal Code (1962) reflects this legal double standard: The code stipulates that prostitution should be treated as a misdemeanor, while patronizing a prostitute should be punished as a mere violation—an infraction punishable by a fine rather than incarceration. The disparity was rationalized even as late as 1980, in the official commentary on the code:

> Authorization of severe penalties [jail time] for such misconduct [patronizing] is wholly unrealistic. Prosecutors, judges, and juries would be prone to nullify severe penalties in light of the common perception of extramarital intercourse as a widespread practice.... This level of condemnation [a violation and fine] would seem far more in keeping with popular understanding than would more severe sanctions. Furthermore, the lenient treatment of customers reflects the orientation of the offense toward the merchandizers of sexual activity.[51]

The prevalence of extramarital sex, a "popular understanding" favoring the clients, and the notion that the law should target sellers, not buyers, of vice are all invoked to justify lenient treatment of clients. Alas, most state penal codes now treat patronizing as a misdemeanor, not a mere violation as the Model Penal Code recommended.

Institutionalized bias persists in law enforcement and is sometimes explicitly condoned by criminal justice officials. In New York City in 1984, the head of the police department's Public Morals Division, Captain Jerome Piazza, defended the policy of not arresting johns on the grounds that, "You can ruin a lot of marriages by making a 'john' collar."[52] And a Phoenix vice detective expressed similar sympathy for arrested customers: "It's really sad. The men are between thirty and sixty, white, with good jobs and families. When their cases go to court, it almost inevitably means a divorce. I hate to see it."[53] Similar sympathies were not extended to the prostitutes.

Since the 1960s the act of patronizing a prostitute has been criminalized by all fifty states in America, though many state laws continue to punish patronizing less severely than prostitution,[54] and law enforcement still falls most heavily on the prostitute. Arrests of johns in most American cities continues to be either sporadic or nonexistent, and the focus remains on supply rather than demand. In very few jurisdictions are prostitutes and their patrons apprehended in equal proportion. The disparity is even more striking when we take into account numbers of participants. Only about 10 percent of prostitution arrests in the United States are male customers, yet customers greatly outnumber prostitutes; hence, the proportions of each population represented in the arrests reveals even more extensive gender bias.

Bias is also evident in what happens after arrest.[55] In most cities first-time arrested customers are routinely offered pretrial diversion rather than prosecution. In 1993 in Seattle, for example, 69 percent of the prostitutes charged with solicitation were convicted, whereas only 9 percent of the customers were convicted, largely because most were offered diversion.[56] Customers who are prosecuted and convicted typically receive lower fines or find themselves less likely to be jailed than prostitutes.[57] Unfortunately, very little research has been done on the treatment of prostitution by the criminal justice system; Catherine Benson and Roger Matthews (Chapter 14) did a unique study of the attitudes and practices of vice squad officers in Britain. They show that many British vice squads now believe it is important to target johns, who are seen as especially vulnerable to legal sanctions, though British law makes arrests of customers fairly difficult. We lack comparable information on American vice squads, but one study documented the frustration of vice officers over the prevailing "revolving-door" syndrome (arresting prostitutes who quickly return to work), though they did not advocate cracking down on customers, as did their British counterparts.[58]

THE SEX INDUSTRY, INTEREST GROUPS, AND THE AUTHORITIES

The central focus of most studies is on *the individual,* and this usually means street prostitutes or the viewers of pornography. This exclusive focus on individual actors neglects the organizations involved in sex work and the larger sex industry. We need more studies of organized sex work—in escort agencies, massage parlors, telephone sex agencies, the pornography industry, and so forth. Some of this book's chapters help to fill this gap—including a unique analysis of Nevada's legal brothel industry; a study of a telephone sex agency; and an examination of strip clubs that offer lap dancing. These are new directions in research, and we need more such studies to make the industry more transparent.

Nor do we have much research on organized intervention in sex work by outreach groups or government efforts to control sex work. Porter and Bonilla (Chapter 7) studied the structure of street prostitution via an outreach organization; O'Neill and Barberet (Chapter 8) examined outreach organizations in England and Spain; and Benson and Matthews (Chapter 14) studied police intervention in street prostitution in Britain.

Similarly, there has been fairly little coverage of the pro- and antiprostitution lobbying groups at the local or national level. American groups have been studied by Jenness and Weitzer,[59] and there are some studies of advocacy groups in other countries,[60] but this is just the tip of the iceberg. Studies have yet to be done, for example, of the Exotic Dancers Alliance, Feminists for Free Expression, the Free Speech Coalition (and its offshoot, Protecting Adult Welfare), and the Adult Film Association of America, which represents 200 producers and distributors of X-rated films and videos. No one has studied antiprostitution organizations in any depth, except Nanette Davis (Chapter 9) on the Council for Prostitution Alternatives in Portland, Oregon.[61]

Antipornography campaigns have been studied,[62] as have blue-ribbon commissions on pornography in the United States, Canada, and Britain.[63] The most controversial of the panels was the 1986 American commission appointed by Attorney General Edwin Meese. Since it marked a turning point in the government's approach to pornography and since it shows how quickly official policy and enforcement practices can change in the field of sex work, it is worth describing the commission's work in some detail here. This commission was the antithesis of the 1970 Commission on Obscenity and Pornography; the two bodies reached diametrically opposed conclusions on the effects of pornography on consumers and on proper public policy in this sphere.[64] For example, while the 1970 commission found no evidence that exposure to pornography contributed to sex crimes, the Meese commission found the opposite, though its evidence was largely anecdotal, based on the testimony of self-described victims recruited to appear before the panel.[65] The Meese Commission has been roundly criticized for its biased approach, including its politically stacked membership, unfair procedures, and neglect of evidence running counter to its sweeping antipornography agenda.[66]

The U.S. Justice Department formally accepted all of the Meese Commission's recommendations and produced a report outlining steps the department was taking to implement them.[67] With a new Obscenity Enforcement Unit and its "Project Postporn," the Justice Department assumed a leading role in the campaign against the industry. Drastic changes were envisioned, as the new unit proclaimed: "Only by removing whole businesses from society…will significant progress be made against the existing industry."[68] The unit used antiracketeering (RICO) forfeiture laws to close adult book and video stores and the novel tactic of simultaneous multidistrict prosecutions of pornography distributors in order to bankrupt and close these businesses. Under this innovative strategy, a company was charged with violations of federal criminal law in several states at the same time. The obvious goal was to force a company out of business under the weight of logistical demands and legal costs incurred in fighting numerous court cases in various jurisdictions. Despite the Obscenity Enforcement Unit's awareness that the multiple prosecution tactic was probably unconstitutional, and despite some opposition within its own ranks and from the FBI, the tactic was used to target not only child pornography and extreme hard-core porn but also distributors of softer pornography.[69] The apparent unconstitutionality of this practice is based on its departure from the prevailing test of obscenity: Under the Supreme Court's landmark 1973 *Miller v. California* decision, local "community standards" are to govern definitions of what constitutes obscene materials (i.e., what appeals to "prurient interests" and is "patently offensive" to the "average person" in a community). Prosecutors working in the obscenity unit typically included Utah as one of the jurisdictions for multiple prosecutions, because its arch-conservative climate virtually guaranteed a conviction. Thus, Utah's community standard in effect became the national standard, arguably violating the test set forth in *Miller v. California.*

Enforcement against the pornography industry increased dramatically after the publication of the Meese report. Whereas only 100 individuals had been prosecuted for violations of obscenity statutes between 1978 and 1986, the number of indictments quadrupled between 1987 and 1991. In 1988 the Justice Department won more than 250 pornography cases against businesses and individuals,[70] and by 1990 seven national pornography distributors had been forced out of business while being prosecuted.[71] Meanwhile, several federal courts denounced the multidistrict prosecution strategy as a form of harassment.

Several changes have taken place under the Clinton administration. The political appointee who served as chief of the Obscenity Enforcement Unit under Reagan and Bush has been replaced with a career civil servant. The unit is now called the Child Exploitation and Obscenity Unit, reflecting a change in emphasis and resources toward enforcement against child pornography, which is now seen as far more dangerous than adult obscenity. And there has been a shift away from multidistrict prosecutions; the current policy is that they are "disfavored," and none has been initiated in recent years.[72] Again, this shows how quickly state policy can change in the area of commercial sex. The advent of the Internet, and the ease with which it makes pornography, including child porn, available, has prompted a new emphasis in American law enforcement circles.

With regard to other types of sex work, the political and law enforcement context deserves much more attention from researchers. Several studies in this vein are offered in Part III of this book.

CONCLUSION

This book contributes to our knowledge of several understudied aspects of sex work and the sex industry—a growth industry that will continue to expand in the future, if the proliferation of services over the past decade is any guide. This book is a beginning, but we need even more research on telephone sex work, off-street prostitutes of all stripes, the porn industry generally and gay and lesbian pornography in particular (its actors, organization, and reception in the gay community), legal prostitution systems, the dynamics of law enforcement, and changes in law and public policy and the social forces shaping such changes. We know precious little about contemporary brothels, transgender prostitutes,[73] and those who work as call girls or escorts.[74] We need much more research on the men involved at all levels—customers, workers, managers, producers, owners. Fresh research is even called for on those topics that have already attracted substantial study. For example, the studies of massage parlors were all conducted in the 1970s; such establishments still exist in many cities. Have they changed since the 1970s? We have a substantial body of research on street prostitution, but even here we need to know more about the dynamics of this trade on the ground (which requires careful ethnographic observation) and about the stratification of street work: that is, variations by status, race, and place and the consequences for the workers. This world does not offer easy access to the outsider, which helps to account for the paucity of research in many key areas; but gaining access should be viewed as a challenge rather than an insuperable barrier.

PERSPECTIVES OF SEX WORKERS AND CUSTOMERS

2

MOTIVATIONS FOR PURSUING
AN ACTING CAREER IN PORNOGRAPHY

Sharon A. Abbott

....

I like the money, and I can do the job. And I am young. I figure, hell, I am going to do it now while I have age on my side.

—*Amy*

In my mind, it is only prostitution if you are compromising your principles. I believe that is true in any walk of life, whether you are having sex or not. If you are doing something for money that you are not comfortable with, you're prostituting yourself.

—*Rita*

Many people choose careers based on what the job can provide for them. Benefits may include money, status and recognition, opportunities for career mobility, and social contacts. Some are drawn to jobs that provide a sense of freedom and independence, jobs in which they can forge their own paths, set their own hours, and be free from rigid demands of authority. Careers in the pornography industry offer several of the same benefits to workers as many other occupations. Despite these similarities, however, jobs in the pornography industry have rarely been viewed as work. Instead, most research on pornography has focused on the effect and reception of pornographic materials once they have been produced and distributed. Numerous experimental studies have addressed such things as gender differences in arousal,[1] the possible links between pornography and aggression, sexual violence, and callous attitudes toward sexual violence,[2] as well as pornography's potential influence on gender equality.[3] This research has treated pornography as a stimulus with little consideration to its content or production.

Similarly, feminists[4] and legal scholars[5] have contributed to debates on erotica and pornography, but have virtually ignored its production. These analysts focus on the "exploitation" of the workers (particularly women), but fail to examine pornography as an industry and career choice, and thus limit a broader sociological understanding of the medium.

As a form of work, pornography requires participants to enter its stigmatized world and, once "in," develop strategies to maintain involvement in the industry. The structure of the industry influences these motivations. Heterosexual pornography production can be broadly divided into three categories: "professional," "pro-amateur," and "amateur." Professional companies are the largest and most organized, typically employing between fifty and one hundred staff members for sales, marketing, distribution, promotion, and production scheduling. Each company releases more than twenty new videotapes per month which feature the most glamorous and popular talent in the industry. Budgets for professional features range from $50,000 to $150,000, averaging closer to the lower end. In contrast, amateur companies consist of a few individuals who perform a variety of tasks, including acting, directing, sales, and marketing. Budgets range from a few hundred to a few thousand dollars. Most commonly, amateur companies do not produce, but rather edit and market "homemade" materials that are sent in by interested participants. Pro-amateur or "gonzo" companies include small companies with large budgets, medium-size companies with small budgets, and subsidiaries of professional companies. Budgets average between $15,000 and $25,000. Unlike the specialized employees of professional companies, the staff at pro-amateur companies perform many functions within the organization. Pro-amateur productions create a bridge between professional and "homemade" productions by offering products with high production quality, relatively low cost, and known performers.

This chapter investigates the work of actors and actresses in the production of pornography.[6] I focus on the motivations for entering a porn career and maintaining subsequent involvement, and I describe the ways in which motives are influenced by two factors: actors' gender and the type of production companies with which they are affiliated.

METHODS

Data were collected in two primary sites of pornography production, Los Angeles and San Francisco. In-depth interviews were conducted with participants involved in all facets of production, including producers, directors, company owners, magazine editors, agents, makeup artists, camera operators, and actresses and actors. Interviews typically lasted between one and three hours. In addition, observations and informal interviews were conducted on production sets, at industry parties, and at an industry trade show.

During the course of fieldwork, I conducted interviews with nineteen actors and thirty-one actresses currently involved in the adult entertainment industry. The sample was drawn using a snowball technique and convenience sampling.[7] I was introduced to a number of the actors and actresses through a key informant, a director involved in the industry for more than a decade. Initial respondents referred me to other people, and to give me a "full picture" of the industry, the director referred me to individuals that he felt represented all aspects of the business. In addition, whenever possible, I sought out interviews with people I met in other situations who were not connected with this director. Both methods helped to increase diversity among the sample.

Whenever possible, interviews were taped and later transcribed. All participants knew my role as a social scientist and were assured confidentiality. Respondents' length of time in the industry ranged from two to fifteen years, with an average of four to five years. As discussed later, this average was higher for actors than actresses. Most had acted in at least fifty videos, with the range being between forty and six hundred (typically corresponding to years in industry).

MOTIVATIONS FOR ENTERING THE WORLD OF PORN

Respondents were asked what jobs they held before working in pornography, and what jobs they would likely hold if they were no longer involved in adult entertainment. These questions often led to discussions about the benefits of pornography over jobs in the "straight" (not X-rated) industries. In addition, actors and actresses were asked a series of questions about their involvement with different companies, their status in the industry, and relationships with their peers. This information shed light on patterns of mobility and organizational culture. Individuals enter the porn industry for several reasons. Five reasons are described below.

Money

Popular beliefs maintain that the lure of "easy money" draws people, particularly the young, to the world of pornography. This belief is supported by trade and fan magazines that glamorize the industry by focusing on the lavish lifestyles of its members. While the industry cultivates the idea of porn as profitable, income varies greatly by individual. Furthermore, rather than "easy money," respondents reported that most of the work is tiring, boring, and physically exhausting.[8] Like prostitutes, a few make a great deal of money while most make a modest or meager living.

While money earned from appearing in pornography videos may seem high compared with many other jobs, annual incomes generated from porn alone typically approximate middle-class earnings. For example, respondents reported that at the "professional level," actresses receive between $300 and $1,000 for an individual scene.[9] The fee is based on the actress's popularity, experience, and audience appeal, as well as what the scene entails. Masturbation and "girl/girl" ("lesbian") scenes pay the least, while anal sex and "double penetrations"[10] generate the most money. The most common scene combines oral sex and penile-vaginal intercourse, and pays, on average, $500. Though the pay is high per hour, income is limited by the amount of work actresses are offered; this money must often stretch between extended periods of no work.

In addition, particularly at the "professional level," actresses must spend a major portion of their income on their appearance. Cosmetic surgeries, such as liposuction and breast augmentation, are the norm in the business, and must be paid for out of the actresses' earnings.[11] Appearances at industry parties and local "gentlemen's clubs" (erotic dancing) often require costumes, which consumes a portion of earnings. While actors do not have these expenses, they do pay to support their images. Males are expected to look good and stay in shape, and are expected to have the status symbols associated with being a porn star (e.g., motorcycles and cars). Even the HIV testing, required every thirty days in order to work, must be paid for out of pocket.

Women earn more on average than their male coworkers.[12] Respondents in this study reported that male talent earn approximately 50 percent less than their female coworkers. Pornography, therefore, is one of the few occupations in which men experience pay inequity. Furthermore, while actors often have more individual scenes per video than do actresses (with the exception of the star), they only rarely appear on box covers (which provide high fees). Therefore, actors' earnings are typically lower for the entire project. Since men in the industry make disproportionately less than women, money alone is an unlikely motivation for actors.

Earnings also depend on the category of porn. While money is a motivating factor at the professional and pro-amateur level, participants in amateur productions are often paid little, if anything at all. Individuals who sell amateur tapes to a distributer are paid, on average, $150. The fee is paid to the individual who sells the tape, not the participants, whose pay is unknown. When videos are produced by amateur companies, talent earn between $50 and $150 per scene. In addition to paying relatively low wages, amateur companies do not have the same connections to such moneymaking opportunities as erotic dancing and modeling, common at pro-amateur and professional levels. Therefore, actors and actresses at the amateur level were far less likely than individuals at higher levels to cite money as a primary motivation .

At the pro-amateur and professional level, the effect of money may be a key factor in keeping members involved in the industry even after they decide to leave.[13] Accustomed to periods of time in which money is plentiful (albeit sporadic), actors and actresses have difficulty finding jobs that offer the (perceived) freedom and flexibility of porn work. This phenomenon is illustrated by the following exchange between a husband-and-wife acting team:

> *Tim*: A friend of mine knew the contacts for porn, and another friend of mine really pushed me into it, and once I tried it, I got hooked into it. I liked the lifestyle. And then I didn't like it. I went through a period where I didn't like it, and it was too late, because I was already in it, and I already changed my cost of living. And that's a mistake that porn actors and actresses make.
>
> *Keri*: They start off making $5,000 a month in the beginning.
>
> *Tim*: They start off and bite off more than they can chew financially a month, and then you're stuck, because most of us can't turn around and go get a CEO job, because now we're in the $80,000 to $100,000 a year bracket. We are used to big houses and nice cars.

The inability to find jobs with similar benefits may keep participants involved in the industry. In addition, talent may begin to "live beyond their means," and the need to support their standard of living serves to keep them in their jobs.

Fame and Glamour

Many respondents report that "becoming known" is a greater motivating factor to enter the industry than money. This motivation is most common at the pro-amateur and professional levels, which have a large distribution of materials, and thus, more opportunities for recognition.[14] Porn stars I interviewed reported being photographed, applauded, and having their autographs requested. Fan clubs offer more opportunity for stars to be admired.

Fan magazines often portray the world of porn as glamorous, and the industry attempts to promote this image. At the pro-amateur and professional levels, the release of high-budget feature films and videos ("glamour pieces") are often accompanied by black-tie parties in highly visible settings (e.g., hotels or convention centers). A key component of these parties are the hordes of photographers from fan, trade, and entertainment magazines who serve as paparazzi for the industry. The mixing of glamorization and advertisement is best exemplified in a recent billboard erected over a busy street in Los Angeles featuring the "contract girls"[15] of a large company. Other examples include the two domestic award shows each year hosted by the industry (a third is hosted abroad). Tickets to these black-tie affairs typically cost $100 apiece. While the focus of these ceremonies is often on high-budget features, amateur productions are also honored. The opportunity for "fame" is therefore available to participants at all levels.

Several actresses, actors, producers, and directors commented that the desire for fame was a desirable trait in talent because enthusiasm for their work increases as popularity and recognition grows. In contrast, if talent is only motivated by money, they are often left frustrated or bored. As one actor argued, "If you are doing it for the money, you won't last long." Production companies similarly assume that interest in money is evident to viewers and disrupts the fantasy that the talent really enjoys their work.

When contrasted with the "straight" (not X-rated) entertainment industry, porn offers a relatively quick and easy means to earn public recognition. Acting in the straight industry is typically characterized by few opportunities, high competition, and waiting for "luck" or "big breaks."[16] Straight actors and actresses often audition for hundreds of parts just to win a few. In contrast, someone aspiring to be a porn star, if attractive enough, can sign up with an agent and appear in a video within days. And fame tends to come quickly in pornography.

Fame and recognition are sought by both actresses and actors. Though actresses attract considerably more attention in adult publications, there are fewer actors overall in the industry, so they become familiar and easily recognized. But while this motivation is not determined by gender, the concept of "fame" varies between the sexes. For females, being famous includes not only being recognized and supported by the industry, but also being desired by viewers, which is much less true for male actors, since the viewers are largely heterosexual males.

Freedom and Independence

Research into the motivations of many other types of sex workers suggests that individuals often become involved in the industry because of their low socioeconomic status and restricted opportunities. For example, in their study of table dancers, Ronai and Ellis[17] argue that women who work in gentlemen's clubs have fewer resources and opportunities than other women. Other explanations for why sex workers enter the trade include poor schooling or job training, broken homes, poverty, sexual abuse, and few opportunities to make money legitimately.[18]

By contrast, a number of my respondents reported that they turned to the adult industry because it offered them what they wanted in a job, namely flexible hours, good money, and fun. It is not blocked opportunity but an understanding of the often inflexible and demanding nature of conventional work that motivates entry into pornography. Porn is appealing because it offers more flexibility and independence. Joanna, a native of France and an experienced actress, said,

> I just can't work in an office. I flip out — I get sick after two weeks. With this, I get to travel and have freedom. I got to come to the United States. I have enough money to take a vacation whenever I want. I just took two weeks off, although I am trying to save money.

Other respondents claimed that they were drawn to the ease of the work. As Kurt explained, "I might be on set from 8 A.M. to midnight, but I don't do a goddamn thing. They pay me to show up, read a book, flirt with girls, and fuck. As far as that goes, it's cake."

A sense of freedom and independence is supported by the structure of the industry itself. While a few dozen actresses and two actors hold exclusive contracts with professional companies,[19] most talent work as "freelancers" or under non-exclusive contracts, in which they guarantee a company a set number of days each month. Not being held to a contract allows talent to select jobs and projects that best fit their schedules, interests, and preferences. As Dane explained, not being under an exclusive contact can also increase overall earnings, because a person is free to work on more projects and spends less time on production sets:

> The reason I accepted a contract is because they are not keeping me exclusively.... I have a guarantee that's just about as big as a normal contract, but I can still work around, and my hours are less. I don't stick around for dialogue and bullshit, I just show up and ba-da-bing, I'm done, like, in three hours. In a contract where I am doing a feature, I sit around for ten, twelve hours. If you spread $500 over twelve hours, it's not as much as if you spread $500 over three hours. Logically, it makes a lot of sense to be non-exclusive.

Producers benefit from this freelance system as well by being able to select participants on a project-by-project basis. Only a few well-publicized stars are needed under exclusive contracts to promote the company.

While porn offers freedom and flexibility in comparison to most other jobs of equal pay, there are certain requirements for being regarded as professional and competent. In order to assure future projects, actresses and actors in all categories are expected to arrive on time, have all necessary paperwork available (identification and HIV test results),[20] be sober and cooperative, and be willing to stay overtime. Being labeled a "flake" is detrimental to a career, and includes everything from forgetting appointments, being uncooperative, and being unable to perform the requirements of the job (for men). Therefore, while the work is unconventional, some aspects of the job are typical to many industries.

Becoming a quasi-professional is possible only at the professional and pro-amateur level. The reasons for this are threefold. First, amateur productions specialize in "new," "different," and "never before seen" talent, leaving little possibility for repeat projects. Second, amateur productions attempt to capture "real" and "authentic" sex, and will not typically hire anyone with a "name" or with experience in the industry. Finally, because amateur productions pay so little (relatively) and are seldom linked to other money-making avenues (such as stripping), it is unlikely that someone could survive financially at this level. Therefore, these participants are motivated by individual interest and opportunity, not a desire for flexible employment, This interest, however, is created by the freedom the industry offers. Many respondents reported that once they made the decision to enter the industry, the doors were open to them.

Opportunity and Sociability

At the amateur and pro-amateur levels, individuals typically find their way into the industry via friends, lovers, and co-workers. For example, amateur companies rely on actors and actresses to invite their friends to participate in a production. Agents are rarely involved with amateur productions because their fees would be too low, but "talent scouts" are used to refer reliable talent (scouts are typically paid $25 to $50). The opportunity to enter pornography therefore often comes from other participants. This avenue of entry applies to both women and men.

Once in the industry, it is easy to make connections that foster sustained contact with the business. On low-budget productions, for example, actresses and actors are often friends, and are brought onto a project specifically because of these relationships. On set, new relationships are formed, which in turn lead to additional projects. On professional sets, stars are given the opportunity to select their co-stars. Having these social ties is therefore critical for success. In addition, these relationships sustain interest and enthusiasm when other motivating factors, such as the lure of money, diminish.

As in many other careers in deviance, once in a subculture, friends and social networks typically become limited to individuals who are also part of the subgroup. Being part of a stigmatized group fosters these relationships. In the porn business, industry parties and less formalized social gatherings provide opportunities to socialize and network. Networking is as vital in porn production as it is in "straight" industries. These parties thus serve to make contacts, form alliances, and provide opportunities to "be seen."

In addition to opportunities via friends, lovers, and acquaintances, other sectors of the sex industry provide an avenue into the world of porn. For women, erotic dancing presents an opportunity to enter the porn industry. Dancers are often informed that they can make more money stripping if they appear in a few pornographic videos, and if a dancer has established a name for herself, she may be recruited by the porn industry. Based on her physical attractiveness and name recognition, a dancer may be offered both an exclusive contract and her pick of directors and co-talent.

If stripping can lead to porn, the reverse is true as well. It is rare for a big-name actress not to "dance" (strip) at least periodically. Dancing provides an opportunity to increase recognition and fan appeal, and thus, to make oneself more "profitable" to the industry. When an actress "headlines" (a featured appearance) at a dance club, the owners advertise that they have a porn star performing, which in turn draws larger crowds. Bigger crowds and increased interest results in higher tips for dancers and more business (and thus more profit) for the clubs. Therefore, actresses, club owners, and porn companies all stand to benefit from this symbiotic relationship.

Porn companies, particularly those offering semiexclusive or exclusive contracts, often encourage actresses to dance in order to advertise the company. Larger companies retain booking agents for their dancers so that arrangements and pay negotiations are handled "in house." In addition, videotapes in which the dancer has performed are often made available for sale. When state laws prohibit such sales, "one-sheets," advertisements for videos with photographs taken on the set, are made available to the customers.

Increased recognition, however, can have negative effects on an actress's career. Porn companies are continually searching for "fresh" faces in order to appeal to both new and old viewers. Actresses who are "overexposed" in videos, magazine layouts, and dancing appearances are assumed to be unable to offer much appeal for viewers since their images become too familiar. Therefore, although publicity is mandatory for a profitable career, it is often a reason for limited company interest. The ingredients for having a successful career are the very things that can end one.

Because magazine spreads and dancing opportunities are far more available for women than for men, actors are not vulnerable to overexposure, and as a result, their careers in porn commonly last twice as long as women's. As one actress explained:

> Girls have a shelf life of nine months to two years, unless you are different. Like me, I am Asian, so it helps. Men stay forever. It is different for a man. If he can perform, he can stay in. There are guys that have been in the business ten or fifteen years.

Furthermore, as Levy[21] found in the "straight" film industry, popular successful actresses are younger on average than their male counterparts, suggesting the beauty norms held by both producers and audiences. In both the straight and adult industries, actors are able to age, while actresses are replaced by younger, newer talent.

Being Naughty and Having Sex

A number of my respondents reported that porn offered them a chance to snub the prevailing norms of acceptable sexuality. Few careers offer the same stigma as appearing on screen engaging in what most people consider a private act. While porn undoubtedly attracts exhibitionists, it is also a vehicle for people who wish to violate, challenge, and refute social norms. This phenomenon is particularly relevant for women, as the double standard offers more stringent norms for female sexual expression, whose violations carry additional sanctions. Male stars in many ways embody sexual norms that equate masculine sex with prowess, adventure, and detachment. A humorous comment by Dane evinced the link between male sexuality and porn: "[An actress] asked me if I had ever thought of being in the adult industry. I am an American male and I have seen porn—of course I have [thought of being in the industry]."

One company in the study catered to and profited from this desire to be "naughty." The owner-director sought actresses and actors interested in being "bad." As he argued, talent interested in money were rarely interested in sex, while those who desired fame were "used up" before they achieved it. Being "naughty" could easily be captured on film and would be appealing to viewers who want to see "real sex" (i.e., not acting). Interestingly, working for this producer offered actresses and actors an additional opportunity to be "naughty" since this particular company was marginal even within the industry (due to personnel, content matter, and geographical location).

In the course of violating social norms, porn offers the opportunity to have sex. Although it is widely assumed that the actresses are "acting" (at least to some degree), many respondents claimed that there was some sexual pleasure in their jobs. Being with "nice" and "gentle" guys was mentioned as increasing arousal. Several also reported that girl/girl scenes were more arousing or erotic because of the interpersonal dynamics between female participants.[22] While female arousal is often exaggerated or faked, it is undeniable that males are obtaining erections and ejaculating in front of the camera (typically constructed as "enjoying" sex). Even when filming soft-core versions,[23] sexual activities are rarely simulated. Furthermore, most scenes end with external ejaculation as a means to suggest that the sex was real. Not surprisingly, most actors cited "getting laid" as a primary motivation for entering a porn career. Once in the industry, sustaining an interest in sex is critical for a successful career. Experiencing sexual problems (inability to maintain an erection or control ejaculation) is the fastest way to end an acting career. As one actor, Chuck, explained:

> If you are the new guy, the first scene is usually no problem. If you have problems in the second scene, don't count on a third and fourth. At first it is fun because it is new. One day you realize it's work. Some guys can't continue.

A vested and sustained interest in "getting laid" is therefore a primary motivation for male actors in all three categories of pornography production.

Being part of the porn world offers sexual opportunities for interested participants off set as well. While many respondents reported that they were in monogamous relationships outside of work, single participants and those involved in swinging reported many opportunities for sex as a result of being involved in the industry. In addition to these opportunities, individuals involved in norm-violating subcultures are likely to hold nontraditional attitudes toward sex and sexuality, and thus be drawn to an arena in which they can exercise these interests. For example, because girl/girl sex is a staple of mainstream productions, actresses have ample opportunity to explore such relationships, which may carry over into private behavior.[24]

MOTIVATIONS FOR REMAINING IN PORNOGRAPHY

Actresses and actors can be divided into those who are forging a career in the adult entertainment industry and those who drift in and quickly out of the industry. Some who assumed it was a "one-time deal" may later decide that they want a career in the industry, while others, planning a long-term career, drop out early. Entrance into the industry, choices made to maintain involvement, and mobility within the industry are all affected by whether the goal is long-term or temporary involvement. Those who "drift" into the industry are more likely motivated by money, sex, desire for independence, and opportunity. Those who are attempting to achieve a long-term career are motivated by success and fame. Achieving and sustaining a successful career is dependent on many factors, including making profitable decisions, having connections, acting professionally, achieving a high status, and being seen. Each factor plays a part in maintaining involvement in the industry.

Making a Name

Just as the desire for fame and recognition motivates actors and actresses to enter the pornography industry, maintaining and increasing fame is a primary motivation for continuing a career in porn. This motive becomes stronger over time as initial fame develops into a respected reputation. In an industry that continually seeks new talent, maintaining fame is hard work. Strategic choices and fan support are crucial to retain one's position as a star. The perks for stardom, however, justify this work. Stars are paid considerably more per project (scenes and box covers), have more say in whom they will work with, spend less idle time on set, receive more recognition for their efforts, and are highly regarded within the industry.

Stars also receive considerably more attention from fans. Individual fan clubs, often maintained by managers, serve to announce local appearances and new releases. They also provide members with such things as personal messages, candid photographs, and trivia about the star. In addition, a well-known producer within the industry has formed a fan club which hosts its own award show and allows members to participate in industry gatherings. Fan clubs serve to make porn stars more accessible to the audience, a primary motivation for "intimacy at a distance."[25] More important, they offer advertisement and support for continued interest, both crucial for a successful career.

Building a fan base is supported by the industry. In an industry that thrives on offering "fresh" faces, actresses frequently appear in more videos during their first year in the industry than in any other year in their career. Generating fan appeal is assisted by the number of projects in which they appear. It is not uncommon for actresses to receive industry awards in their first year due in part to the sheer number of videos they appear in.[26] Actors have a different experience. Because there is a small pool of male talent, their involvement continues as long as they do not experience any problems (usually sexual) on set. While actors do not typically have fan clubs, they achieve star status because of their longevity and recognition.

Fans occupy a peripheral position within the industry. Because most consumption of porn is anonymous, producers, directors, actors, and actresses rarely know who their audience is. Although the industry is dependent on fans for survival, many of the respondents reported a fairly negative image of the imagined viewer. Comments about viewers ranged from "lonely" and "hard-up" to "stupid" and "disgusting." Ironically, then, actresses and actors are motivated in part to receive recognition from a group they know little about and often disparage. In addition, they reported little pride in the products they produce.[27] Like most artifacts in the "sleaze industry," porn is disposable, mass-produced, fungible, and easily forgotten. "Classics" (such as *Deep Throat, Devil in Miss Jones,* and *Behind the Green Door*) are rare, but are highly regarded and carry the promise of "getting your name known." The reward for appearing in more successful (and profitable) productions is fame, not money. Unlike the "straight" industry, actors and actresses are paid a flat fee for their performances, and receive no royalties for successful projects.

While striving for admiration from the "outside," actresses and actors are also motivated to be successful in the eyes of their peers. "Having what it takes" to succeed in porn is dependent on both internal and external approval and admiration. Conformity and peer pressure are as common in the adult entertainment industry as they are in most jobs. Although achieving status in the industry is critical for success (particularly in regard to securing work), it also provides a primary motivation for staying in the business. Building a reputation among peers and being famous in regard to fans were the most commonly cited motivations for maintaining a career in pornography.

Achieving high status serves multiple functions for both participants and organizations. The porn industry forms a closed community in which members rely on one another for both social activities and professional connections. As in other deviant careers, relationships take on a dual function because the deviant lifestyle limits interaction and sociability with "nondeviants." Furthermore, many respondents claimed that the industry was much like a family, albeit one full of competition and gossip. Achieving status within this group is dependent upon many factors, including being well-liked and/or respected, being recognized as competent, and achieving career longevity in the business. While networks and friendships are crucial for careers, they also offer support, social opportunities, and validation.

Career Strategies

Compared to many jobs, porn offers more freedom, independence, money, and sex. Once in the industry, many respondents reported that they were motivated to make a successful career of it. Some respondents commented that being involved in porn had hurt their chances of working in mainstream jobs, making them even more motivated to make porn work profitable. While most recognized that the career was short-term, they engaged in strategies to prolong their involvement and to make their careers more lucrative.

For actresses, one means to achieving a career in pornography is to make themselves consistently desirable and available (at least visually) to the public. This includes erotic dancing, modeling, being photographed, granting interviews, responding to fan groups, appearing at award shows, and signing autographs at trade shows (such as the Video Software Dealer's Association and the Consumer Electronics Show). In addition, computer technology has led the pornography industry to offer fans interactive software, CD-ROM, and online chat sessions. A pornography career thus can extend beyond acting in videos.

For actors, a successful career is dependent almost exclusively on one's ability to perform sexually. There is little supplemental work an actor can do to boost his career beyond being dependable, consistent, and available. Because there are few opportunities in related settings, some actors support their careers by holding other jobs in the industry. For example, one actor I interviewed also worked as an editor for a pro-amateur company. His goal was to use these skills to make a leap into the straight industry, although a number of respondents reported that this type of mobility is difficult due to the stigmatized nature of porn. Other actors advance within the industry to directing videos and working in other aspects of production. Although they often make less money than when acting, they achieve some degree of "professionalism" and prolong their careers by developing other skills.

In addition to building fan appeal or recognition, building a career requires making sensible choices and decisions throughout one's involvement in the industry. Working with the "right" (successful) companies increases one's chances of both being famous and developing a career. Regardless of the point of entry, to "make it" in porn, actors and actresses must quickly move up to professional companies. Those who are unable to break into the professional scene are unlikely to achieve fame. As previously discussed, while some recognition is afforded to those in amateur productions, there are simply not enough opportunities for exposure to achieve fame. Furthermore, working with reputable companies with high budgets (for both production and advertising) increases the chance of winning industry awards, which in turn offers fame and recognition.

A successful career is also dependent on having the right connections within the industry. For example, although several respondents claimed that talent agents were relatively useless in the industry, connecting to a reputable agent[28] increases the possibility of a porn career. For example, two producers I interviewed reported that although virtually all of the actresses and actors are known to them beforehand, they continually pay an agent fee. In return, agents contact them first when "hot" talent enters the industry. This relationship is also advantageous to actresses and actors, who subsequently enter at the highest level possible. In addition, agents often provide opportunities for modeling, as they are connected with both pornography and adult magazine companies.

Beyond agents, decisions about who will work on a particular film are made by directors, producers, actresses, and occasionally actors.[29] It is not uncommon, for example, for arrangements about future work to be made while on the set of another project. Furthermore, the directors refer reliable talent to other directors, and the participants request and refer each other for upcoming work. It is mandatory therefore to have high status and a good reputation within the industry. High status, however, is different from being well-liked. Competition for desired projects and publicity further affect these social relationships. These relationships are enmeshed with the interpersonal politics of the culture. Most respondents reported that knowing and pleasing the right people, being in the "in crowd," and competing with adversaries are key components of the work. Since project opportunities often come via informal networks, being involved in the porn subculture is essential for continued involvement in the industry. Actresses and actors who remain peripheral to the culture and/or who are excluded from it are more likely to drift out of the pornography industry because of limited opportunities. Maintaining a career is therefore dependent on being involved in the porn subculture.[30]

Mobility and Commitment

Mobility in the industry is difficult to measure in its traditional sense, partly because of the organizational structure of the industry. For example, upon entry, actors and actresses often move up from the amateur to the professional level. This is particularly true for actors who must prove themselves sexually in amateur productions before they are allowed to advance to pro-amateur and professional features. Because of the higher budgets, higher number of participants, and tight production schedules in professional features, directors need to be assured that there will be no unnecessary delays on the set because of sexual difficulties.

In contrast, some actresses enter at higher levels. Those who enter via modeling or dancing typically start at the pro-amateur level and, after proving their commercial value, are advanced to professional productions. Actresses who are considered exceptionally attractive and individuals with preestablished public recognition often start at the professional level. Once established in the professional scene, however, actors and actresses often appear in pro-amateur productions with no repercussions to their careers. Furthermore, because pro-amateur organizations are often owned by professional companies, this movement is supported by the industry.

Actresses who display little interest in moving up are often criticized by their coworkers and others as "fuck bunnies," "sluts," or "skags," and are seen as lacking ambition, skills, or knowledge.[31] This judgment is encouraged by the assumption that any pretty woman can make it in porn if she wants to. As unskilled laborers, the work of actresses is regarded as fairly easy, even in comparison with their male coworkers, who must "perform" to remain employed. In addition, because of higher pay and higher levels of publicity and fame, females reap more benefits in the industry. Therefore, those who cannot make it despite these advantages are assumed to be lacking personal ambition, with little consideration given to structural constraints.

Mobility is facilitated by longevity and commitment. "Sticking around" and "taking it seriously" are observable qualities, and are often translated into "having what it takes." Moving between pro-amateur and professional productions and working outside the porn industry are essential for a freelance career, suggesting the importance of horizontal rather than vertical mobility. The phenomenon of "working the circuit" is common in other industries where employers' commitment to employees is low and employees operate as independent contractors. In sum, those who wish to stay in the industry must display a continuous interest in forming networks, choosing the right projects, "looking good," being seen, and getting along with others.

CONCLUSION

Actors and actresses who are searching for quick money and/or sexual adventure quickly leave the industry once those goals are met, as do those who take one-time opportunities to act in porn videos. Those who remain must build a career for themselves in an industry that centers on the temporary. Motivations change with experience and are replaced with other goals. Of the motivations that are associated with entry into the industry, fame and recognition appear to be the most sustaining. In addition, although the construction of fame differs between actors and actresses, the desire for admiration and renown does not appear to be limited to women.

Initial motivations may be replaced by more substantial goals once talent is established in the industry. For example, although many respondents reported that "being naughty" was a primary motivation for entry, this goal is met in a relatively short time. It does not take many video appearances to establish one's rejection of traditional values. Over time, those interested in challenging mainstream societal values forge a career in which they receive approval for their actions and opportunities for recognition and exposure. Being "naughty" gives way to longer-term career goals. Those motivated by sex quickly learn that they must be able to preform on command in order to remain in the industry. Having sex becomes work, and actors and actresses are motivated to remain in the industry because they are among those who can "do the job." The motivation for sex is replaced by the desire to keep the job.

The careers of porn actors and actresses share some similarities with other deviant careers, such as drug dealing.[32] Participants often have a difficult time "going straight" (or leaving the business) after growing accustomed to the money associated with their work. In addition, being part of a stigmatized group reduces one's chances of achieving success in the "legitimate" world.

The motivations reported by porn talent are also salient for other types of sex workers. Research has suggested that strippers and prostitutes often enter the industry following economic crisis, yet remain in the industry because of the rewards (financial gain, independence) of sex work.[33] Success in the pornography industry requires the same qualities as success in other sectors of the sex industry. For example, being perceived as a "professional" is required for porn actors and actresses, call girls, prostitutes, and madams.[34]

Other studies of mobility within the sex industry identify two conditions necessary for movement.[35] First, information must be disseminated among the members. The participants must know that mobility is possible, and be informed about how to move through the hierarchy. Second, mobility requires an open system in which rank is based on achievement. To make moving up in rank possible, there must be high turnover or the market must be able to support many individuals at a given rank. Mobility in the porn industry is dependent on networks, informal relationships, availability, and demands in the market.

Finally, gender differences are also evident in other sectors of the sex industry. For example, research on male strippers suggests that males experience less social stigma than their female counterparts.[36] In the porn industry, male respondents reported less stigma and higher status, along with greater opportunities for certain kinds of career advancement within the industry (e.g., working as editors or directors). And just as most female strippers have held previous jobs that required some display of their body (modeling, go-go dancing, topless waitressing),[37] porn actresses were far more likely than their male counterparts to have had previous ties to the sex industry. A final comparison comes from a study comparing male, female, and transgender prostitutes.[38] The authors found that male and transgender prostitutes were more likely to report sexual enjoyment with clients than female prostitutes. Porn actors, similarly, were more likely than actresses to report sex as a motivation, and were more dependent on enjoying the sex in order to maintain their careers.

CHAPTER

3

SMART GIRLS WHO LIKE SEX: TELEPHONE SEX WORKERS

Grant Jewell Rich and Kathleen Guidroz

Mr. Jordan asked what phone sex was. Ms. Lewinsky stated that she may have explained it this way: "He's taking care of business on one end, and I'm taking care of business on another."

—Excerpt from the Starr report

Though phone sex is ubiquitous—virtually all men's magazines as well as numerous newspapers contain ads for this lucrative industry[1]—very little research has been done on the topic.[2] This chapter focuses on commercial telephone sex work, specifically how phone sex operators attempt to create and maintain a positive self-identity while employed in a socially stigmatized occupation.

Prevailing stereotypes about phone sex and phone sex workers are evident in certain fictional treatments of telephone sex, such as Spike Lee's 1996 film *Girl 6,* or Nicholson Baker's 1992 novel *Vox.*[3] The Lee film promotes the false notions that phone sex workers are extremely beautiful and that they work in glamorous phone sex offices filled with pricey, state-of-the-art computer equipment and are located in expensive luxury business suites. The real world of phone sex business is more mundane.[4] Baker's novel also distorts the nature of commercial phone sex, since it suggests that phone sex is emotionally deep and sexually gratifying to both parties, and may lead to future contacts, perhaps even romantic encounters.

In this chapter, we move beyond common stereotypes of phone sex work by examining workers' actual experiences. We focus on the specific ways in which telephone sex operators' identities both shape and are shaped by phone sex work. We are interested in examining how phone sex operators view themselves and their personal lives in relation to working in an occupation considered by many to be deviant.[5] Do they see themselves as "bad girls" involved in degrading work or do they have more positive views of their work?[6]

In his study of deviant subcultures, Becker[7] notes that members of such cultures use techniques such as secrecy, isolation, and self-segregation to maintain a positive self-image and to protect themselves from legal and social sanctions. In *Stigma,* Goffman[8] describes the methods by which deviant people strive to conceal or manage their "discredited" and "spoiled" identities. Our findings indicate that phone sex operators also employ several strategies to maintain self-esteem, to protect themselves and their families from social censure, and to keep future career options available. Finally, workers are aware of the distinction between "home" and "work" and use this distinction to help define their identities. Thus while modern society and modern technology have created a situation that for many has blurred the distinction between home and work,[9] most phone sex operators maintain very separate home and work identities. For instance, workers will adopt phone personae and false names that they do not use at home. Furthermore, most of the workers in our sample do not take phone sex calls at home. This helps the worker to distinguish the work self from the home self, the "stage" self from the "real" self.

METHODS

The study is based on interviews with twelve female phone sex operators[10] employed by a company owned by a former phone sex operator in an urban area of the United States. The sample was augmented with observations at the work site as well as with conversations with phone sex operators in other cities. The agency, Smart Girls Who Like Sex,[11] serves primarily male callers located throughout the country. The agency advertises its services through men's sex magazines and provides services via 800 and 900 numbers (for $3.99 per minute), and credit card, direct, and prepaid calls (for $1.99 per minute). Our initial contacts were made through personal acquaintances, and snowball sampling provided referrals for interviews, which were conducted between 1996 and 1998. Since our sample was not a random one, it may not be typical of all phone sex operators. Additionally, the male callers may not have been typical, since the advertisements for the agency stressed the education and intelligence of the phone sex operators. An advertisement for the agency appearing in one of numerous pornography magazines features a young white woman holding a telephone in one hand and a book in the other. She is bare-breasted and wearing a plaid skirt that is hiked up to reveal white lace panties. To fully communicate the phone sex operators' youth, sexiness, and intelligence, she is wearing lace socks, high heels, and glasses.

The study uses qualitative methods for a number of reasons. First, since access to sex workers is limited (due to the stigmatized nature of the profession), a large sample of workers is not available. A large sample would have been necessary for quantitative analysis of the data. Second, little research has been done on phone sex work, and thus there is a need for exploratory, qualitative investigation. Our study aims to give the workers a voice through in-depth interviews. Despite the upscale appearance of the agency and our modest sample of workers, the sparse existing work on phone sex workers[12] lends support to our basic findings.

We conducted interviews in a variety of settings, ranging from the respondent's home to the work site. Interview questions focused on why and how respondents entered phone sex work, their day-to-day experiences on the job, what they liked and disliked about the job, their views of the male callers, and whether phone sex work had affected their personal lives. Most of the interviews were tape recorded. Some respondents were interviewed more than once and some interviews were conducted over the phone, though the researchers had face-to-face contact with all respondents at least once.

THE AGENCY

Approximately forty workers are employed by the Smart Girls Who Like Sex agency, ranging in age from twenty-one to forty-five. Most of the operators work part-time, but several work up to forty hours per week. The agency rents a small basement office suite in an otherwise drab office building near a part-residential and part-warehouse section of the city. Since most of the requests for phone sex calls come in at night, work shifts are typically between 11 P.M. and 5 A.M., when seven operators at a time work in the office, and one or two may work on a scheduled or on-call basis from their homes. Visits to the agency revealed a typical office space, with a main reception desk containing the "caller list" (a binder with an estimated 13,000 names), file cabinets, a water cooler, microwave, and the agency's policies and procedures for receiving and verifying callers' credit card numbers. The office contained none of the pornographic fliers and posters seen by Flowers[13] in her phone sex research. The phone sex operators sit in small rooms with doors that may be closed but do not eliminate sound. One of the authors, for instance, heard Debbi speaking in a loud yet recognizable girlish voice, "Oh Daddy, I want your big cock inside my little pussy!" From the hallway outside the office, one could hear an operator screaming loudly in an approximation of having an orgasm. Like the phone sex company Flowers[14] worked for, security measures are stringent. The door to the building is kept locked, as is the door to the office inside it, twenty-four hours a day. Only employees are allowed into the office.

Although the agency presented itself as a telemarketing company, most of the other occupants of the building know or suspect it is a phone sex company. The people who work in the building are rude to the women coming in and out of their office. Chrissy said,

> Regardless of how quiet we try to be, they do know what we do. They are disrespectful to us. They leer; they jeer; they make comments. I don't even like going out of this office to go upstairs to get something to drink.

Other workers had varying opinions about the offices. Debbi in particular liked the anonymity of the office location in addition to the structure of the office phone-sex rooms:

> I like the way the office is set up. I don't have to do my calls in front of anybody. I'm over by myself. Guys say, "I bet you're at a table with a bunch of girls with phones." And I reply, "You'd be able to hear them, for one." I also like the security of it. I talk to people in other services, and they're not like that. To me, that would be very scary. To have some guy show up who thinks I'm into being beaten into a bloody pulp and being raped by twenty different guys. It would scare me for someone like that to find me.

Like most office workers, the phone sex operators gave their office homey touches. They put up personal decorations, copies of slogans and poems, vegetarian recipes, and even humorous artwork depicting their least favorite caller at the time (e.g., a little voodoo doll in a suit with a huge phallus). These personal touches indicate that, to some extent, the workers attempted to humanize the office.

IDENTITY CONSTRUCTION AND JOB SOCIALIZATION

Phone sex companies have difficulty recruiting and retaining employees. The women Flowers interviewed had worked at an average of three companies each.[15] Though our respondents reported fewer phone sex jobs, they had been employed in fairly short-term capacities. In our sample, no operator had been working for the agency longer than eighteen months.

Our respondents' educations ranged from high school graduates to college graduates, but none of them thought that she got her job due to her level of education. Typically the women found the job via an advertisement in the newspaper or through a referral by a friend or acquaintance who already worked for the agency. As a potential phone sex operator, each worker had to ask herself whether she could do the work. Would she be able to have phone sex with male callers, where the goal is the caller's orgasm? One worker, Heart, recalled:

> You had to be comfortable talking about sex. Obviously anyone with serious hang-ups wouldn't call for an interview—or they'd quit after the first weird call—which happened a lot. Some people just can't deal.

When asked why they decided to become phone sex operators, several workers told us they thought it would be fun, in addition to providing the income they needed. Chrissy said,

> I was going through a divorce. I had a real job because I do have a bachelor's degree, and I was burned out. So I quit that job ... and I saw this ad in the paper. And I thought, "Phone sex, ha ha. Oh my God, how funny. That would be really fun to do at night while I was looking for a better job."

Annette added that the setting or environment was as important as the type of work when considering employment with the agency:

> I always thought that it would be such a hoot, so much fun to do; and I'll do domination calls. Then I saw it in the newspaper.... The other job I went to was run by a man—a sleazy-looking fat guy with dead deer and knives all over the place. I decided there's no way I'm going over there. And also the girls at that place were a little more like what I thought phone sex girls would look like, you know, a little more white-trashy kind of girls. I thought, this place is sleazy.

Annette indicated that a sense of the agency's normalcy and integrity was important to her:

> Over here ... all the women look like normal, wholesome-looking women. This boss weeds for this. I don't think many places weed out to try to get smarter, more wholesome, and normal women.

Phone sex workers typically have not aspired to their career for years, nor do they typically have relatives involved in the sex industry. Our data suggest that women seeking phone sex work share the following: (1) they need money, (2) they see phone sex as their most lucrative option, and (3) they feel reasonably sure they would be comfortable discussing sex over the telephone.[16]

Another difference between socialization to conventional professional careers and phone sex work is the amount of formal training given to a worker. Most phone sex operators receive very little training.[17] The phone sex workers in our study were typically interviewed once by the employer and then immediately put to work. Almost all of the learning was on-the-job, and much of it was unsupervised. Heart noted:

> They just stick you by the phone and you talk. They probably give you an easy call. You just pick it up as you go, and you can talk to everyone else if you have questions.

Another worker, Spice, commented, "You're on your own.... The manager was there for the first call—that's it." Annette listened in on others' calls and learned from the other operators which words to use during a call. She said callers get turned off if operators use the word "penis" rather than the word "cock." To learn about possible scenarios with callers, Annette also purchased pornography magazines to learn phrases like "come on my face" and to incorporate them into her phone sex repertoire.

Most of the socialization was informal, and given that working hours were around the clock, many informants rarely saw the boss. Part of this informal socialization included talking with coworkers about working conditions, how to deal with problem callers, how work affected personal life, and future plans. In one spirited conversation, Spice gave Heart tips about the sexual preferences of certain callers, including methods to keep the caller on the phone for longer periods of time. Such professional exchanges are frequent at a phone sex office.[18]

None of the workers we interviewed envisioned phone sex work as a long-term job or career. Most had plans to return to school to complete college, obtain additional degrees, or move to another city and find work in "respectable" fields. For example, Hannah planned to continue with phone sex work only while she was in college, and Debbi stated,

> Do I see myself as a phone sex operator for the rest of my life? No, I do not. When I started this job I was not looking for my career goals. Maybe I'll do it for the next year or two if I can't find something better.

It may be tempting to view phone sex work as a route into the world of exotic dancing and prostitution, but our data and the available literature suggest that this is rare.[19] Only one worker in our sample reported being involved in other kinds of sex work.

IMPRESSION MANAGEMENT AND STIGMA

Every worker was aware that she was employed in a stigmatized occupation, and all reported being embarrassed at times by the nature of the work. When asked about the number one stereotype of phone sex operators, most respondents mentioned the notion that they are "sluts" in real life, willing to perform any sexual act with anybody. Several operators expressed contempt for callers who called the agency expecting the operators to act like "brainless bimbos" and were pleased when callers appreciated their intelligence or education.

The women had various strategies for telling others about their work. Many selectively revealed some but not other details about their work, and the details revealed varied by person. Elle noted that she was "more honest with her credit card company" than she was with her family about her job. Pepper noted that her brother, cousin, and close friends knew, but not the rest of her family or acquaintances. Chrissy said that telling her family would "rock their world":

> I just couldn't tell them. I have dreams sometimes that they find out because truly I have a lot of guilt over it, like, because of my upbringing. A lot of girls tell their parents; they don't care. I know a girl who does calls in front of her father.

Heart said that when asked about the nature of her employment she typically told people that she did "telemarketing." In fact, the agency manager would verify workers' cover stories. For instance if a woman stopped working at the agency and wrote on her résumé that she was employed in "sales," the manager would verify this story.

Concealing the nature of the work was often difficult. For instance, many workers did not want friends or family driving them to work. Even when concealment was not an issue, some women kept home and work entirely separate. Heart commented:

> When my car broke down I either didn't work or had to have a coworker pick me up. I could have taken calls at home but—even though she can't talk yet—I would have felt weird doing it with my daughter around.

Debbi feared that her identity would be revealed through the course of a call. She explained:

> What I like the least about my job is the fear that callers could identify me in some way. Once I got a call from a guy who dated one of my cousins. That was so weird.

And Star noted, "When friends visit and want to see where I work, I flip out."

Leading these "double lives" can be time consuming, stressful, and mentally exhausting. Spice, for instance, has told her family she is employed in telephone sales at a place where she formerly worked. She often reports worrying that she will slip and reveal the true nature of her work in an unguarded moment, or that she will forget the details of her story and be caught in a lie. The guilt of lying takes its own toll. Spice says she sometimes "feels really bad about the whole thing—my family is proud that I have a steady job and a good income, but a lot of it is a lie."

One turning point is when the worker reveals her job to a new significant other. Star commented:

> I don't do it at first—otherwise they either leave or get horny. I start the relationship and within a month or so, I feel trusting enough to open up about it. The guy usually asks a million questions and wants me to do it with him, which gets old fast.

Annette used disclosure to test her dates:

> If it's a man and you tell him you do phone sex, how they react is a good way to know whether or not you can go out with them. If they say, "Oh, give me a sample," then I think they're a pervert. I'm not gonna do it.

And Pepper noted:

> They're fine with it at first, because they think it means I'll be loose in bed, but after a while some of them just think I'm low class—not marriage material. I've got to weed them out earlier.

Most of the workers had unconventional relationships—not one was married, and several were divorced. Many had lovers who were either married or were seeing multiple partners, and only one was engaged at the time of the interview. Some were lesbian or bisexual. Given the nature of our data, it is difficult to determine whether the nature of the job precluded long-term monogamy or marriage or whether the job self-selected for candidates who preferred nonstandard romantic lives. As Mint put it:

> What's the guy gonna say, "Mom, Dad, let me introduce you to Mint. She's a phone sex worker, and we are going to get married"? My lover is a lawyer. What's he going to do, say to the [law firm] partners, "This is Mint. She's a phone sex worker, and we like to have phone sex from my office"? It's screwed up.

Being a phone sex worker is socially stigmatized, and each respondent invoked elaborate impression-management techniques to deal with this stigma. From renting apartments, to meeting new boyfriends or girlfriends, to applying for new jobs or to school, to fully disclosing the true nature of one's job, the workers soon realize that their work affects all aspects of their lives.

Maintaining Self-Esteem

Phone sex workers often feel as though they are degraded by persons who become aware of the work they do. One way of preserving their self-esteem is to distance themselves from women working in other sectors of the sex industry and, at times, other women doing phone sex.[20] Heart commented:

> We're not like those streetwalkers—crawling down the street in the middle of night in the middle of winter. We work in an office. I never touch a cock. I can't get a single disease. I can't get attacked. I'm not a prostitute. I can sit here, read a magazine and just moan occasionally … and still get paid. I don't have to wash my hair or wear makeup; I can wear jeans; I can eat on the job. I can even work at home if I want.

Mint added:

> I don't have sex. It's just pretend. I'm not like some escort girl, spreading my legs—this is more classy. Most of the job is just sitting around waiting for a call.

Another technique is to professionalize their work. Gretchen, for example, indicated it was important to respond appropriately to the agency's "professional and executive callers" by assuring their anonymity and responding to their upscale tastes. Our respondents also capitalized on the agency's name, which offered "smart girls." Workers also emphasized the demanding nature of the work. Star said,

> The worker must be open-minded, aware, and intelligent. And she must listen, listen, listen. A good phone sex worker finds something in common with the caller, even if it's small. She treats the caller like a person. She participates. It's 50 percent performance and 50 percent real.

Debbi, too, emphasized that the work is not mindless:

> It's a lot harder than you think it is. I think people think that we get on the phone and we moan and grunt and make coming sounds. Some of these calls are very challenging. Really! And that wears on you emotionally. I've worked hard jobs, and I've done difficult things before and never gone home as tired as I do from this job because of the mental exhaustion some days.... Well, we do a lot more than they give us credit for.

Workers also stressed the economic benefits of the job and sometimes acted as if anyone not involved in phone sex was missing a grand economic opportunity. Not only was the income good—$10–$15 per hour—but workers also received gifts from callers.

Thus, workers maintained self-esteem by distancing themselves from socially undesirable "hands-on" sex work and by embracing a socially desirable goal—namely, a stable job with a decent income, plus perks.

Male Callers and Worker Identity

One important aspect of the work was the influence of male callers on workers' self-perceptions and behavior. Callers had both negative and positive effects on the workers.[21]

On the positive side, several respondents said they obtained a new self-awareness by working as a phone sex operator. Hannah, for example, expressed a greater respect for herself and other women. Additionally, some workers reported that working in the business had made them more knowledgeable about and comfortable with their sexuality, both in fantasy and in real life. Heart commented:

> Sometimes I hear something from a caller that I've never tried before. It sounds cool. I ask the caller about it and then try it out with my real-life lover —sometimes my lover is like, "Where did you learn that?" I just laugh.

Star said,

> I used to be pretty shy. In my love life, I let the guy start everything. Now I'm in control. Some guys are even intimidated by me sexually. Phone sex

opened me up—the worst thing that can happen is the guy hangs up. Big deal. I felt comfortable experimenting with new things in fantasy and then tried the things I liked in real life.

Mint added:

Phone sex has made me more liberated. I got tied up by my boyfriend for the first time this weekend. It was great. I also want to try sex with another woman. I never would have thought about that before this job. Now I really want to experiment.

Worker self-esteem and job satisfaction may be increased by the actions of certain callers. Spice reported with great pride that when she returned from a vacation there were forty-two messages waiting for her from callers who specifically requested phone sex with her.

Another self-esteem booster is gifts. Flowers reports that phone sex agencies have ways for callers to mail the operators gifts, letters, and photographs.[22] Callers of the Smart Girls agency may send gifts to the workers through a post office box. The manager documents and photocopies or photographs gifts and letters for security purposes. Workers also sell panties to callers, which usually bring $25 to $50. Heart said, "Sometimes I wear them before I send them, usually I don't. I tell them I get them at Victoria's Secret, but I just get them from Sears." Workers have received flowers, candy, and cash ($100 is common). Spice showed an engagement ring a caller had sent her (his real-life engagement did not work out) along with the appraisal form; the ring was valued at about $4,000. Another worker received a new stereo system.

Positive experiences with callers were mentioned less frequently, however, than negative experiences. As in Flowers'[23] study, callers with interests in rape fantasies, other violent sex, bestiality, and incest were common. Most of the respondents had negative feelings about these calls, and they had much latitude in accepting or refusing calls. The operators at this agency are provided a list of the types of calls they can refuse. Examples include calls referred to as "children calls, anal calls, animal calls, domination calls, rape calls, etc." And although the operators are not supposed to criticize callers during a phone sex call, many of the respondents engage in what could be considered insidious "acts of resistance" against objectionable callers. Olga attempted to discourage callers from requesting distasteful fantasies, while Hannah simply refused calls involving torture or mutilation or children. Regarding a particular caller who had been requesting dismemberment fantasies from several of the operators, Spice said,

I hate "Mr. Mutilation." Wants to cut my head off. He's big into kidnapping, dungeons. He says it's not real and that he is just curious. I don't know. I hate it, but at least I figure if he is talking to me he is not out there really doing it.

Chrissy uses a "good touch–bad touch" response during her "little girl" calls to demonstrate the wrongfulness of adult sexual contact with children. When a caller says to her, "You know I'm going to touch you," she responds with a high-pitched voice, "My mommy taught me about good touch and bad touch. That's bad touch, and I'm going to tell my mommy."

Some of the other workers viewed this aspect of their work as "community service," meaning that they hoped to send a message to callers that certain sexual fantasies and practices were unacceptable or immoral, such as sex with children and animals and physical and sexual violence against women.

Another type of community service involves instructing callers that a real phone sex operator does not match the stereotype of a brainless, sex-crazed woman masturbating during the call. Some of the respondents believed they are educating men about women and female sexuality. Annette wanted men to care about women's bodies and women's pleasure:

If the guy doesn't care about female orgasm, if the guy says he doesn't like to eat pussy … that probably gets me more than anything does. I go on with these guys, "Do you know that the clitoris is like the sexual counterpart of the male blah blah blah…?" So many callers could [sic] care less about female orgasms.

Many workers reported that they lost respect for men as a result of the job. While workers reported with pride that doctors and lawyers called the line, they noted that a lot of callers were "pathetic" and "losers." Pepper noted that prison inmates tried to make collect calls all the time. Spice said there were a lot of "pussy boys" and "whiners" who were passive and complainers. At the same time, she reported that many callers were "nice, sweet, sensitive guys who were lonely, desperate, or shy."

Clearly, phone sex workers felt that the callers influenced their lives—not just financially, but also in terms of how they viewed their own real-life relationships, and how they viewed men in general. Workers tended to report an improvement in their own sexual lives (though they noted obstacles to forming new, or long-lasting romantic relationships due to the stigmatized nature of the job), but also a distaste for the men's frequent interest in rape, incest, pedophilia, and bestiality. Workers also viewed as "idiotic" callers who phone when children, a spouse, or an employer is nearby, or who call excessively, such as the basketball coach whose wife divorced him over a $10,000 phone sex habit. Workers tended to feel that the men were "putty in [their] hands," and this perception bolstered their self-esteem and empowered some women. Pepper said, "I used to get trampled over by men. Now I know they're just stupid."

SUMMARY AND CONCLUSIONS

This analysis of the world of phone sex points to several important findings. First, phone sex workers have developed sophisticated methods of impression management. Being in a stigmatized profession, the workers have learned techniques to conceal or misrepresent the nature of their employment to family, friends, and new employers who may disapprove of the nature of the work. These methods include lying, maintaining friendships with others in deviant subcultures (who might aid in corroborating cover stories), and maintaining clear boundaries between home and work.

Second, this study notes the particular ways in which workers are able to maintain self-esteem while working in a deviant job. One way in which phone sex operators reconcile their work with their identity is to view the job in exclusively economic terms. Thus the women may note that though the job may be at times distasteful, the pay is excellent, the hours are flexible, and there are other benefits, such as gifts. Another way self-esteem is maintained is for the worker to distance herself from other types of sex workers, who have physical contact with customers and who risk AIDS, beatings, and arrest. The phone sex operator frequently notes that no "real" sex ever occurs.

Third, this research sheds light on workers' perceptions of the callers and the callers' treatment of the workers. A number of women were disturbed by the violence and degradation in some of the men's calls—fantasies that include rape, dismemberment or mutilation, sex with animals, and child molestation. As in other forms of sex work, even longtime workers report days in which a particular man has said or done something troubling to the worker. The workers report having learned much about the nature of male sexuality, in terms of fantasies and insecurities. These types of calls are frequently noted as a negative aspect of the workplace and are often a challenge to the worker's willingness to do the job. Callers are often perceived as "idiotic," "silly," "typically male," or as completely enslaved to their sexual desires. While most callers are viewed negatively, occasionally a worker will experience a caller who has had a positive effect upon her. Being called by doctors, lawyers, business executives, and professors can help to reinforce a worker's identity as a skilled, talented employee, as well as a person who is valued by powerful, educated, and wealthy people.

Finally, the fact that at this agency all of the workers and the boss are women had a powerful effect on the employees. In an occupation in which employees are frequently subjected to degrading male comments, the opportunity to work in an all-female environment was viewed positively. The workers benefit from the bonding and support they receive from their co-workers at the agency, and they view the company owner as a role model—a strong, intelligent woman who has created a successful business in a male-dominated world. Several workers reported they have learned more about the ways a business works, and that they aspire to run their own business someday. Still others said they are treated with respect by the owner and could never again work for a male boss. These working conditions, coupled with the financial rewards of the job, present a challenge to the theorists who argue that sex work is inherently oppressive and demeaning to the workers.

GAY MALE VIDEO PORNOGRAPHY: PAST, PRESENT, AND FUTURE

Joe A. Thomas

Though gay porn makes up a disproportionately large segment of the pornography market (by some estimates one-third to one-half of the $2.5 billion adult industry is gay sales and rentals)[1], it has generally been neglected in the fierce debate over pornography during the past two decades. Perhaps the fact that the debate has largely been driven by feminist claims about pornography's exploitation of women has led to gay pornography's neglect. Yet our understanding of pornography cannot be defined solely in heterosexual terms, and an analysis of gay pornography may help to expand our knowledge of pornography in general.

What distinguishes pornography from other types of expression is its primary goal of sexual stimulation. Richard Dyer has noted that the goal of the pornographic narrative itself is sexual climax;[2] there is a parallel between the activities depicted and the activities they are intended to inspire. Pornography, as opposed to other forms of sexual representation, is recognized by both its creators and its consumers as an instrument of sexual arousal. Such sexually explicit material has a long history, dating back to prehistoric images of stylized male and female deities and continuing through classical antiquity, but despite pornography's Greek etymology, its current classification as a media genre began during the nineteenth century. While the content of pornography has usually reflected the heterosexual orientation of the dominant culture, same-sex imagery and narratives have always found a place in the history of erotic expression. In the last twenty years gay porn has developed into a significant force in the pornography industry and in gay cultural life.

Understanding the history of gay porn in film and video is vital for understanding the gay video phenomenon of today. Many of its unique qualities (as well as those that it shares with straight porn) can be explained by tracing the stylistic and iconographic evolution of the gay porn film. In many respects the development and growth of gay porn mirrors the political ascendancy of gays and lesbians. As the struggle for gay liberation expanded and gained a higher profile during the 1970s, so did the gay segment of the pornography industry. Similarly, the belated adoption of condom usage in gay films reflected the advent of AIDS in the 1980s. Gay porn also expressed changing gay cultural ideals of masculinity and beauty. Ultimately, because the sexual activity that is depicted in gay porn represents the basic difference that creates the homosexual identity, gay porn's popularity can be seen as an important affirmation of gay life and culture.

This chapter focuses on the history, production, and content of gay male video pornography. Video is chosen because it is the most popular and prominent pornographic medium in the gay subculture. Most print magazines in the past two decades have assumed a supporting role to video, commonly featuring layouts of video performers, or even stills taken from videos.[3] Many magazines—such as *Skinflicks* or *Unzipped*—focus overtly and exclusively on videos in both their imagery and their content (featuring video reviews and interviews with industry luminaries). The contemporary gay pornography industry thus centers around live-action features.

This chapter is based on an extensive review of the literature on gay pornography and my analysis of a number of videos produced in the 1970s, 1980s, and 1990s. Part of this study focuses on the historical development and stylistic evolution of the videos. It also examines the culture that has developed around the production of gay videos, as well as the distinguishing characteristics of gay video and its role in gay culture.

HISTORY

With the advent of the motion picture in the late nineteenth century, pornographers immediately seized the opportunity to utilize this new medium. While explicit heterosexual films were made in the 1890s, the earliest surviving filmed depictions of gay sex date back to the 1920s. Al di Lauro and Gerald Rabkin mentioned incidental homosexual relations in two heterosexually oriented French films: *The Chiropodist* and *Je Verbalise*.[4] Thomas Waugh's research showed that about 8 percent of surviving stag films contained some sort of gay content, usually in a bisexual context.[5] The first known exclusively gay stag film was *Three Comrades* from the 1950s. This short film concluded its three-way male action with an intertitle proclaiming, "Aw Shit. I'm Disgusted. So Let us Quit," leading one to wonder if it might be intended not for a gay audience, but as a bit of exotic slumming for the stag's usual male heterosexual viewers.[6]

During the 1960s, gay sex films were largely limited to soft-core posing and wrestling movies made for home projection, along the same lines as the older stags. However, the number of sexually explicit films did increase in the decade; Thomas Waugh has documented about one hundred explicit all-male stag films from the 1960s, (in contrast to a handful from earlier years),[7] but most of these were amateurish at best.

Gay subjects did not, however, share in the surge of popular "sexploitation" films characteristic of the 1960s. Instead, while straight viewers were subjected to an onslaught of "nudie" and "nudie-cutie" films from prolific producers such as David Friedman, gay viewers found their own tastes reflected in the more rarefied air of underground art films. Many of the prominent underground filmmakers in New York in the early 1960s were gay (Kenneth Anger and Andy Warhol), and their avant-garde works, while generally nonnarrative, often contained suggestive or overtly homosexual content. Anger's *Scorpio Rising* (1963) was a dreamlike, impressionistic, homoerotic montage involving a motorcycle gang; Warhol's *My Hustler* (1965) told the story of two bitchy queens who fought over a handsome young prostitute. What made these rather esoteric art films appealing to a gay audience was their open representation of the eroticized male body presented within the relatively safe (for closeted gay viewers) context of avant-garde art. And according to Richard Dyer, the precedent of such avant-garde underground films often provided important formal and narrative models during the early days of gay porn in the 1970s.[8]

Developments in jurisprudence also contributed to the growth of gay pornography. John d'Emilio and Estelle Freedman have explained how a series of U.S. Supreme Court rulings between 1957 and 1967 helped to open the floodgates for increasingly explicit sex movies. The famous *Roth v. United States* case of 1957, which sustained the conviction of a bookdealer for selling pornography, paradoxically cracked open the door for more explicit materials by proclaiming that "sex and obscenity are not synonymous." By 1967, the infamous book *Fanny Hill* was found not to be obscene because it was not "*utterly* without redeeming social value."[9] Although these two court decisions laid the initial framework, the early-1970s explosion in sex films was likely triggered by the Supreme Court victory of the Swedish film *I Am Curious (Yellow)* in 1969; a startling number of erotic film festivals followed.[10] A simultaneous growth in eroticism in mainstream media was exemplified by Hollywood productions such as *Midnight Cowboy*, which chronicled the story of a male prostitute; as Hollywood moved into new sexual territory, the sex film industry moved from cheap stags to more lavish and explicit productions. Waugh has attributed the increased production and quality of cinematic porn to the newly liberalized legal environment created by the court decisions of 1969–70, which made it possible for cinematic professionals to enter the industry, thereby creating not only a better product, but broader distribution.[11]

John Burger has traced commercial exhibition of hard-core gay sex films in cinemas to at least as early as 1968, when the Park Theater in Los Angeles began screening the features of pioneering filmmakers Pat Rocco (*Sex and the Single Gay*) and Bob Mizer (the creator of the famous Athletic Model Guild porn production company), along with the avant-garde underground films of Kenneth Anger and Jean Cocteau.[12] However, the climax of pornography's rise as a popular phenomenon was reached in the early 1970s, most obviously characterized by the unexpected popularity of the hit movie *Deep Throat*. Made in six days for $24,000, it opened in June of 1972 in New York City and grossed $33,033 its first week. In a significant change from earlier sexploitation movies, *Deep Throat* was reviewed by all the famous movie critics: Judith Crist, Vincent Canby, Andrew Sarris, and others. By the end of 1973, it was among the top ten moneymaking films of the year.[13]

Ironically, even as pornography became more explicit and *Deep Throat* heralded the arrival of "porno chic," new court decisions during the decade allowing "local standards" to be used for judging obscenity contributed to the decline of porn's popular appeal and availability and to pornography's eventual retreat from mainstream culture. The "X" ratings of Hollywood productions of the 1960s soon came to be seen as highly undesirable for mainstream films, but were a badge of honor for the newly emerging porn films. The adult film industry began labeling its products "XXX," as if its hard-core content deserved more than just the single "X" of earlier years.

Deep Throat's emergence as a hugely popular hard-core phenomenon actually followed the earlier example of the first widely distributed, hard-core gay release: *The Boys in the Sand*. While its potential audience was naturally smaller, it nevertheless grossed $800,000 shortly after opening in December 1971 in New York at the 55th Street Playhouse; and with a production cost of only $8,000,[14] this film was the gay prelude to the straight porno chic of the following two years. Directed by Wakefield Poole, it starred soon-to-be gay superstar Casey Donovan, also known as the professional actor and model Cal Culver. Vaguely episodic, the movie had a dreamlike quality that betrays the influence of the earlier underground films of the 1960s.

The Boys in the Sand showed the enormous market potential of gay porn. Wakefield Poole followed up on his successful first feature with *Bijou* (1972), a moody, lyrical exploration of a "straight" man's discovery of gay sex. This film used many of the technical tricks of the art films and demonstrated well the intimate connections between underground films and the early days of gay porn.

The production of gay porn films continued to expand during the 1970s. Companies such as Jaguar and P.M. Productions began producing a stream of hard-core features for release in a limited number of gay porn theaters. As the industry diversified, it also became more commercialized than before. Gay porn lost its early formal references to art films and its occasional aspirations to being something more than "just pornography." In many ways it converged with straight pornography. Both genres began to minimize narrative and aesthetic content in favor of increased explicitness.

By 1981 there were 20,000 adult bookstores and 800 sex cinemas in the United States.[15] However, the proliferation of home VCRs during the following decade made video pornography readily accessible, and video soon became the primary medium for pornography. As prices of home VCRs fell during the 1980s, the market became increasingly lucrative and producers began shooting films directly on video, aimed at the domestic market of home viewers. More VCRs led to more videos and more viewers.

Gay porn soon made the transition into the video age of the 1980s. Initially gay porn videos were collections of the earlier short films or video versions of hard-core features. Anthologies such as the Falcon Videopacs brought together some of the popular, usually silent, short features from the 1970s and early 1980s. Whereas many early-1970s films were made on a shoestring budget by semiprofessionals, in the 1980s the well-funded producers and distributors of straight pornography took a role in gay porn as well. Gay porn companies such as Vivid or HIS were subsidiaries or divisions of large straight-porn manufacturers. By the mid-1980s features shot directly on video were the standard; simultaneously, the old gay porn theaters (and their straight counterparts) largely disappeared.

The pioneering early-1970s gay porn films often used whatever models were available. The typical work from P.M. Productions, for instance, featured a couple of handsome stars (such as Eric Ryan or Jack Wrangler) in a cast of average-looking, even homely amateurs. Later in the decade, companies such as Colt produced a few silent shorts with especially handsome, beefy men (which became their specialty), but most of the decade's production suffered from man-on-the-street casting—a definite problem when representing sexual fantasies for an audience of gay men highly attuned to particular standards of physical beauty.

Gay videos of the 1980s were dominated by exceptionally young performers, smooth and sleek, in contrast to the everyman of average 1970s films, or the bodybuilders of Colt. The performers' body hair was minimal, the "swimmer's build" predominated, and models' ages never seemed to exceed twenty-two or twenty-three. Youth was at a premium. Directors William Higgins and Matt Sterling set the standard for the new 1980s gay porn model. Higgins's work, ranging from *Sailor in the Wild* in 1983 to *Big Guns* in 1987, epitomized this change from the gay porn of the 1970s. Higgins's films generally starred a cast of slightly built, smooth-skinned, youthful men with an occasional muscular, mature performer. Matt Sterling's work, such as 1984's *The Bigger The Better,* also starred boyish performers but with more emphasis on muscularity. The change to younger models was seen in print pornography as well. David Duncan's analysis showed that during the 1980s more than 90 percent of the oldest models appeared to be only in their teens or twenties; in the early 1970s almost half had appeared thirty or older.[16]

Videos of the 1980s also tightly defined actors' sexual roles as "tops" or "bottoms." The top was the insertor in anal sex, and the bottom was the recipient. The top might occasionally engage in a little oral sex with his partner, but that was not typical. John Summers' *Two Handfuls* is a good example, as Brian Maxon is serviced by three different men, but hardly lifts a finger himself until the final scene. One could usually predict what roles the performers would play only a few seconds into the scene. The top was usually the more muscular, tan, and athletic of the two; he also had the bigger penis. Exclusive tops held a privileged position both within the industry and in the narrative of the video;[17] most of the major porn stars of the 1980s were exclusive tops.

One would think that a medium that flouted societal taboos about sexuality would itself be less subject to taboos. Instead, both gay and straight pornography is bound by unwritten rules of representation. Restrictive sexual roles (e.g., tops and bottoms, often determined by physical type) are only one aspect of pornography's strange dedication to tradition. The "cum shot" is another necessity. The unspoken rule would seem to read, "No male may climax out of view of the camera. The ejaculate must be clearly visible, and preferably land on the body of his partner." Yet another rule is, "Any third party who discovers a couple having sex must immediately disrobe and join in."

CONTEMPORARY GAY VIDEO PORNOGRAPHY

Despite lingering stylistic conventions, during the early 1990s the industry changed in certain respects. The performers no longer all looked alike; the image of the Calvin Klein underwear ad was no longer the single canonical standard of beauty in gay pornography. Moreover, production values seemed to have improved, especially editing. For instance, in productions from reputable studios viewers were no longer subjected to a six-minute, continuous close-up of anal sex. Lighting became more sophisticated; and following the lead of straight porn, exotic and more expensive locales began to crop up, such as Hawaii in *The Man With the Golden Rod* (1991).

The trend toward professional refinement in videos was largely due to the arrival in the late 1980s of former performer Kristen Bjorn into porn production. Bjorn's work possessed an unusually distinctive, signature style. He was said to film everything himself, without a crew, and to spend days or weeks shooting each feature[18] (when most of the industry considered a two-day shoot an extravagance). His longer shooting schedule enabled him to create the illusion that his performers were multi-orgasmic, sometimes climaxing as many as five times in one scene. He was also the master of the "handless cumshot": capturing images of performers ejaculating profusely, seemingly from sheer sexual excitement, without masturbating or being touched by anyone else during orgasm. Each film focused on an exotic locale with exotic men. Early works such as *Carnaval in Rio* (1989) and *Island Fever* (1989) were shot in Brazil; later videos moved to the beaches of Australia, the forests of Canada, and the newly accessible cities of eastern Europe. More often than in straight films, gay porn was usually racially segregated into all-black and (more commonly) all-white features. Bjorn broke decisively with this convention, using attractive men of various races and ethnicities, and especially mixed-race performers. The success of Bjorn's videos proved that there was a market for racially integrated gay pornography.

Bjorn's high production values threw down the gauntlet for the rest of the industry and set a new, higher technical standard. As a former still photographer,[19] Bjorn carefully framed every scene, using props extensively. Combined with his carefully chosen sets and locations, his meticulous productions resulted in lush, visually striking videos that consistently have been among the most popular rentals reported by video outlets. As a result of Bjorn's efforts, production values, especially photography and editing, improved immensely across the industry as other producers attempted to keep up and compete with him. Of course, a lot of low-quality videos were still produced, but high-end studios generally paid more attention to lighting, casting, and cinematography than in previous years.

Other unexpected changes took place in the casting of videos in the 1990s. In most top-of-the-line productions (often from Catalina or Falcon), the actors were more professional and actually seemed to enjoy their work.

They represented a much broader range of ages and body types than in the 1980s. Although young performers were still frequently seen, it was no longer uncommon to find performers in their thirties and even early forties. Realtor Cole Tucker began appearing in videos in 1996 at forty-three.[20] Body hair began to make a major reappearance with the success of models such as Zak Spears and Steve Regis.

In their performances many actors of the nineties were sexually versatile, overturning the porn conventions of the 1980s. Superstars of the 1980s were nearly always tops; the most famous performer of the decade, Jeff Stryker, never bottomed, and almost never performed oral sex. Rarely did an actor change his role from one feature to another, and almost never in the same scene.[21] In the late 1990s, however, many videos from Falcon (the largest producer of gay porn) as well as from most other companies, contained at least one scene with mutual anal sex (Falcon's 1998 release *Current Affairs* being just one example).

Similarly, sexual "types" in general were less pronounced in the 1990s videos. A big bruiser like Steve Regis surprisingly turned out to be primarily a bottom. The late bodybuilder Steve Fox usually bottomed as well, defying the 1980s stereotypes of "bigger build on top." Even the straight "trade" tops of recent years (such as Ty Fox and Ken Ryker) actually were active participants in sex, even giving oral sex to their partners before proceeding to their standard top roles in anal sex. In *Playing with Fire* (1996) Fox did everything except passive anal sex, including kissing; the same goes for Ryker in *Matinee Idol* (1996). More tops in the 1990s actually seemed to be gay men as opposed to "gay for pay"—for instance, Brad Hunt or Aidan Shaw. These two were never penetrated on camera, but performed their roles with relish, kissing, sucking, and doing everything else short of anal penetration. Shaw has had a subsequent successful career as a writer and has vocally self-identified as gay both in interviews and in his writing.

Another 1990s development was the vast increase in foreplay, kissing, caressing, and frottage. In the 1980s performers dropped their drawers and went straight for the dicks. With some notable exceptions 1980s videos showed little kissing or affection. Actors in the 1990s commonly kissed even before removing their clothes, and kissing frequently continued throughout the scene. Both Kristen Bjorn and Falcon Productions have been notable in this regard. In fact, the extensive kissing would seem to distinguish gay porn from straight porn, which has rarely focused on such romantic content. Gay porn actors of the 1990s also seemed more interested in each other's bodies than before. A scene with Steve Regis and Ace Harden in *Club Sexaholics* (1996) was a good example, as these two men kissed and caressed each other's bodies before proceeding to have sex.

Safer sex standards have also been established in the industry since the 1980s. In 1988 condom usage began to appear in gay videos, but only sporadically.[22] However, because of growing AIDS activism in the late 1980s, by the early 1990s most actors consistently used condoms in anal sex scenes (although not in oral sex). The gay adult film industry is far ahead of heterosexual pornography in this regard. Only in 1998 did the straight industry begin to consider condom usage instead of relying on periodic HIV testing, and then only in response to several performers' seroconversions.

Plot and acting have rarely played an important role in video pornography. However, increased production values (perhaps due to the higher revenues that have come with videos' increasing popularity as well as to consumer demand for higher quality videos) have resulted in an emergent sense of style. For example, *The Other Side of Aspen 3* (1995), contained an unusual scene that exemplified the new stylishness in gay videos. Two men had sex in a car in a scene filmed in near-darkness without bright lights or explicit close-ups. The realism of the dark, cramped quarters and quick, frantic copulation lent a stylish sense of voyeurism to the video.

Producers experimented with new subjects in the 1990s. *Bad Boys' Ball* (1995) was a well-directed documentary that combined interviews with performers along with scenes from their stage act as they put on an X-rated strip show in London. Another video, *Master Strokes* (1996), took the form of an anthology, with several directors (including Bjorn) filming soft-core vignettes that were directly inspired by the gay pornography of the 1950s and 1960s, and including narration and collages of vintage images.

What caused these recent changes in porn videos' style and content? I would argue that in this case, art imitates life: Changes in video porn reflected a changing gay identity. As the AIDS crisis brought together divergent parts of gay culture, the rise of queer radicalism brought a renewed openness to diversity and a recognition of the value of difference. One of the tenets of the early-1980s radical group Queer Nation was the recognition of diversity within the gay community. The increasing consciousness of diversity seemed to be reflected in the new range of ages, ethnicities, and physical types within porn videos in the 1990s.

A sort of mini sexual revolution took place as well. During the late 1980s and 1990s sex and sexual orientation were scrutinized from new perspectives by a diverse range of scholars from Judith Butler to Camille Paglia. Paglia's ideas about the sexualized nature of Western culture[23] were popularized through extensive media attention. The popular columnist Susie Bright launched a lively media campaign against sexual repression. In articles and books[24] she promoted the open enjoyment of pornography, sex toys, and kinky sex, and discouraged and ridiculed sexual stereotyping of any kind. Pat Califia issued collections of her own question-and-answer columns[25] in which she, a butch lesbian, forthrightly answered the technical and emotional sex questions of America's gay men. These popular authors were part of a new sexual liberation that celebrated diversity, openness, and sexual pleasure. This new attitude was also reflected in the loosening of conventions in video porn.

THE CONTEMPORARY GAY VIDEO INDUSTRY

Video pornography's explosion in popularity in the 1990s (with the production of between fifty and seventy videos a month)[26] included the birth of a complex, interactive subculture of industry players and fans: an array of celebrity directors such as drag queen Chi Chi Larue and Falcon director John Rutherford (who has a college degree in film production); influential critics such as Mickey Skee, who has written a variety of books on the industry as well as numerous reviews; a variety of industry magazines and Internet Web sites; and a vast number of popular performers who made profitable appearances as featured strip acts in gay clubs. Some also worked as professional escorts (the commonly used euphemism for male prostitutes).

Among the many directors of the 1990s, Chi Chi Larue (perhaps the heir apparent to the incomparable drag queen Divine) was a prolific director who has worked for many of the major studios. A drag queen originally from Minnesota, Larue appeared on the porn scene in the late 1980s and quickly rose to *auteur* status while amassing a prolific and respectable body of work. Larue freely incorporated drag into his public persona, appearing with his considerable retinue of buff performers as the emcee during their club dates. Larue gained remarkable influence as one of the few directors who consistently worked with a variety of the top gay porn production companies. While the quality of his work remained somewhat uneven, at his best Larue was one of the premier producers of hard-core gay porn. Being a drag queen, Chi Chi had a flair for camp that showed in his popularity with gay actors. As he put it, "I just happen to be a drag queen in my private life, which I've brought out and made more visible. I've turned myself into a personality that goes along with directing these movies."[27] In interviews some performers have credited him with creating a new respect and consideration for actors on the set[28] that seems to have extended beyond his own productions. Not coincidentally, Chi Chi came on the scene in the late 1980s, as major changes were taking place in the industry.[29] Gino Colbert, for instance, had by that time become a major director of epic gay porn videos notable for their elaborate plots, high production values, and emphasis on acting.

Gay print pornography focused on the stars of videos, but so did the rest of the gay media. Popular gay men's magazines such as *Genre* have featured interviews with gay performers such as Ken Ryker.[30] The most popular gay magazine, *Out*, has featured several articles on the porn industry,[31] as has its rival, *The Advocate*. *The Advocate* is an interesting case. Dating back to the beginning of the gay movement in the early 1970s it long included—along with news and editorials—various sex advertisements and columns, including splashy ads for pornographic movie and video releases. In 1993, in an attempt to become more like its glossy new rival, *Out*, *The Advocate* relegated its potentially controversial material to a new publication, *Advocate Classifieds*, which included the sexually oriented commercial and classified ads as well as sex columns and a sprinkling of nudes and sex stories. Dave Kinnick, who worked in video production, wrote a biweekly column for *Advocate Classifieds* as well as numerous interviews with performers.[32] The presence of Kinnick's column was clearly a sign of the acceptance of porn videos as a staple of the gay erotic diet. He was later replaced by a series of other columnists who continued his porn gossip column. *Advocate Classifieds* has since evolved into *Unzipped,* the most widely circulated magazine focusing on the gay porn industry, replete with gossip columns, interviews, pictorials, video reviews, and other features. Many local gay periodicals also began to run video review columns, usually humorous and tongue-in-cheek. Most prominent among these was the biweekly "Rick and Dave's Excellent Video Review" in the free L.A. gay magazine *Frontiers*. The gay porn industry even developed its own awards shows, which were reported on in the numerous industry magazines such as *Starz* and *Skinflicks*. The two most prominent among these shows were the *Gay Video Guide*'s Gay Erotic Video Awards (GEVA) and the Gay Adult Video News Awards (GAVN), sponsored by the adult film industry's primary professional publication, *Adult Video News*. The GEVA prizes were chosen by video critics and a celebrity panel, the GAVN awards by an international panel of gay judges.[33]

Actors making the dance circuit in the nation's gay bars became an integral part of the gay porn industry—and a major boost to performers' incomes. Go-go boys had been around for years, but in the late 1980s, following the lead of the popular Chippendale's dancers for women, roving troupes of muscular male dancers began making the circuits of America's gay bars. Most bars seemed to have dancers on the menu at least once a week by the early 1990s.[34] These dancing boys represented the same peak of physical perfection that one found in contemporaneous videos. In the 1990s many gay porn performers used their video work primarily as a means to make a name for themselves to obtain work on the dance circuit in gay bars, where they could make much more money.[35]

Additional work was necessary because working in gay sex films did not pay a living wage. Pay varied tremendously depending on the popularity and experience of the performer and the company and kind of work they were expected to do. Performers generally were paid by the scene; the per-scene rate ranged from about $500 to $2,000.[36] Tops usually were paid more than bottoms because, as in the straight porn industry, reliable erections were a scarce commodity. There were no fringe benefits such as medical insurance.

Many gay porn performers pursued careers or had jobs outside the industry. The magazine *Unzipped* published an article on performers' "day jobs," which included Realtor, hotel clerk, personal trainer, financial consultant, and registered nurse.[37] However, prostitution was not uncommon as a means of supplementing a performer's income. Indeed, for many, "escorting" was their primary source of income.[38] According to porn star Blue Blake, as an escort he made "more money than God."[39] Magazines such as *Unzipped* (national) and *Frontiers* (southern California) contained hundreds of ads for escorts, which often included pictures of the "product." Many ads made note that the advertiser was a "porn star" or "former porn star" or "Colt model." Thus the videos became an important means of building a market for their escort services. With an average charge of $250 per hour, this could be a much more profitable occupation than working in videos. In fact, escorting is so intimately involved with the pornography industry that the largest online discussion boards on gay porn include an entire section on "Sex with Pornstars, Escorts, Etc."[40] Here, men could exchange information and recommendations about male prostitutes (always referred to as escorts) both in and out of the pornography industry.

The gay porn industry had important parallels with and differences from straight porn. The two branches of the industry saw similar growth during the expansion of the video market in the 1980s. Both gay and straight porn had a well-developed "star system" in which certain popular performers received higher salaries and better working conditions. Both segments of the industry were also geographically centered in Los Angeles, and used the same sound stages in some instances. Some performers even crossed over between genres: Straight male performers occasionally performed masturbation scenes in gay videos, and female performers such as Sharon Kane had frequent cameos or nonsexual roles. Gay videos joined in the straight industry's boom in "niche" videos. These videos included such specialized genres as amateur, wrestling, transsexual, bondage, and others. Longtime straight-porn performer Nina

Hartley has maintained that the development of highly specialized niche-market videos was the most dramatic new development in adult films of the 1990s.[41]

In straight videos, however, women are always the primary focus. Men are purely supporting characters. The box covers always feature women; the male may be represented by a cropped body and a penis, if that. Men's subordinate roles in straight porn (and their correspondingly lower salaries) have occasionally led male performers to turn to gay videos. Another important difference between the gay and straight video industries was the lack of a gay market for "soft-core." Many straight videos were released in two versions: a hard-core version for the home video market and a soft-core version for adult cable television channels. Gay videos have been scarce in the lucrative cable market, although a few studios do occasionally make soft-core versions of major gay features. Some companies, such as the now-defunct Greenwood Cooper, focused exclusively on soft-core, which included nudity and sometimes physical contact, but no penetration.

Who watches gay porn videos? Statistical studies are scarce, but judging from its prominence in gay media and entertainment, viewership in the gay community appears to be quite high. Even in 1979, when print pornography was the main form of pornographic expression, one informal survey found that more than 50 percent of 1,038 gay male respondents said that they sometimes used pornography for sexual stimulation.[42] When *Frontiers* magazine held a survey of its readers in 1997, about one-quarter said they watched porn videos once a month, and about 15 percent viewed them once a week. About half viewed porn with others, and the other half alone. Almost half claimed to use porn as a prelude to having sex. When asked about their thoughts while viewing porn, almost 30 percent imagined having sex with the performers. A much smaller group imagined being the performers, and another 25 percent imagined both.[43]

SIGNIFICANCE

In many ways gay porn has become a microcosm of contemporary gay life. With its improved production values and increased diversity it reflects changes in attitudes and lifestyle in the gay community. Porn also plays an important role in the social and cultural life of gay America.

A major difference between gay and straight pornography is that gay porn is thoroughly integrated into gay life, whereas straight porn is considered deviant and stigmatized by the mainstream heterosexual world. Porn has always held a more exalted (and accepted) position in gay culture than in straight; as sexual outlaws, gays were less concerned about being called perverts. As Michael Bronski pointed out, straight culture generally considers pornography to be highly dangerous, and gay pornography doubly so.[44] Despite the changes wrought by the sexual revolution, mainstream America remained highly discomfited by the open display of sexuality, even heterosexuality. What better way to assert a gay identity than by the open, casual acceptance and celebration of homophobically dreaded sex acts? The omnipresence of sexual imagery in gay media—even beyond pornography—has been explained as a way for gays to create a "positive definition" for themselves.[45] Charles Isherwood has written that porn came "out of the closet" in the late 1980s in conjunction with a politicization of the gay community that found a vehicle in groups such as ACT-UP; thus porn became a personal assertion of gay identity.[46] Heterosexual society's continued discomfort with sexuality in general and pornography in particular meant that gay men's casual acceptance of pornography provided another tool for thwarting the norms of the dominant culture. The celebration of pornography confronted straight culture head-on with one of its most dreaded repressions.

In the gay community, video porn has become as common and quotidian as bar-hopping. Or, as Bradley Moseley-Williams put it, "That pornography is so accepted in the gay community that we are almost blasé about it, is a cliché."[47] Along Santa Monica Boulevard in West Hollywood, a predominantly gay neighborhood in Los Angeles, a large billboard was twice used to advertise newly released porn films: for *Idol in the Sky,* superstar Ryan Idol's last movie, and later for *Ryker's Revenge,* the comeback film for the popular early 1990s star Ken Ryker. Porn star Tome Chase's image graced two billboard advertisements for an adult video store in the gay quarter of Houston in 1998. Such public advertisements are hard to imagine for a straight video outside of the immediate vicinity of a porn store.

While straight porn long ago lost the chic appeal it had had with early hits such as *Deep Throat* (1972) and *Behind the Green Door* (1973) and is now fairly marginalized in straight culture, gay videos have achieved an almost respectable position in gay life. The swapping of gay porn videos has become common, and rental outlets are no longer the sleazy adult bookstores and arcades that were the initial locus for pornography. Legitimate gay bookstores such as the Lobo chain in Texas or Gay Pleasures in New York began to rent and sell porn videos alongside pride flags and *New York Times* bestsellers. Robert Hofler reported that porn stars have been seen regularly at disco openings and various public and private parties. Porn work could even provide an entry into influential West Hollywood circles—ones available to those with the proper abs and pecs but without other credentials.[48] Producer and director Ronnie Larsen has made a cottage industry creating dramas and documentaries about the gay porn industry. His play *Making Porn* opened in Los Angeles in 1994 and has since toured across the country, often to sell-out crowds of primarily gay men. He followed up with an informative documentary film in 1997, *Shooting Porn*. German director Jochen Hick's 1998 film *Sex/Life in LA* documented several socioeconomic levels of gay sex work in Los Angeles; it made the rounds of all the major gay film festivals. Porn videos themselves had an inordinate number of stories involving the industry itself: from *Giants* (1983) to *The Making of a Gay Video* (1995).[49] *Bad Boy's Ball* was a behind-the-scenes story of a traveling stage act of gay porn models. It included extensive, revealing interviews with the performers. While a number of behind-the-scenes straight videos have been made, the straight industry has seen nothing like the regular, broad-based media attention lavished on gay porn and its stars. The gay press has frequently printed interviews with porn performers alongside articles on relationship building, travel, and politics. The straight media are more likely either to condemn pornography or to treat it as an exotic and mysterious artifact.

Gay videos themselves sometimes demonstrate a connection between porn and gay life. In *Show Your Pride* (1997) scenes from an actual gay pride parade centered around the float of director Chi Chi Larue, who was surrounded by hordes of scantily-clad, muscular porn models dancing to the disco beat, much as they might during their frequent club performances. This montage played out against the sound of a plaintive voice wailing "Show your pride" to a repetitive disco tune. This scene, sandwiched in the middle of the video, segued abruptly to a massive orgy, completely without transition. This video illustrated the exalted position of porn stars in gay life through their prominent position on a float in a real pride parade; and through its quick jump cut from scenes of a cultural event to hard-core sex, it was also a metaphor for the casual ease with which many gay men approach pornography.

Despite its integration into gay life, gay porn has not been without its critics. Writers such as Michelangelo Signorile and Daniel Harris have vilified gay porn and its muscular bodies as presenting destructive and impossible models of beauty and sexuality.[50] Gay porn has also been subjected to much of the same criticism applied to straight porn: that it is sexist, degrading, and violent, especially to women. These arguments have depended largely on the assumption that pornography, per se, was degrading and aggressive, and that in gay pornography one partner (the bottom) was inevitably subordinate, submissive, and "degraded," and was thus merely a stand-in for a woman. In this way (the argument goes) gay pornography merely reproduced heterosexual norms of violence and sexism.[51] Convincing arguments have been made against this position, especially by Thomas Waugh[52] and Scott Tucker.[53] Gay men may easily identify with both performers in a sex scene; and the performers themselves do not always adhere to such rigid role identification. When performers slip easily between the roles of penetrator and penetrated, even within a single scene, the identification of the penetrated as subordinate and oppressed becomes purely syntactical and without relevance to social realities. While the straight porn industry has been criticized as exploitative of women, the lack of female performers in gay male porn argues against a simple extrapolation from straight to gay pornography. In fact, the pornographic depiction of a forbidden gay sexuality serves to subvert, rather than emulate, the highly gendered strictures of straight culture. Carl Stychin makes a strong argument for the liberatory potential of gay pornography, and he takes issue with the sweeping claims of the feminist critique of porn, which "when extended to gay porn, completely fail[s] to consider the basic differences and needs of a culturally and socially marginalized sexuality, and in fact mimics the traditional patriarchal views of sex and eroticism."[54]

The casual acceptance of pornography into gay life also creates something of a political conundrum: When right-wing religious extremists are continually defining gays primarily in terms of radical sexual practices (such as in the "documentary" *The Gay Agenda*), does the popularity and broad acceptance of pornography play into the hands of right-wing religious extremists? To some degree, it probably does; but this negative should be balanced with the positive value of having one's own sexual identity—rejected and stigmatized by the status quo—validated by seeing it played out in front of one's very eyes. Public displays of same-sex affection like those enjoyed by heterosexuals are dangerous and generally forbidden for gays. Whereas the mass media constantly and openly affirm heterosexual identity, gay pornography is one of the few venues for seeing gay sexuality presented in a positive light.

THE FUTURE OF GAY VIDEO PORN

The 1990s saw technical improvements in the production and manufacture of gay videos as well as a continuing expansion of the market. Increased diversity among the models and an experimentation with new approaches contributed to this expansion. For the next decade, it seems likely that, while a plateau has been reached in terms of market saturation, producers will continue to broaden the range of products available. The diversity of physical types among performers is likely to expand. Increasing numbers of models over thirty are emerging as a major trend, even while videos featuring young performers remain popular.[55] The industry is likely to become more ethically diverse as well.

The "gonzo" film phenomenon that has become such an important part of straight porn is likely to surface in gay porn as well. Gonzo videos break down the "fourth wall" between the filmmaker and his or her subject, and, by extension, the wall between the viewer and the performer. Technical values are minimal; the camera is usually hand held, and the cameraman is also the director. The camera moves freely among the performers, and the cameraman occasionally makes comments, gives direction, or even joins the action. This type of video is closely related to the amateur videos that preceded it, and which continue to be an important market. As the numbers of amateur gay videos have increased, gonzo seems likely to follow.

Gonzo and amateur videos are important examples of the growing role of the niche market. The niche market is composed of specialized videos focusing on a particular taste or fetish. Gay video already has a healthy market for wrestling, sadomasochism, bondage and discipline, scatological, ethnic, and other kinds of video. Altomar Productions creates videos featuring men from their mid-forties up through their seventies. This company also produces a line of fetish videos focusing on uncircumcised men and foreskin.[56] The niche market is likely to become a larger proportion of the gay porn industry as more men realize that videos catering to their particular tastes are available.

One of the primary means by which this knowledge will become available is through the Internet and the World Wide Web. Adult products already represent a significant proportion of business conducted on the Web; despite government efforts to curb Internet pornography, online pornography will certainly continue to be a major factor in the growth of gay porn. Most studios already maintain extensive Web sites, and many performers—especially those who escort—have home pages. New technology (such as interactive online audio and video, digital video disks, and interactive CD-ROMs for computers) will grow in importance as the price and accessibility of the necessary equipment move into the reach of the average consumer.

While explicit sex will always be the most important factor in gay videos, recent trends suggest that films with a sense of style and an inventive narrative are on the rise. The 1997 GEVA and GAVN Video of the Year awards went to *Naked Highway*, an on-the-road story that borrowed from sources as diverse as Jack Kerouac, *Thelma and Louise*, and *Easy Rider*. It used flashbacks, sophisticated camera angles, and stylized editing to create a video with a clear narrative and a sense of style. While the mainstay of the market will continue to be videos focusing almost entirely on sex, more sophisticated and complex productions such as *Naked Highway* seem likely to become more common. In both of these genres, gay video pornography seems likely to continue as an important force in gay culture.

WHY MEN SEEK OUT PROSTITUTES

Martin A. Monto

Stay in the Tenderloin area. There are hookers in the Mission district, but almost without exception they are I.V. drug users and at higher risk to be AIDS carriers. Also this is a rough area; lots of crime and police hassles. You can usually negotiate a pretty good deal with the street whores.... Prices start at $40 and go up. (San Francisco, California)

She was lovely without clothes on. However, some creep had been rude and obnoxious towards her; she had bruises and scrapes on her thigh and elbows from when this guy didn't have the courtesy to stop a moving car so she could get out.... I think that we should be treating these girls with the respect and dignity that some of them pay us and that everyone else gets. (Portland, Oregon)

—*Clients' comments in* The World Sex Guide,
a Web-site providing information to consumers about prostitution opportunities

When thinking about prostitution, the general public, policy makers, and researchers alike have focused on prostitutes rather than their clients. One-sided efforts to reduce prostitution by arresting prostitutes have been decried as unfair and discriminatory.[1] Though state laws are now phrased in gender-neutral language,[2] the vast majority of those arrested are female prostitutes.[3] Only a tenth of arrests for prostitution are of the clients,[4] virtually all of whom are men.[5] Though there have been calls for research into the motivations of clients for several decades, very little research has focused on this population.

This neglect of male clients reflects a sexual double standard in which women are seen as responsible for male deviance.[6] But there is also the difficulty of contacting clients, who make an effort to conceal their activities.[7] The problem of accessibility is compounded by the fact that both researchers and lay persons tend to assume they already know the reasons men seek out prostitutes.

Even in comparison with the limited knowledge we have of prostitutes, our knowledge of their clients is meager. Current conceptions of the customers are based primarily on cultural stereotypes,[8] anecdotal information,[9] second-hand accounts,[10] and small qualitative studies.[11]

Early estimates of the percentage of men who visit prostitutes were flawed and exaggerated the number of men involved.[12] Pioneering research by Alfred Kinsey in 1948 estimated that 69 percent of men had visited prostitutes at some time in their lives.[13] However, because his research was based on a convenience sample rather than a probability sample, his findings could not be generalized to American men. Nevertheless, his figure was widely reported, and it became the basis for estimates by others, such as Benjamin and Masters, who used Kinsey's data and their own impressions to estimate that about 80 percent of men had visited prostitutes.[14] These high estimates have served as ammunition for both antiprostitution advocates, who have used the figures to emphasize the scope of the problem, and pro-legalization activists, who have used the figures to show that prostitution is inevitable.

Recent, high-quality research, conducted as part of the National Health and Social Life Survey in 1992, provides a very different picture: Only 16 percent of men in the United States have ever visited a prostitute, and only 0.6 percent of men visit prostitutes each year. Further, the study found that the percentage of men whose first sexual experience was with a prostitute declined among men who came of age in the 1990s (1.5 percent) in comparison to men who came of age in the 1950s (7 percent).[15]

Though the proportion of men who visit prostitutes is lower than had been thought and may be diminishing, prostitution remains a matter of concern in the United States, where about 90,000 prostitution arrests are made each year. Over the past five years, several cities have launched educational programs for arrested clients designed to discourage reoffending. The existence of these programs allows unprecedented access to a population that has been long hidden from view. Relying on questionnaires administered to 700 men attending workshops in San Francisco, California (N=588), Portland, Oregon (N=82), and Las Vegas, Nevada (N=30), I evaluate the attitudes and motives of clients. The subjects of the study are not a representative sample of prostitution clients. Virtually all were arrested while trying to hire a street prostitute, rather than patronizing escort services or indoor establishments. Additionally, they were arrested in three Western cities that may not be representative of the nation. Nevertheless, the data allow us to move beyond anecodotal accounts, and to evaluate popular views of prostitutes' clients in light of information collected from a previously inaccessible population.

JOHNS SCHOOLS: A NOVEL RESPONSE TO PROSTITUTION

In 1995, programs in San Francisco and Portland began providing classes for men arrested while trying to hire street prostitutes. While Portland's Sexual Exploitation Education Project is now defunct, San Francisco's First Offenders Prostitution Program continues to provide monthly classes, usually to more than fifty men.

These programs represent a fascinating social phenomenon. They are based on the idea that the current practice of arresting prostitutes but not their customers is ineffective and reflects a double standard in which women but not men are held accountable. Focusing on the demand side of the equation and holding men responsible for prostitution helps to redefine the prostitution encounter, in which men are seen as having a choice as to whether to buy sex and female prostitutes are seen as having less of a choice. Proponents argue that instead of being an act between consenting adults, prostitutes, many of whom are not adults, may feel compelled to participate due to threat of violence, drug addiction, or dire economic circumstances.[16] Additionally, these programs represent a redefinition of prostitution from a victimless crime to a crime with victims, namely prostitutes, neighborhood residents, local businesses, and unsuspecting partners who are put at risk of sexually transmitted diseases.

Many of the ideas underlying these programs emerged out of the experiences of women and men who were in direct contact with women attempting to leave prostitution. San Francisco's program was designed by Norma Hotaling, herself a former prostitute and heroin addict, and San Francisco police Lieutenant Joseph Dutto and is run by the local district attorney's office.[17] Men who attend the program are able to have their arrest record expunged. Fees charged to the men offset costs and support Standing Against Global Exploitation (SAGE), a nonprofit organization run by Hotaling and staffed by former prostitutes, which provides programs and support to assist women leaving prostitution.

The one-day program includes a variety of presentations designed to discourage future prostitution encounters. Among the presenters are a representative of the district attorney's office, who explains the legal penalties that await men who re-offend; a health educator, who presents a slide show about sexually transmitted diseases that may infect clients and be transmitted to their loved ones; and a panel of community residents, who describe the detrimental effects that prostitution has had on their neighborhood. The most intense and powerful component of the program is a presentation by former prostitutes, referred to as "survivors," who describe how they came to be prostitutes, the violence they experienced, and their feelings about their customers. The message that is conveyed is very different from the ones the men may have received as paying clients, as the presenters have no incentive to support the fantasy that they were sexually aroused by past prostitution encounters.

These testimonials are followed by a presentation on pimping and the trafficking of women and children in the United States and worldwide. The day concludes with a presentation by a counselor who discusses "sexual addiction" and suggests strategies for coping with urges that may seem uncontrollable.

Portland's Sexual Exploitation Education Project (SEEP) emerged out of the experience of Peter Qualliotine and other men and women belonging to a pro-feminist organization called Stopping Violence Against Women. Their close relationship with Portland's Council for Prostitution Alternatives, an organization providing support for women seeking to leave prostitution, and the Portland Women's Crisis Line, a hot line for victims of violence, provided them with resources and ideas for developing the SEEP program. Instead of working directly through the police department, SEEP was an independent, community-based organization. Men were required to attend the program as one of the conditions of their probation, and their arrest and conviction remained on their record.

While the ideas that served as an impetus for Portland's program are similar to those that inspired San Francisco's, the educational format was different. SEEP was an interactive, 17-hour workshop that lasted Friday evening through Sunday afternoon, never with more than thirteen offenders at a time. Four workshop coordinators, two men and two women, led the offenders through a series of exercises and educational presentations. As in the San Francisco program, a "speak out" by former prostitutes was one of the highlights. Consistent with its longer duration, the program had more comprehensive objectives, including

- reframing prostitution from a victimless crime to a form of violence against women;
- showing how men's sexual socialization leads to acts of violence against women;
- stressing the choice and responsibility men have to create egalitarian relationships without coercion.

Portland's program ceased operations because it stopped getting referrals from the courts, apparently because of waning support from the district attorney's office San Francisco's program, however, continues to thrive and has served as a model for programs in several other U.S. cities, including Las Vegas, Nevada, and has been copied internationally as well. In January 1999, the National Institute of Justice presented a demonstration program in San Francisco to allow interested agencies and organizations to view the First Offenders Prostitution Program and to provide resources and information to those considering such a program.

METHOD

Anonymous questionnaires were administered to men immediately prior to the first session of each day's johns school. More than 80 percent agreed to participate. Though refusals constitute the largest proportion of the remaining 20 percent of men, late arrivals and language or reading barriers account for many of the noncompletions.

FINDINGS

Who Are These Men?

Table 5.1 describes the background characteristics of the men arrested for trying to hire prostitutes. The majority were white, 18 percent Hispanic, 13 percent Asian, and 4 percent African-American. In general, the men were fairly well-educated. Forty-two percent had completed a bachelor's or higher college degree, and 35 percent reported some college work. Forty-one percent were currently married, 36 percent never married, 16 percent divorced, 5 percent separated, and 2 percent widowed. Ages ranged from eighteen to eighty-four, with a mean of thirty-eight. Most worked full time. A quarter had served in the military, similar to the proportion of adult men in the United States who have served. A third reported that their parents divorced when they were children. Fourteen percent reported that they were physically hurt for no reason as a child, and the same percent said they were touched sexually by an adult during childhood.

A number of questions were worded identically to items on the nationally representative General Social Survey, allowing for comparisons between clients and the general population of American men.[18] Clients were significantly ($p<.05$) less likely to be married and more likely never to have been married than were the national sample. Of those who were married, clients reported less marital happiness than the national sample. These differences suggest that pros-

TABLE 5.1 CUSTOMERS' BACKGROUND CHARACTERISTICS

ETHNICITY	(N= 676)
White	61%
Hispanic, Chicano, or Latino	18%
Asian	13%
Black	4%
Other or Combination	4%

LEVEL OF EDUCATION	(N= 692)
Did not graduate from high school	8%
High school graduate	15%
Some college training	35%
Received bachelor's degree	28%
Received graduate degree	14%

MARITAL STATUS	(N= 689)
Married	41%
Never married	36%
Divorced	16%
Separated	5%
Widowed	2%

WORK STATUS	(N= 666)
Working full time	81%
Working part time	7%

titution serves as an alternative sexual outlet for some men who do not have a partner or who do not get along well with their partners. In addition, clients were much more likely to report that they had more than one sexual partner over the past year (56 percent) than the national sample of men (19 percent).

Sexual Behavior

Clients' responses to questions about sexuality and the sex industry are provided in Table 5.2. Almost all of the men reported having exclusively female sex partners during their lifetime. Asked the number of partners the men had in the previous year, a tenth said they had had none, a third had had one, another third had had from two to four, and 23 percent had had five or

TABLE 5.1 (CONTINUED)

WORK STATUS	(N= 666)
Student	2%
Other	10%

AGE:	(N= 648)
18–21	3%
22–25	10%
26–35	32%
36–45	34%
46–55	16%
56–65	4%
66 or older	1%

PARENTS DIVORCED AS A CHILD	(N= 659)
Yes	34%

TOUCHED SEXUALLY BY ADULT WHILE A CHILD	(N= 660)
Yes	14%

PHYSICALLY HURT FOR NO REASON AS A CHILD:	(N= 657)
Yes	14%

SERVED IN ARMED FORCES:	(N= 659)
Yes	26%

more. Though some might expect men arrested for soliciting a prostitute to be regular users of pornography, fully 70 percent of respondents reported viewing pornographic magazines or videos "never" or less than once a month.

Seventeen percent claimed never to have had sexual relations with a prostitute, indicating that their only experience had been propositioning the police decoy. Twenty-one percent reported having had sexual relations with a prostitute one time during the past year, 31 percent more than one time but less than once per month, 9 percent one to three times per month, and 3 percent once or more per week. The average age of first experience with a prostitute was twenty-three, although some had had their first experience as early as age nine or as late as age sixty. Fellatio was the most common activity with prostitutes (47 percent), followed by vaginal sex (14 percent) and "half and half"

TABLE 5.2 CUSTOMERS' SEXUAL BEHAVIOR

SEXUAL ORIENTATION	(N= 659)
Strictly heterosexual	94%
Experience with both	5%
Strictly homosexual	1%

NUMBERS OF SEXUAL PARTNERS OVER PAST YEAR	(N= 683)
None	10%
1	34%
2	15%
3 or 4	18%
5 to 10	15%
11 or more	8%

FREQUENCY OF SEX OVER PAST YEAR:	(N= 680)
Not at all	9%
Once or twice	9%
About once per month	15%
2–3 times per month	21%
About once per week	18%
2–3 times per week	17%
More than 3 times per week	7%
Do not know	4%

HOW OFTEN LOOKS AT PORNOGRAPHIC MAGAZINES	(N= 668)
Never	31%
Less than once a month	40%
One to a few times a month	20%
One to a few times a week	7%
Every day	2%
Several times a day	0%

HOW OFTEN WATCHES PORNOGRAPHIC VIDEOS	(N= 668)
Never	35%
Less than once a month	35%
One to a few times a month	21%
One to a few times a week	6%
Every day	3%
Several times a day	0%

TABLE 5.2 (CONTINUED)

AGE AT FIRST SEXUAL ENCOUNTER WITH A PROSTITUTE	(N= 531)
9–17	18%
18–21	33%
22–25	20%
26–35	21%
36–45	7%
46 or over	1%

CIRCUMSTANCES OF FIRST SEXUAL ENCOUNTER WITH PROSTITUTE	(N= 547)
Buddies set it up	22%
Prostitute approached	31%
Approached prostitute without others knowing	31%
Family member set him up	5%
Visited a brothel	3%
Other	8%

MOST COMMON SEXUAL ACTIVITY WITH PROSTITUTE	(N= 518)
Oral sex	47%
Vaginal sex	14%
Half and half (oral and vaginal)	12%
Hand job	6%
Other	5%
Two or more are equally common	16%

HOW OFTEN USE CONDOM WITH PROSTITUTE	(N=530)
Never	3%
Seldom	3%
Sometimes	9%
Often	10%
Always	75%

PROSTITUTION SHOULD BE LEGALIZED	(N=551)
Agree somewhat or strongly	74%

PROSTITUTION SHOULD BE DECRIMINALIZED	(N=545)
Agree somewhat or strongly	72%

(both fellatio and vaginal sex, 13 percent). In contrast, a study of Camden, New Jersey, found that vaginal sex was slightly more common than oral sex among its sample of frequent clients.[19] Regarding condom usage, three-quarters reported that they always used a condom when having sexual relations with a prostitute, a figure similar to the New Jersey study.[20]

In terms of their views on American prostitution policy, three-quarters thought that prostitution should be legalized, and 72 percent thought it should be decriminalized (the terms "legalized" and "decriminalized" were not defined in the survey). Clients' support for legalization and decriminalization is much higher than that of the general public (documented in Chapter 10 by Ronald Weitzer).

Do the Clients Accept Common Rape Myths?

Research consistently shows that many street prostitutes are victims of violent crime, including beatings and rapes,[21] most of which are never reported to police.[22] Does it follow then that clients are more likely than other men to endorse myths about rape? Rape myths are "prejudicial, stereotyped, or false beliefs about rape, rape victims, and rapists"[23] that serve to justify or support sexual violence against women and diminish support for rape victims.

Respondents were asked questions that assessed their views of rape myths. They were not, in general, more likely to endorse rape myths than other samples of men.[24] Twenty-two percent thought that "if a girl engages in necking or petting and she lets things get out of hand, it is her own fault if her partner forces sex on her"; 15 percent agreed that "in the majority of rapes, the victim is promiscuous or has a bad reputation"; and 7 percent agreed that "women who get raped while hitchhiking get what they deserve."

While these findings suggest that most clients do not hold views that might support violence against prostitutes, they also do not invalidate the substantial evidence that prostitutes experience extensive violence. The findings suggest that a relatively small proportion of clients may be responsible for most of the violence against prostitutes.

Why Do Men Go to Prostitutes?

As noted earlier, people tend to assume that the motives of johns are obvious, not worthy of serious exploration. Kinsey's research[25] supported the assumption that most men would take advantage of the services of a prostitute if they had the opportunity. However, more recent research contradicts the notion that buying sexual services is conventional behavior among men.[26] Why, then, do some men seek out prostitutes?

A few researchers have conducted in-depth interviews with the clients of prostitutes.[27] McKeganey and Barnard conducted sixty-six telephone interviews of men responding to an advertisement in a tabloid newspaper and nine in-person interviews of men contacted on the street. They also obtained information from sixty-eight men attending a health clinic specializing in sexually transmitted diseases. They argue that men are attracted to paid sex because they desire sexual acts they cannot receive from their partners; they are able to have sex with a larger number of sexual partners; they are attracted to specific physical characteristics; they like the limited emotional involvement; and they are excited by the illicit nature of the act. The authors also suggest that some men seek prostitutes in order to inflict violence on them.

Holzman and Pines interviewed thirty men, contacted through the snow-ball sampling of acquaintances, in an effort to capture the subjective experience of the prostitution encounter. This sample was one of regular users who had paid for sex an average of more than fifty times. They argue that men's primary motivations for having sexual relations with a prostitute are the desire for sex or for companionship. Men are also motivated by the mystery and excitement associated with the risky encounter, the belief that prostitutes are women of "exceptional sexual powers," and an interest in avoiding emotional involvement or the risk of rejection.

Jordan's in-depth interviews of thirteen clients in New Zealand suggest that men's reasons for seeking prostitution vary depending on their personal circumstances and their ability to meet their needs through conventional relationships. Older married men, especially, indicated that their wives were unwilling or unable to satisfy them sexually. Others sought prostitutes because they wanted to avoid committed relationships or felt unable to enter into conventional relationships. Some were motivated by the desire to satisfy intense sexual urges or to have sex with a large number of different women, while others sought prostitutes for companionship, intimacy, or love.

In the present study, clients answered thirteen questions that assess possible motives for seeking prostitution. All of the items are personalized "I" statements, such as "I have difficulty meeting women who are not nude dancers or prostitutes," and "I like to be in control when I'm having sex."

Table 5.3 reports the percentage who agreed with each statement. In addition, I compared the responses of repeat customers (at least two encounters in the past year) to first-time customers; the responses of married men and unmarried men; and the responses of college graduates and nongraduates.

TABLE 5.3 MOTIVES FOR SEEKING PROSTITUTES

(PERCENTAGE AGREEING TO THE STATEMENTS)

STATEMENT	TOTAL	REPEAT USER	FIRST-TIMER	COLLEGE GRAD	NON-GRAD	MARRIED	NOT MARRIED
I have difficulty meeting women who are not nude dancers or prostitutes.	23.4%	29.2%*	14.0%	17.1%*	28.5%	19.9%	26.1%
I think most women find me unattractive physically.	23.3%	24.7%	21.0%	16.0%*	29.1%	21.0%	25.1%
I want a different kind of sex than my regular partner [wants].	42.6%	49.6%*	31.3%	49.1%*	37.4%	50.2%*	36.7%
I am shy and awkward when I am trying to meet a woman.	41.9%	47.4%*	32.9%	35.7%*	46.8%	36.2%	46.1%
I would rather have sex with a prostitute than have a conventional relationship with a woman.	19.3%	24.3%*	11.2%	19.6%	19.1%	20.5%	18.3%
I am excited by the idea of approaching a prostitute.	46.6%	55.9%*	31.4%	56.1%*	39.3%	48.7%	45.1%

TABLE 5.3 (CONTINUED)

(PERCENTAGE AGREEING TO THE STATEMENTS)

STATEMENT	TOTAL	REPEAT USER	FIRST-TIMER	COLLEGE GRAD	NON-GRAD	MARRIED	NOT MARRIED
I don't have the time for a conventional relationship.	33.3%	38.4%*	25.0%	31.1%	35.2%	25.7%	39.0%
I don't want the responsibilities of a conventional relationship.	29.5%	34.8%*	20.6%	26.4%	32.0%	23.9%*	33.7%
I like to have a variety of sexual partners.	44.1%	53.9%*	27.9%	54.1%*	36.3%	41.9%	45.9%
I like to be in control when I'm having sex.	41.8%	45.5%*	35.6%	37.2%*	45.3%	41.6%	41.9%
I like to be with a woman who likes to get nasty.	53.9%	60.4%*	43.2%	52.7%	54.8%	53.1%	54.3%
I need to have sex immediately when I am aroused.	36.1%	40.7%*	28.6%	33.5%	38.4%	37.8%	35.1%
I like rough hard sex.	20.2%	21.9%	17.4%	17.6%*	22.3%	15.7%	23.5%

* Pearson chi-squared test significant at p<.05

The most frequently endorsed statements, by around half the men, were "I like to be with a woman who likes to get nasty"; "I am excited by the idea of approaching a prostitute"; "I like to have a variety of sexual partners"; "I want a different kind of sex than my regular partner"; "I am shy and awkward when trying to meet women"; and "I like to be in control when I'm having sex." All of the remaining items were endorsed by at least 19 percent of respondents.

Though the most frequently endorsed item (Table 5.3) would seem to best explain men's reasons for sex with prostitutes, the "woman who likes to get nasty" is not explicitly defined as a prostitute. Still, this item, in conjunction with the second most endorsed item, "I am excited by the idea of approaching a prostitute," supports the idea that one of the attractions of sex with a prostitute is that it is illicit or risky. According to a client interviewed by Holzman and Pines, part of the attraction was the "element of risk ... the gambling element."[28]

Several other questions point to a commodified perspective toward sexuality, in which sex is analogous to a consumer product rather than an aspect of intimate relationships. The desire to "have a variety of sexual partners," the need to "be in control during sex," and the urge to "have sex immediately when I am aroused" all point to this kind of self-focused sexuality that Blanchard calls "McSex" in his popular exposé on "young johns."[29] According to one man he interviewed, "It's like going to McDonald's; most people are looking for a good quick cheap meal. It's satisfying, it's greasy, and then you get the hell out of there." The idea of shopping for a sex partner with particular physical attributes, such as hair color, body type, or ethnicity—a motivation described by McKeganey[30]—also reflects a conception of sex as a commodity rather than as part of an intimate relationship.

Wanting a kind of sex different from what one's regular partner wants (43 percent) supports the idea that some men seek out prostitutes because they can do things with them that other women might find unpleasant or unacceptable. In contrast, liking "rough sex" (20 percent) may be not only a sexual preference but also a reflection of the desire to dominate women during sex. According to one client, if "you've got the money in your pocket, then you've got the dominance over them."[31]

The data also suggest that some men pay for sex because they have difficulty becoming involved in conventional relationships. Forty-two percent agreed that they were "shy and awkward" when trying to meet women, 23 percent felt unattractive physically, and 23 percent had "difficulty meeting women who were not nude dancers or prostitutes." For some of these men, patronizing prostitutes may be an attempt not only to have sex, but also to establish a kind of intimate relationship with a woman. Jordan describes one very shy client who felt desperately alone and eventually fell in love with a prostitute. When she quit working, he was disappointed. Though he continued to visit prostitutes, he claimed, "It's not sexual relief that I go for—it's to relieve some loneliness that I feel."[32] These responses indicate that, for a minority of clients, frequenting a prostitute may be a way of establishing an intimate connection with a woman.

Finally, some of the clients felt that they did not have the time, energy, or interest to invest in a conventional relationship with a sexual partner. Though only 19 percent said that they preferred sex with a prostitute to a conventional relationship, 30 percent wanted to avoid the responsibilities of a conventional relationship, and a third said that they did not have time for a conventional relationship.

Further support for these motives for patronizing prostitutes is found in the fact that each item was more likely to be endorsed by repeat-users than first-time offenders. (For all but two of these items a chi-squared test of independence indicated significance at the $p<.05$ level.) Repeat users were more than twice as likely as first-timers to report that they had difficulty meeting women who were not prostitutes or nude dancers and were also more likely to say that they were shy and awkward when trying to meet women. A commodified approach to sexuality—that is, an interest in variety, control, and immediate satisfaction—is also more evident among the repeat users.

Motives for buying sex differ according to social class, as indicated here by respondents' education level. College graduates were more likely than non-graduates to indicate an interest in sexual variety and excitement, to want sexual acts different from those their regular partners offered, to want a variety of sexual partners, and to feel excited by the idea of seeking a prostitute. Non-college graduates were more likely to report difficulty meeting women, awkwardness, and feeling physically unattractive. Some of these men may buy sex from prostitutes because of their inability to form conventional relationships with women. Additionally, non-college graduates were more likely than college graduates to say they wanted to be in control during sex. Prostitution may be one way in which they gain some control in their encounters with women.

Married clients were more likely than unmarried men to report wanting a different kind of sex than their regular partners. Among unmarried men this may reflect the lack of a regular sexual partner. A married man who has a sense of entitlement to sex may see patronizing a prostitute as justifiable should the wife not meet his perceived sexual needs. Unmarried clients were more likely to report shyness, a liking for rough sex, and a desire to avoid the responsibilities of conventional relationships, all of which could limit their success in forming conventional relationships.

CONCLUSION

The act of approaching a prostitute is a product of many factors. These are likely to include the availability of prostitutes, knowledge of where to find them, access to sufficient money to pay them, risk of being caught or of contracting disease, and ease of securing services. While these practical issues may be important in influencing whether a man *seeks* prostitutes, they tell us little about the needs that the man is trying to fill through prostitution. This chapter sheds light on these motivations.

There is no single or simple reason men patronize prostitutes. Even the conventional notion that "they go for sex" falls short, as some men visit prostitutes in an effort to experience emotional intimacy, and many men who want sex do not patronize prostitutes. Rather, seeking the services of a prostitute appears to reflect a number of motivations, including an attraction to the illicit nature of the encounter, a desire for varieties of sex that may not be provided by regular partners, defining sex as a commodity, and a lack of interest in or access to conventional relationships. All of the influences are more pronounced among repeat users than among first-timers. Motivations appear to differ depending on the backgrounds of the men, with college graduates more likely to seek the excitement of illicit sex, and nongraduates more likely to report difficulty in forming conventional relationships. Additionally, married men were more likely to be seeking sexual behaviors they could not experience with their wives, and unmarried men were more likely to avoid conventional relationships or report difficulty in securing them.

Few men were motivated by the most destructive reasons for patronizing prostitutes—because one likes rough sex or because one holds beliefs conducive to rape.

This is the first large-scale study of prostitutes' clients in the United States. Many of the respondents would not have volunteered to participate in face-to-face interviews and would not normally be accessible to researchers. Nearly all of the men were arrested while trying to hire a female street prostitute. Future studies comparing these arrested clients with patrons of escort services, indoor prostitution establishments, and male prostitutes would be especially helpful. A critical issue that deserves further study is why some men but not others choose prostitutes as a means of meeting their sexual desires. After all, many men sometimes "feel awkward and shy when trying to meet a woman," "want a different kind of sex than their regular partner" provides, or "get excited about the idea of approaching a prostitute." Interviews comparing clients to nonclients are needed to explore how socialization regarding sexuality and masculinity leads some men to consider prostitution as an option.

CLIENTS AND CALL GIRLS: SEEKING SEX AND INTIMACY

Janet Lever and Deanne Dolnick

The old fascination with female prostitutes as purveyors of "sex without responsibility"[1] neglects the possibility that some female prostitutes may also be purveyors of intimacy without responsibility. A closer look at the content of prostitute-client interactions should yield a better understanding of prostitutes' occupational requirements, as well as highlight some clients' motives that are rarely recognized.

Arlie Hochschild in her book *The Managed Heart* defined "emotional labor" as "the management of feeling to create a publicly observable facial and bodily display; emotional labor is sold for a wage and therefore has *exchange value*"; she defined "emotion work," by contrast, as "these same acts done in a private context where they have *use value*."[2] Dealing with conventional work, Hochschild does not have to reconcile the contradiction presented by the unusual case of sex workers who may feign the emotions connected to sexual acts, signs of arousal, or flirtation for a set fee—the kinds of emotional display linked with physical intimacy that are normally part of the unpaid emotional work done in the private sphere by women in noncommercial relationships.

The prostitute, by definition, sells sexual services. Intimacy—a close, affectionate, or loving personal relationship with another person—is not necessarily offered by the prostitute. The hypothesis we test here is that clients expect and receive more emotional services in the form of intimacy from call girls (a term we use to refer to both call girls and escorts)[3] than from street prostitutes. The basis for this hypothesis rests on the higher cost of call girls' services, which restricts their clientele to fairly affluent men. Because the men seeing call girls can pay more, they get more time, as well as settings more conducive to extended intimacy services, such as nongenital caressing or kissing and companionship.

There are, of course, other occupations where opportunities for personal disclosure or intimate touch are part of what the patron pays for, at least implicitly. Scholars refer to the receipt of these services as the commercialization of intimacy, citing the clear-cut cases of the psychotherapist and therapeutic masseuse.[4] More broadly, we can think of feigned or real expressions of caring and interest as part of the "emotional labor" expected of those in the "listening occupations," such as barber, hairstylist, and manicurist, as well as the fabled bartender who lends an ear while he or she pours a drink.

The variable among these "listening occupations" is the degree to which a client may assume that the service provider is genuinely concerned about the client or the intimate revelations the client has unilaterally offered. Among the occupations mentioned, the psychotherapist—explicitly seen as a "caregiver"—is assumed to care the most while the barber, bartender, and nonsexual masseuse are expected to care the least; expectations about the call girl's caring probably lie in the middle ground.

Perhaps what the call girl is really selling is the *illusion* of intimacy. Hochschild states that, "Once an illusion is clearly defined as an illusion, it becomes a lie."[5] But part of the emotional labor performed by the call girl is to keep the illusion alive; she defines her behavior as a playful "fantasy" rather than an illusion to keep it from being a lie. As the buyer of fantasy, the client is absolved from any responsibility to reciprocate displays of intimacy to the call girl. The client understands that being intimate is part of the call girl's work and that he is not her only client. Both client and call girl *agree to pretend* that her caring and sexual attraction for him are real.

To clarify the separable components of sex work, it should be noted that just as there are prostitutes who sell sexual but not emotional services, there are other sex workers who sell emotional but not sexual services, if the latter are narrowly defined as intention to arouse to climax. Examples include the classic "taxi dancer"[6] (whose real occupational title is "dance hostess") who in contemporary Los Angeles sells her companionship and close access to her body as a dance partner for 35 cents a minute, and the Asian hostess who also gets paid by the number of minutes spent attending to clients in the 200 Hostess Clubs that have sprung up in Southern California.[7] Researchers describe the Asian hostesses' duties as including attentive listening and flirtatious talk that alludes to, but does not actually include, sex acts.[8] Again, the question to be addressed here is whether different strata of "prostitutes" sell sexual services, emotional services, or both.

METHODS

The analysis presented here draws on data and personal contacts from the Los Angeles Women's Health Risk Study, which was conducted by RAND in 1990–91. One author was a member of the senior staff and the other a member of the junior staff on the project. Understanding the emotional labor of female commercial sex workers was *not* one of the study's goals. Instead, the study had three stated goals: first, to estimate the size and demographic composition of the female prostitute population in a large metropolis, namely Los Angeles County; second, to collect self-reported data on sex and drug-taking behaviors that put one at risk of AIDS and other sexually transmitted diseases (STDs); and third, to collect blood samples from the prostitutes to test for the presence of antibodies to HIV, syphilis, and hepatitis B.

Two subpopulations of female prostitutes interested the researchers. First and foremost, we targeted the numerous and visible prostitutes on the streets. Second, we targeted the various groups that make up the less accessible subpopulation of off-street prostitutes.

Unlike other studies of female prostitute populations that are based on convenience samples, the RAND study utilized an "area/day/shift" design to draw a probability sample of 998 street prostitutes. Los Angeles was divided into seventy-nine geographical areas where there was a probability of prostitution taking place, and these areas were randomly sampled; interviews also took place during a random selection of days and times.[9] Women were eligible to participate if they said they had traded sex for money, drugs, or something of value in the last year. The response rate for the street prostitute sample is 61 percent (assuming all women who refused screening or denied eligibility were simply refusing to participate) or 89 percent (if all such women were in fact ineligible).

Unlike the street prostitution sample, it proved impossible to randomly sample from the hidden and complex off-street prostitute population,[10] but we were able to interview eighty-three call girls. These women were recruited in three ways: We called their numbers advertised in sex tabloids or phone directories (n=30); they responded to our ads, fliers, and mass-media campaign (n=26); or we got their names and numbers through referrals from informants or other women whom we had previously interviewed (n=27).

Response rates varied by mode of recruitment: The response rate of the women we contacted through their ads ranged from 12 percent, assuming those who denied eligibility were simply refusing to participate, to 17 percent, if all such women were in fact ineligible. Although we don't know how many eligible women saw our ads and fliers or became aware of our study via radio and newspaper coverage, we interviewed twenty-six of the fifty-three women (49 percent) who called us and claimed eligibility. When personally referred to us, women were very cooperative, and we interviewed twenty-seven of thirty women (90 percent) who came to us via this snowball technique. The authors interviewed nearly half of the call girls (Deanne interviewed thirty-four and Janet interviewed seven) and the remainder were interviewed by two other interviewers; nine of the interviews took place over the telephone, thirty-eight were conducted in person at a RAND office, and thirty-six were done at a location chosen by the respondent, usually her home.

There were notable demographic differences between the call girls and street samples. Nearly 70 percent of the street sample was African-American, whereas nearly 80 percent of the off-street sample was white. The average educational was 11.6 years in the street sample, a little less than required for a high school diploma, and 13.5 years, or some college, in the off-street sample. Median age, on the other hand, was the same, between twenty-nine and thirty years old in both samples.

Women in both the street and off-street samples were paid $25 in cash to participate in a 45-minute interview. One section of the instrument included questions about sexual activities with *all* clients within the previous week, and another section focused exclusively on the sex worker's *last client,* including a sociodemographic description of him, details about the time and place of the interaction as well as what was done, whether there was any prior relationship with him, whether she or he drank alcohol or used drugs during time together, whether a condom was used, and what was given in exchange for the woman's time and services.

None of the items in the lengthy survey was designed to operationalize the concept of emotional labor. In effect, what follows is a secondary analysis of a data set, much as Marks used items from the General Social Survey to test his idea that Americans find some intimacy—defined as friendship, emotional support, or companionship—with coworkers in the workplace.[11] In the L.A. Women's Health Risk Study, the detailed information that respondents provided about their interaction with the last client lends itself to a univariate comparison of street prostitutes' versus call girls' services that can be taken as proxies for intimacy.

How long and how often the client and prostitute have been seeing each other suggests their levels of familiarity and comfort; what type of setting was used also suggests level of comfort and sharing of personal environment; the amount of time spent together and whether alcohol or drugs were shared are both measures of companionship provided; whether conversation occurred implies at least the opportunity for personal disclosure and detailed knowledge of the other; whether or not nonsexual massage, caressing, kissing, and hugging occurred tells us about affectionate or nongenital touching; and whether the man touched or performed oral sex on the woman's genitals indicates whether there was the type of sexual reciprocity that characterizes most noncommercial sexual relationships.

Although we rely most heavily on the quantitative data described above, we also draw on qualitative data in our analysis. First, because we knew so much less about the modus operandi of call girls, we instructed the interviewers to make marginal notations of any commentary offered by the respondents that elaborated on their answers to survey questions; usable marginal notes were available from seventy-five of the eighty-three respondents. Second, in the last stages of drafting our results, we found ourselves wanting even more detail and recruited a clique of four call-girls to keep a one-week diary in which they recorded how much time they spent with each client, what was discussed prior to and after any sexual activity, and whether the woman engaged in any "acting" or emotion work to feign intimacy or whether any real intimacy had occurred. We also draw on informal talks about this subject with five male clients and two call girl informants we have known for years.

RESULTS

The reader should keep in mind that characteristics of the client and details of his transaction with the prostitute are based on her perception and unilateral report. Further, the reliance on data about the "last client" may limit generalization to all clients, although we do not know whether that is so or how much it distorted the data.

Table 6.1 presents a demographic summary of the last client of the street prostitutes and the call girls. Racial differences are striking: Nearly all (more than eight in ten) of the call girls' clients are white, and the second largest racial group is Asian, whereas the streets host a more democratic array of clients of different races and ethnicities. The majority of call girls believed their last client was from the upper income brackets, whereas the majority of street prostitutes believed their client was middle-class. These class and race differences were predictable insofar as not all men can afford the higher fees for a call girl's services; the median amount paid by the last client of the call girls was $200, compared to $30 spent on the street.

TABLE 6.1 CLIENT CHARACTERISTICS

	STREET CLIENTS (N = 998)	CALL GIRLS' CLIENTS (N = 83)
PERCEIVED RACE/ETHNICITY		
White	34%	82%
African-American	40%	1%
Hispanic or Latino	23%	5%
Asian	2%	7%
Other	1%	5%
ESTIMATED AGE		
Age 20 or less	1%	1%
Age 21–35	35%	32%
Age 36–40	26%	26%
Age 41–50	27%	21%
Age 51–65	10%	16%
Over 65	1%	4%
Could not tell	0%	0%
ESTIMATED INCOME		
Upper	26%	65%
Middle	50%	27%
Lower	12%	4%
Don't know	12%	5%
PERCEIVED MARITAL STATUS		
Married	44%	36%
Not married	32%	59%
Don't know	25%	5%

Totals may not equal 100% due to rounding.

The demographic variable most related to the need for companionship as well as sexual services is marital status. In their pioneering study of the sexual behaviors of males, Dr. Alfred Kinsey and associates found in 1948 that single men (especially those who were divorced and in their thirties) were more likely than married men to have had extensive experience with prostitutes. Just as it is presumed that most wives are sexual partners, it is presumed that most also provide companionship.

Of course, some single men are dating or living with someone, and some married men have an equal or greater need for companionship and intimacy, but on average, we can assume that single men's relationship needs are greater than married men's. The fact that a larger percentage of call girls (95 percent) than street prostitutes (75 percent) believed they knew their last client's marital status can be taken as another indicator of greater familiarity, although the majority of all sex workers felt they knew their client's marital status. Many married men seek services from call girls and street prostitutes—at least 36 percent of the call girls' last clients were married, and 43 percent of street prostitutes' were. But a much higher percentage of call girls' clients were reported to be single—59 percent, compared with 32 percent for street prostitutes.

Some men spoke of time with a call girl as superior to the dating scene. They explained that an encounter with a call girl guarantees sex for the equivalent of the price for a nice dinner for two on a regular date in which sex may or may not follow the man's outlay of cash. One attractive, unmarried young Ph.D. in chemistry who worked in industry, when asked why he doesn't date at all, replied, "I am married to my company." And one call girl made the generalization that her single clients have a great time—they like "to party"—while her married clients are more awkward and more inhibited by guilt.

Table 6.2 shows the sex worker's relationship to her last client. Some people may be surprised to see that street prostitutes have their share of regular clients (more than one-quarter of last clients), but the call girl is far more likely to set up an ongoing relationship with a man (just under half were men they had "seen" enough to consider "regulars"). Note, however, that call girls had sexual relations for the first time with 40 percent of their last clients. If indeed emotional services are more expected of the call girl, then she may be under more pressure than her street counterparts to create a comfortable feeling with total strangers a good portion of her working time.

In terms of length of relationship with "regulars," there is less difference than expected. Among the men described as previous or regular clients, 49 percent of the call girls' clients have seen them for longer than a year, compared to 43 percent of the street prostitutes' clients. In fact, the longest relationship was reported by the street prostitute who claimed she met one "regular" thirty years ago, whereas the longest relationships described by call girls were ten years in duration. For those relationships that had lasted longer than a year, the mean length was 3.8 years for street prostitutes' clients and 4.5 years for clients of call girls. Perhaps because the cost of the interaction is less prohibitive, a majority of regular clients saw street prostitutes as recently as last week, a frequency that only a quarter of clients of call girls could match.

TABLE 6.2 STATUS AND DURATION OF RELATIONSHIP WITH LAST CLIENT

	STREET PROSTITUTES (N = 998)	CALL GIRLS (N = 83)
New client	59%	40%
Previous client	13%	11%
Regular client	28%	49%
First saw previous or regular client		
Last week	4%	2%
Last month	15%	4%
Within last year	38%	45%
Over year ago	43%	45%
Last saw previous or regular client		
Last week	63%	26%
Last month	25%	36%
Within last year	9%	34%
Over year ago	3%	4%

Table 6.3 shows a dramatic difference in setting for the interaction with the last client. Virtually none of the call girls reported "car dates," in contrast to roughly one-third of the street prostitutes. Contrary to the stereotype of a call girl arriving at an out-of-towner's hotel room, only one in six call girls saw her last client in a hotel; by contrast, more than a third of the street prostitutes saw the last client in his hotel room. Nearly two-thirds of call girls' last interactions took place in the privacy and familiarity of either her home or the client's. Surrounded by personal artifacts, the setting is likely to be pleasant and clean, perhaps even luxurious. Equally important as the lack of impersonality in the setting is the fact that sex on regular dates typically occurs in someone's home, so the setting for intimacy with a call girl is often more like that of noncommercial intimate interaction than a commercial one.

Table 6.3 also shows a dramatic difference in the amount of time spent with the client. Although close to one-quarter of the call girls spent less than a full hour with their last client, compared to more than half of street prostitutes, only one in seventeen call girls spent less than fifteen minutes, compared

TABLE 6.3 CHARACTERISTICS OF LAST TRANSACTION

	STREET PROSTITUTES (N = 998)	CALL GIRLS (N = 83)
Where interaction with client last took place		
Your home	2%	30%
His home	10%	33%
His hotel/motel	38%	16%
Your hotel/motel	9%	0%
Car or limo	32%	2%
Other	8%	19%
How much time spent with last client		
Less than hour	56%	23%
(less than 15 minutes)	(32)%	(6)%
One hour	19%	38%
2–4 hours	16%	19%
5 or more hours	10%	20%

Totals may not equal 100% due to rounding.

to one in three street prostitutes. One in five call girls had spent five or more hours with the last client, much as one might on a regular date. One in ten street prostitutes spent that much time with her last client.

According to information offered by some of the call girls we interviewed, long "dates" sometimes include having lunch or dinner together, much like a regular date. Our informants say that some women charge for each hour of their time—even for non-sexual activities—whereas others cultivate the fantasy of wanting to be in a man's company by not charging for time spent dining. Some regular clients even get "sleepover" privileges, which accounts for some call girls' reports of long hours for their last interaction.

As stated, the median cost of an encounter with a call girl was $200, nearly seven times the median of $30 spent on a street prostitute. In a society that believes "you get what you pay for," it can be assumed that clients who spend more expect to get more time and services. Answers to our survey item about whether the last client gave the woman anything else besides money or drugs, either as a gift or as part of her payment, 21 percent of the call girls got some-

TABLE 6.4 DRUG AND ALCOHOL CONSUMPTION BEFORE AND DURING INTERACTION WITH LAST CLIENT

	STREET PROSTITUTES (N = 998)	CALL GIRLS (N = 83)
Woman consumed substance before interaction		
Alcohol	39%	21%
Drugs	51%	6%
Alcohol/drugs shared with last client		
Alcohol	7%	18%
Drugs	8%	4%
Both	5%	4%

thing material, but so did 14 percent of the street prostitutes. The gifts most frequently reported by call girls were jewelry (one let her clients know her preference for antique jewelry), perfume, flowers, and champagne—the type of gifts a man might give to a girlfriend or wife. When street prostitutes reported receipt of something material, it was most often food, cigarettes, or alcohol, but a few reported receiving jewelry or flowers.

Table 6.4 shows that the use of drugs and alcohol often precedes or occurs during the interaction with a client. Sharing the same substance while together is an activity typical of real dates. "Partying together"—at least in terms of sharing alcohol—is more frequent with call girls than street prostitutes, yet it characterizes only a minority of interactions. Also, many more street prostitutes than call girls used drugs or alcohol prior to seeing their last client.

Table 6.5 highlights responses from a list of twenty possible activities engaged in with the last client. Respondents were shown a card listing sex acts and asked to indicate *all acts* they did during their last encounter. Table 6.5 shows the most common sexual activities performed, whether unusual sexual requests were granted, and the prevalence of sex acts performed upon the prostitute's genitals, as well as nonsexual activities that arguably sustain a feeling of intimacy.

The most common sexual activities are also considered among the most intimate sexual activities—vaginal intercourse and fellatio (oral sex performed on the male). These acts were the ones most common for both call girls and

TABLE 6.5 ACTS OF SEX OR INTIMACY ENGAGED IN WITH LAST CLIENT

	STREET PROSTITUTES (N = 998)	CALL GIRLS (N = 83)
Give him "hand job"	7%	26%
Give him oral sex	57%	45%
Vaginal intercourse	51%	66%
Anal intercourse	0%	1%
Domination/B&D	0%	8%
Two or more sex workers together	1%	7%
Touch woman's genitals	4%	26%
Give her oral sex	4%	17%
Nonsexual massage	2%	30%
Conversation	5%	51%
Caress, kiss, and hug	3%	42%

street prostitutes. Vaginal intercourse was more common with call girls, but call girls also supplied more manual stimulation of the client's genitals—possibly instead of oral or vaginal sex, but more likely in combination with other acts. About two-thirds of both the call girls (64 percent) and the street workers (68 percent) reported that they had used a condom with their last client.[12]

The incidence of anal intercourse, domination fantasies (B&D abbreviates "bondage and discipline"), and group sex is very low in both samples, although more frequent with call girls. The low incidence of these acts (see Table 6.5) may dispel one myth about why men use prostitutes. Kinsey suggested that men go to prostitutes to obtain types of sexual activity that they cannot get elsewhere, and his examples included oral sex, sadomasochism, fetishes, and group sex.[13] Letting 732 male clients explain their own motives, Winick found that when men said a prostitute "gives me something different" or "what I want," they were mostly referring to a variation in body type from their regular sex partner rather than a variation in sex acts.[14] More recently, interviews with 164 clients in Camden, New Jersey, also indicate that most clients seek vaginal and oral sex, rather than unusual variants of sex acts.[15] Commenting on what men ask for (not necessarily what they get), some women characterized requests as "normal" or "straight" sex.

Clients who purchase sex acts may or may not engage in acts intended to arouse the female partner. While some men's own arousal is heightened by stimulating a woman's genitals orally or manually, another motive for these acts may be to give pleasure and not just receive it. When we look at sex acts performed upon the female partner, the differences between samples are strong. Over a quarter (26 percent) of call girls had their genitals touched, compared to only 4 percent of street workers; 17 percent of the call girls but only 4 percent of the street workers received oral sex.

The comparison to the frequency of cunnilingus in noncommercial encounters is interesting. In the recent national probability study reported by University of Chicago researchers, 17 percent of the married women surveyed reported that they had received oral sex during their last sexual event with their husbands.[16] In other words, call girls were just as likely as wives to receive oral sex.

When we focus on the intimacies of nonsexual massage, conversation, caressing, kissing, and hugging, the differences are even stronger. Nonsexual massage performed on the client is done to relax and arouse him, and this sensual touch adds to the sense of intimacy of the encounter; 30 percent of call girls' clients received this personal service compared to only 2 percent of street workers' clients (the third who were in a car were obviously limited, but two-thirds had the same spatial opportunities of most call girls). A few call girls explained how the massage is as much for their sake as the man's because it fills time so the client will think he got a lot for the high fee. As one call girl stated, "If we jumped right into sex and he came in five minutes, he'd want to come again for his $200."

For most women intimacy includes talk—small talk and deep talk—and research on gender and marital relationships indicates that many men resist this aspect of intimacy.[17] But some men want more talk, too. A *Washington Post*/Kaiser Family Foundation/Harvard poll found that 16 percent of married men said they were dissatisfied with "the amount of time [they and their] partner spend talking openly about things that are on your mind."[18]

Whether clients get and give verbal intimacy in the form of self-disclosure or listening to the other's disclosures in their noncommercial relationships is not known, but talk *is* included in what most men get in the situation of limited reciprocity with a call girl. Half of the last clients got conversation as part of their interaction with a call girl, compared to only one in twenty on the street. The men's work was the most common topic discussed with the four women who kept postsession diaries, and they claimed it was discussed in great detail. In contrast, a primary complaint of the divorced wives studied by Riessman was that their ex-husbands had refused to relate what goes on in their work world.[19] The diaries revealed that the clients also discussed their children and politics; one talked about his wife and bad marriage. One informant believed she created a "safe space" for her clients, many of whom alleviated their insecurities by asking about the adequacy of their penis size or asking advice about their sexual approach with women, presuming a professional has expertise on these subjects..

Several call girls interviewed in the L.A. Women's Health Risk Study described having at least one client who only wants to talk, or only wants to be held. One woman told of holding a client who cried for his entire hour. Another described a new client who cried during his screening interview when he revealed that his wife had left him a year before. Several call girls recognized a parallel between their work and the psychotherapist's; in fact, seeing oneself as a type of therapist is one source of pride for some call girls.

Although most call girls say that they do not like to kiss clients, and that they keep "necking" to a minimum with other diversionary tactics, 42 percent reported that they did "kiss, caress, and hug" their last client, compared to only 3 percent of street prostitutes. The literature on street prostitutes consistently shows that they avoid kissing precisely because they perceive it as "too intimate" or as a feature of romance. Kissing is more difficult for call girls to avoid. As one call girl explained, "The street women are just selling sex, they don't have to play the games we do. We make believe we want to be with the guy, and if you want to be with him, then you'd want to kiss him, right? Guys expect a lot for a lot of money."

CONCLUSION

We hypothesized that call girls provide greater emotional services to clients than street prostitutes. In particular, clients expect call girls to create at least the illusion of intimacy in the exchange. The data culled from the L.A. Women's Health Study show that call girls are more likely to establish ongoing relationships with regular clients (regardless of their marital status), and some of these relationships last for years. Interactions with call girls are far more likely to take place in settings that are personal, and these settings seem conducive to conversation and affectionate touching as well as sex acts. Call girls are more likely to have their own genitals touched or to receive oral sex, akin to normal intimate relationships, although most clients are more focused on receiving than reciprocating sexual pleasure.

It seems that call girls, like the hostesses described earlier, in effect are selling increments of their time, more typically measured in hours than in minutes, while street prostitutes offer only as much time as needed for the particular sex act agreed upon. Call girls' higher prices could be justified by access to cleaner, more comfortable, safer, and more private environments as well as more attractive sex partners but, in addition to all those advantages, male clients have come to expect more time and affect as well as sex. Because there is more time, greater familiarity can develop, and there is opportunity to do more "ordinary" things together, such as sharing a meal or drinks.

While call girls appear to offer more intimacy than street prostitutes, the data suggest a surprising amount of time and personal service may be offered by the latter to some clients, especially to their regulars or those they see in motels rather than cars. The qualitative data we collected are limited, and we know more about call girls than street prostitutes because we interviewed them in off-street environments that allowed more time and comfort to elaborate answers. Had our interviewers on the street been instructed to collect qualitative data, we might have found fewer differences between the two groups on some of the questions.

Use of diaries was experimental, and we cannot offer detailed analysis from more than a few call girls; however, they yielded enough interesting data to support their use more extensively by future researchers. In particular, diary data and our informal talks with informants are better suited than our survey data to answer this important question: Is the intimacy offered an illusion, or does real intimacy develop over time?

Our limited qualitative data suggest that not all the call girls are being "phony" or acting all of the time. Most women we asked said that they really like some of their clients, especially those they have seen for years. As one informant said, "You cannot know someone that long without it being a real relationship." Some claimed to be genuinely interested in being updated on a "regular's" life. As in other commercial relationships, the likelihood of intimate exchange typically increases over time and is one reward of customer loyalty.

Call girls should be added to the list of "listening occupations." Several women described what is known as the "stranger on a train" phenomenon where the talker can be more openly revealing because the listener is not part of one's social network. Or perhaps it is the lack of reciprocity and controlled environment that encourage some clients to reveal more to the call girl than they do to friends and family. Encounters with sex workers may offer the "instant intimacy" that some men say they find in bars.

Also, a woman's reaction to sexual stimulation can sometimes be real. Although we know this intimate detail only from one of the women who kept a diary, she noted that she has orgasms with some of her clients. But she noted that when she is busy (it is not uncommon to see three men over a short period of time when business is good), she fakes orgasms, too—a clear-cut example of emotional labor. Another woman's diary entries, also documenting emotional labor, describes how the "affect" during sex may be in large part for show or ego-boosting. Her diary included notations like "I did the usual moaning thing" or "I made typical 'into-it' sounds and 'that feels good' remarks."

Our qualitative material includes one example of a call girl's self-conscious preparation for emotional labor. One informant described "psyching herself up" from the moment she takes off her blue jeans to take a shower, put on her makeup, and get into her sexy miniskirt and halter top (if she's going to client's place) or her lingerie (if he's coming to her place)—both costumes for her fantasy performance. Sex workers have to conjure up the "feminine" demeanor of "niceness" and "sexiness" even when they are not in the mood.

The blanket notion that these men owe no reciprocity because a woman's services are paid for is also called into question by one informant—a well-educated, upper-middle-class twenty-nine-year-old—who continually calls her lawyer, doctor, and accountant clients for help with her personal problems. And some clients desire a real and reciprocal relationship with a call girl. While many enjoy the lack of responsibility in a commercial relationship, other men either have not been able to find intimacy elsewhere and fall in love with a call girl, or they indulge real-life "Pretty Woman" rescue fantasies and try to save a woman from "the life."

Is emotional labor involved when the prostitute is male? Applying Nieva and Gutek's notion of "sex role spillover,"[20] one would expect that the emotional requirements of the job are greater for women than for men doing the same personal service work because "stroking"—supplying socioemotional support—is a gender-based role. West reports minimal expectations for emotion work by male prostitutes in London, who mostly have an aloof attitude, or by their clients, most of whom are seeking nothing more than sexual release.[21] However, some of the young men—especially those who work for higher wages through advertised services—view clients as friends and see conversation as part of what they do with clients. Just as some call girls in our study observed, one male escort noted that "sometimes it's like giving therapy."[22] But in general, emotional requirements are minimal for men. Caukins and Coombs suggest that clients of male prostitutes tend to seek out masculine types who cater to the client's fantasy of having sex with a supermasculine male.[23]

Understanding the personal consequences of the emotional component of the job of prostitute is beyond the scope of this paper. Wharton and Erickson describe how women with emotionally demanding jobs suffer negative psychological consequences, including "burnout" and detachment, that can diminish their ability to be emotionally available in their personal relationships.[24] When thinking of "burnout" in doing sex work, researchers are far more likely to focus on physical fatigue, repercussions on self-esteem, or loss of attractiveness. Yet burnout and alienation among call girls may also involve the toll of coping with the emotional demands of clients. More research on the emotional dimensions of sex work would heighten the appreciation of the many interpersonal skills required in this occupation.

2

VICTIMIZATION, RISK BEHAVIOR, AND SUPPORT SERVICES

DRUG USE, HIV, AND THE ECOLOGY OF STREET PROSTITUTION

Judith Porter and Louis Bonilla

Women who engage in sex work have a wide range of lifestyles and can work in vastly different settings. An understanding of this is important in order to promote AIDS prevention in this population. Street prostitution is the form of prostitution most closely related to HIV/AIDS in the United States because of the connection with drug use. Although patterns of prostitution may be different across regions of the country or cities, much of the research assumes that patterns of street sex work are similar.[1] This chapter demonstrates that street prostitution varies considerably by race, drug use, and locale within one city, and on the basis of these differences we suggest targeted strategies for education and service delivery to this population to prevent the spread of HIV/AIDS.

BACKGROUND

Epidemiological models of AIDS risk behavior tend to address prostitution as individual sexual behavior but often ignore its social context, which provides little insight for AIDS prevention.[2] The label "prostitute" includes a variety of women. Although it is difficult to provide precise data and it is not clear how these figures were derived, some researchers have estimated that about 20 percent of prostitution in the United States is street prostitution and the remainder is spread among massage parlors, bar prostitution, outcall services, and brothels.[3] Injection drug use is most common at the street level, with one-third to one-half of street prostitutes in the United States injecting drugs. Most street prostitutes who are injection drug users used drugs before beginning sex work.[4] In addition, street sex workers are most likely to be poor, disproportionately members of racial minorities, substance addicted, and the most likely of any group of sex workers to be arrested.[5] The category "prostitute" also obscures the fact that many are not full-time prostitutes, but exchange sex for money or drugs only occasionally and in certain contexts, with the increasing exchange of sex for crack.[6]

Prostitutes are popularly viewed as vectors of HIV infection. Although the importance of HIV transmission through prostitution has been demonstrated in Africa, prostitution is not a major vector for the transmission of HIV infection in the United States, in part because street prostitutes are more likely to perform oral sex (a lower risk practice for HIV infection than vaginal sex) with their clients and also because they frequently use condoms with them.[7] Among U.S. prostitutes, as well as among prostitutes elsewhere,[8] HIV infection is related to injection drug use, especially long-term drug use, or to large numbers of nonpaying sex partners. Studies have found significant differences in HIV seropositivity between sex workers who inject drugs or engage in sex with drug injectors and those who do not.[9] Not only are prostitutes who inject drugs at higher risk generally, but they may not identify their steady, nonpaying partners as being at risk and will thus often share drug injecting equipment or not use condoms with them.[10] One recent study of New York street prostitutes indicates that almost half have a history of injection drug use, and more than one-third of this sample was HIV positive.[11]

Crack cocaine has destabilized the structure of street prostitution in urban areas.[12] The entry of large numbers of crack-addicted women into street prostitution has driven the price of sex down, especially in African-American areas where crack use is prevalent,[13] increasing the level of competition and diminishing prostitutes' bargaining power over price and condom use.[14] Also, before crack, pimps were more likely to house, clothe, feed, and pay for the fixed expenses of the women in their "stables," and indeed this was part of the informally structured arrangement between prostitutes and their pimps.[15] At least on the street level, this is less the case today. Crack-addicted women often do not have pimps or lookouts to protect them because they cannot afford them; they must spend what they earn to maintain their addictions.[16] Also, more prostitutes barter sex for drugs.[17] Because of the presence of frequent and unprotected sex among female crack users, crack use has been viewed as a risk factor for HIV/AIDS among female sex workers.[18] Inconsistent condom use during oral sex, given the lip damage caused by crack smoking, is associated with HIV seropositivity among crack-addicted sex workers.[19]

Ecological and cultural factors are related to differences in drug- and sex-related risk of HIV/AIDS among different subgroups of Latina sex workers.[20] Thus, the type of strategy likely to be effective in reducing HIV risk may differ among different groups of sex workers. While the literature does give some indication of the effect of type of drug used, much of it does not examine sources of variation in the structure of street prostitution by race and locale within one city, nor have the implications of such contextual variations for HIV/AIDS prevention among sex workers been widely studied. Our study addresses this very issue.

METHODS

Data were obtained from informal, unstructured interviews conducted with prostitutes in North Philadelphia over a twelve-month period. We were trained as street outreach workers and trained and certified as AIDS educators by a local Latino community-based organization which serves the North Philadelphia area. We volunteered as an outreach team one afternoon a week for this organization, doing street outreach with female sex workers. As outreach workers, we distributed condoms, bleach kits, written material on HIV/AIDS, information on HIV testing, and lists of soup kitchens, housing, drug treatment, and other essential services. An important part of our work was to discuss with the women the services they needed and to give them information to connect with these services. The interviews usually lasted several minutes, since the women were often in the process of soliciting clients, but repeated contacts gave us the opportunity to discuss their needs and the context of their work. We taped detailed field notes after each outreach session which were then transcribed. The quotes we utilize are from our transcribed field notes (names have been changed to protect anonymity). Our taped information is reliable because we taped the field notes together, verifying each other's perceptions and noting where we differed. Our observations validated the information the women gave us, because we saw the type of supplies they took and physical signs like needle track marks or blistered lips from crack smoking. McKeganey and Barnard have also used street outreach observations to validate self-reports in their study of prostitution in Glasgow, Scotland.[21] We validated our outreach observations in other ways. We did weekly group AIDS education presentations at two major local welfare offices and a hospital drug detoxification unit in the area we serviced. In addition, we volunteered at a weekly needle exchange program located in one of these areas. In these venues, we were able to confirm our observations by extended personal conversations with the women when they were not at work, with their pimps or male partners, or with staff of these programs.

We conducted interviews in North Philadelphia, the poorest area of the city, with a high rate of drug use, extremely poor health indicators, a high rate of sexually transmitted diseases, a large percentage living in poverty, high unemployment, and morbidity and mortality rates far above the city average.[22] Though the area is predominantly African-American, there are also large low-income Latino and white neighborhoods there.

The sample is a nonrandom, convenience sample of street prostitutes who worked in the three major stroll areas in North Philadelphia on Friday afternoons. In all three areas, the women actively solicited clients by standing on the street or by waving down cars. The areas are several miles apart from each other. One area is the major stroll area for white prostitutes. It is located underneath an elevated railway line in a racially transitional but still largely white, extremely low-income neighborhood on the edge of a commercial district. The area is full of abandoned buildings and factories. Another area is a park in a low-income African-American and Latino neighborhood next to a major expressway. The park is frequented mostly by African-American prostitutes. Neither area has easily accessible hotels or rooms where the women can take their clients; sex is performed mostly in cars. Another area is adjacent to a major urban thoroughfare in a black community. Although the area is primarily a low-income residential area, it is surrounded by commercial establishments, including cheap hotels where the prostitutes can take their clients. Sex is performed in hotels or row houses or in cars, although for privacy the prostitute picked up in a car must leave the area with the john. This area is frequented solely by African-American prostitutes.

We saw an average of six to seven African-American prostitutes every week in the park area (ranging from two to thirteen per week over a twelve-month period), ten African-American prostitutes a week in the hotel area (ranging from two to thirteen), and six white women (ranging from one to eight) underneath the elevated train, though the number of white prostitutes we contacted every week was actually higher because the needle exchange program, heavily frequented by white prostitutes, was in this area. Every week, from one-third to one-half of the women in the park or under the elevated railway were women we had seen at least once before. The women in the hotel area were a more stable population, though some left temporarily and some permanently and were replaced by new sex workers. Over time, the number of prostitutes in the areas varied with the weather, police actions, number of clients on the street, and movement of the women themselves into and out of "the life." We spoke with at least 150 women over the course of the year.

It is important to note the limitations of this type of research. The research was conducted during street outreach efforts and is not a formal series of highly structured interviews. Much of the data was gathered during the women's working hours, limiting the amount of time they could spend talking to us. This sometimes yielded incomplete interviews when, for example, the women would leave because prospective clients drove by or their pimps or male partners were watching them. It is also important to note the limitations of the sample. The majority of women were full-time street prostitutes who were working in public stroll areas on late Friday afternoons, and hence our sample does not include women in bars, crack houses, or shooting galleries, call girls, part-time prostitutes, or women who work in the areas we covered either late at night or earlier in the week (though the weekend is the busiest time of the week). Our sample is limited to white and African-American prostitutes and to three areas of North Philadelphia—the target areas of the agency for which we volunteered—and thus these women may not be representative of women who do prostitution elsewhere in the city.

Research of this type has certain benefits. We interviewed women during their working hours and in their work environments, enabling us to observe the context in which their activities took place and the social networks existing among the women. Also, our work as service providers gave us access to these women in a non-threatening situation. Race and gender did not seem to seriously affect the quality of information we received. We consistently appeared each week, represented a known and respected minority organization, and delivered needed supplies and service information in addition to offering a sympathetic ear. Outreach work also provided an excellent opportunity to compare differences in the context of street prostitution by stroll area.

VARIATIONS IN STREET PROSTITUTION

White Prostitutes

The white street prostitutes usually worked alone or occasionally in groups of two on the edge of a commercial district underneath an elevated railroad (the "El"). They were almost all addicted to injectable heroin. We knew this because they frequently told us and also accepted the bleach kits used to sterilize needles that we distributed. They had visible needle track marks and we saw many of them returning used needles at the needle exchange program in this area. An excerpt from our field notes illustrates this:

We approached a white sex worker and asked if she wanted condoms. She took them, and when we asked if she needed bleach, she said, "I'm a drug addict." She said she'd shared needles with someone who was HIV positive and knew she should get tested, but she was afraid to find out her status.

Most of the white prostitutes' business occurred in cars, although occasionally they worked out of abandoned buildings, where they were more isolated and vulnerable to assaults by their clients. Although there was some variation, the white prostitutes were likely to work for themselves and their boyfriends (who were usually addicted to heroin themselves); prostitution supported the woman and her partner's heroin habit. The white prostitute (usually in her late twenties) was generally older than the African-American prostitutes we met and worked as an isolated individual rather than with a small group of other women. The structure of male control did not involve one man managing several women, but rather consisted of a couple in a steady relationship where the man was the lookout for the woman while she solicited. A similar pattern of male partners as lookouts, with the woman's prostitution supporting both her and her partner's heroin habit, has also been observed in Glasgow, Scotland.[23] The following field note describing the white male partner of one of these women summarizes the relationship between the white prostitute and her male partner and her working conditions:

Tony says that the girls out here are usually working for their husbands or boyfriends and they split the profits. The woman has the man looking out for her; they wait in their cars. Tony's wife tells him to which location she will take her johns and how long she will be gone with each. He always takes the license number of the car and if his wife doesn't come back, he'll contact one police officer who is friendly. He says the money is good and it's easy money. He says that 90 percent of the work the women do here is blow jobs (oral sex), which go for $20. Vaginal sex is $50, but it's rare. Most johns are white businessmen in their fifties who come in for quick blow jobs. A girl can make $200 on a good day. Tony said that the women hate the job. They do it because they have to; they need the money for drugs. The girls work a regular area. He stated that life under the El is very dangerous. He's seen five girls die this year; three were killed by clients and two died from drug overdoses. The cops also entrap and bust the girls regularly.

As crack dealing increased in the area, many of the women became addicted to crack as well as to heroin. The pattern of the woman's working to support her boyfriend's habit as well as her own appeared to be shifting by the end of the research. If a woman broke up with her male partner, she might work on her own without a male lookout in order to use the money to support her addictions:

> Mary said that although many of the girls still had boyfriends, she herself had recently broken up with her longtime boyfriend, who had worked as her lookout. She was using large amounts of heroin and crack, though heroin was still her primary drug. She made enough money to support both her drug habits and pay for her room and food. She said she would accept only older white men as customers, since she was working without a regular male lookout, and she had to be more safety conscious as far as selection of clients was concerned. She encouraged many of her steady customers to page her at home when they wanted her services, though she still worked on the street by herself if she needed the money.

White prostitutes usually did not have extensive family or supportive friendship networks on whom they could rely. They rarely spoke to us about their children. We do not know whether they had children or whether they were simply cut off from contact with them. Some told us that they sometimes acted as lookouts for one another if their male partners were not around or they did not have a male partner and that they would share condoms with other women who did not have them. However, according to our interviews, these relationships were typically informal and did not constitute structured friendship networks. Some of the women told us they came from outside of Philadelphia and had no family networks. Others were rejected by their families and had no contact with them. "With us as we are, our families don't want us," one said.

These women appeared to be in bad health with visible signs of dental problems and skin conditions, and they appeared undernourished. They were often dirty or disheveled, and bore signs of being physically assaulted. They were often battered not only by the clients but also by their male partners, as some of the women told us, and they were at risk physically from the health problems associated with drug addiction. In addition, they were generally not connected with social or welfare services. Few of the white prostitutes, for example, had medical cards, welfare, or health insurance. The staff of the local drug detox program at which we gave HIV/AIDS presentations told us that these women tended to enter drug detoxification programs only after a major crisis, like the discovery that their partners are HIV positive, or after they hit bottom, an observation confirmed by our interviews. The effects for addicted women of being so extremely isolated from health care are partially revealed in the following excerpt from our field notes:

One white woman was battered, beaten with fresh bruises on her face. She said she was three months pregnant and showed us her stomach. She said she didn't have any family in Philadelphia. She came from a southern state two years ago. She does not have a medical card, she's homeless, and when I asked her what services she wanted, she implied she needed prenatal care (she pointed to her stomach and said "for the baby"). She didn't know where to get prenatal services because she didn't have a medical card or relatives to provide any kind of support structure.

These prostitutes were also at very high risk of HIV infection. Although other research has indicated that injection drug use is common among minority prostitutes, in North Philadelphia the white street prostitutes were more likely to be injection drug users than the African-American street prostitutes, thus putting them at risk of HIV infection through drug use. Since at least 20 percent of injection drug users in Philadelphia who were not in treatment tested HIV positive in one study,[24] the chance that these women were already HIV-infected was high, a suspicion confirmed by the staff of the local drug detox program. Although they preferred to use clean needles, they sometimes shared needles either because they were "sick" (in withdrawal) and didn't have clean needles available or because their living conditions caused inadvertent sharing. A common problem, for instance, arose from several injection drug users living in the same place:

A white prostitute told us … the people in her house all injected drugs and they take her needles when she isn't there. She came back to her room and found the needle obviously used in her absence and the cooker (where drug is melted) full of blood.

These women told us that they often shared needles with regular sex partners or did not use condoms with them, even though they used condoms on a more frequent basis with their johns. Condom use with johns, however, appeared to be inconsistent:

A white prostitute said a lot of the girls didn't use condoms consistently. She was the only one, she said, who used them regularly. She wouldn't service a date if they didn't use condoms; she didn't care if she lost the money, but she already had endocarditis (inflammation of the heart valve, a common illness among injection drug users) and she was afraid for her health. She said that a lot of the girls were HIV positive or had sexually transmitted diseases and they still didn't consistently use condoms.

These observations on inconsistent condom use were confirmed by other white women we interviewed.

African-American Prostitutes

Our data on African-American street prostitutes were gathered primarily from the two main African-American stroll areas: a small area that contained several hotels and row houses, which the women used for their work; and a park area, where business usually occurred inside parked cars. Although there were behavioral differences between the two locales dictated by social context, there were also some similarities in behavior that transcended location and which may stem from race. Although both groups of black prostitutes reported that their clientele was interracial, many of the johns we observed were black men.

Most of the African-American prostitutes we saw in these two stroll areas were addicted to crack and did not inject drugs. They were open about telling us that they were "on the pipe." Many did not know why we were offering them bleach. When we explained that it is used to sterilize needles, we were often told "I don't do that shit." The women frequently displayed blistered or injured lips, visible signs of heavy crack use, but we did not see the needle tracks that we did on the white sex workers. Weiner has also reported that in New York City, African-American sex workers were more likely to smoke crack than whites, and white women were more apt to use injectable heroin than African-Americans.[25]

Crack seems to have driven down the price of sex for these women, in part because of competition among the women and in part because of informal competition with the women who exchange sex for drugs in crack houses. We were repeatedly told by prostitutes how the influence of crack-addicted women had driven down the price of sex. The field notes below reflect a conversation with one African-American prostitute in the park:

> The going rate for a blow job was $20, which is what she charged. Some girls out here give men a blow job for $1.50. They're "real ho's." They drive the price down for the other girls. She could understand it if they were doing it for food or kids, but one girl gave a blow job for $1.50 and bought crack with it and smoked it. She strongly disapproved of this; this was disgusting and she should be driven out. She was giving the girls a bad name because the price was too low. If she knew someone who was giving $1.00 blow jobs, she'd "beat the shit" out of them.

Although women were working for money to purchase drugs, some reported they were also working for money for food or child support:

> The African-American prostitute in the park told us that she was cut off General Assistance which [at the time of the research] only lasted three months

111

in Pennsylvania. As a result she has no money to pay her rent. She said she has a drug problem and prostitutes for drugs, but now she also has to prostitute for money for food and rent, which is why she's out early today.

Many of the African-American prostitutes we interviewed, both in the park and in the hotel area, were born in Philadelphia and had networks of relatives in the city with whom they were in contact. Some lived intermittently with different relatives (especially mothers, sisters, and grandmothers). Others lived in abandoned buildings or rented cheap hotel rooms, and still others lived in the row houses out of which they worked. Even in the latter case, however, they often returned to relatives to stay for short periods of time. Many of the African-American prostitutes had regular or semiregular contact with female family members, usually their mothers

Rita, for example, saw her mother regularly. Her mother did not approve of Rita's prostitution but accepted it, and Rita lived with her mother and two of her children during the week in another part of North Philadelphia. At the time of the study, nineteen-year-old Danielle had been working for two years in the hotel area and alternated between living with her sister and mother every several weeks. Shakwana became pregnant by (she said) one of the male hangers-on around the hotel but was still able to return to her mother's to have her baby.

At least some of the women had families of their own in other parts of Philadelphia and worked only on the weekends to supplement their incomes or maintain their addictions:

Denise lives in West Philadelphia with her two children and her mother. She said she never stayed overnight at the hotel. She goes home when she's done. She said the scene is different in West Philadelphia, a lot slower. In North Philadelphia, it's busier and you make more money. She takes the El every day to "work" here and takes it home after work.

Most of these women had children. When they discussed their children with us, one common theme was guilt about being "bad mothers," a finding also reported by other researchers.[26] Although the women maintained contact with their families, it was often intermittent, and though some of their children were with female relatives, some were often in foster care:

LaVerne had a court appointment. The Department of Human Services wanted to put her daughter in a mental hospital because her behavior was bizarre. She was currently in foster care. LaVerne said she didn't feel the child needed to be in a mental hospital; she wanted the child with her mother.

LaVerne felt that if she were with her family and got the attention her grandmother would give her, she'd be better. She said the social worker "just wants to take my child away permanently." She lives with her sister and goes home occasionally to see her mother. She says her mother will always accept her. She always brings her mother a little money, because she's taking care of two of the children. Her mother deserves to get her welfare, LaVerne said, "because I'm not in any condition to take care of the kids. The family is the most important thing. I feel really sad when I think of my kids."

Among both groups of African-American prostitutes, many were on welfare because they had children, and many had medical cards. A number of African-American women told us that they had been in drug treatment programs or received medical examinations for sexually transmitted diseases on a regular basis, and many reported having been HIV-tested. Most of these women were also aware of free health services provided at local district health centers, which were available to them even if they did not have medical cards. The majority of African-American prostitutes indicated that they were aware of access to some health care services, however minimal.

Although there were similarities in crack use, family networks, and awareness of services among the African-American prostitutes in the two different social settings (the park and the hotel area), there were also differences by locale. The prostitutes who worked primarily in the park and those who worked in the hotel area differed in type of sex practiced, the type of client they saw, their relationship to male pimps or lookouts, the type of violence to which they were exposed, and to some extent, their ability to network with services.

African-American Prostitutes in the Park

The prostitutes in the park worked primarily out of cars. They tended to perform oral sex, which is quick, and the park provided the privacy for them to do so in a car. The women in the park were more likely to be in a formal relationship with a pimp; in fact, many of the women had pimps watching them as we talked, which made it difficult for us to interact with them and to learn as much about them as we could with the other groups. Although some of the women in the park appeared to be working on their own, more typical was the presence of men who were managing several women in a formal business relationship. For instance, as an example of a behavior frequently encountered, one man came up to us to get condoms for "his girls." When we asked how many he had, he said "three." The men often sat in cars with several women, and the women stood outside the cars and solicited clients. Prostitutes in the park area needed to work out of cars because there were no buildings or wooded areas in the park to conceal their activities. Thus, women were more reliant on working in pimps' cars. Also, because of the transient and unprotected nature of the locale, they told us they needed a pimp for occasional protection from customers, muggers, or other prostitutes. Women also frequently worked in the cars of men who picked them up, and they needed someone to note the license plate numbers of the cars in case they failed to return.

The park prostitutes appeared physically battered. And because they were controlled by pimps, they were restricted in their ability to informally network with other women about social services. Although our interviews indicated they knew about some social or medical services and used them, they were not aware of as wide a range of service options as were the African-American hotel prostitutes.

African-American Prostitutes in the Hotel Area

The prostitutes who worked in the hotel area occasionally worked out of cars, but since this area is adjacent to a major thoroughfare and is in a heavily traveled residential/commercial area, privacy in a car was extremely difficult unless they left the area. Thus, many brought the clients they solicited on the street to rooms in hotels that rented by the hour or half-hour, or brought the clients to row houses in which some of them lived either regularly or intermittently. We were told by the women that most of the women in the hotel area had regular customers, a practice that was somewhat less frequent in the park, which had a more transient population. Also, they reported more vaginal sex than the park prostitutes, in part because of the privacy granted by the hotel room.

Whereas previous literature indicates that most of the men involved with female street prostitution were pimps or proprietors of business establishments, in the hotel area male roles were more fluid, and many women worked on their own. The presence of so many women working independently had increased because of the widespread use of crack. The women binged on crack, often hitting on the pipe a number of times a day.

Because of this bingeing, many women wanted to spend their money on drugs rather than on male protection. This observation was confirmed both by the women themselves and by men who worked as bouncers in the hotels. As one bouncer told us:

> The girls (in the hotel area) work for themselves. There's no pimps around here. They watch out for each other. They're independent here. They use the money they get for themselves for drugs. They take whatever they can get. The rates went down around here; whatever they can get, it's enough. If they

were using once in a while, they would charge a little higher. But they're using [crack] so much now, they take what [money] they can get.

The bouncer's observations are verified by entries in our field notes:

> Tamika looked exhausted and said she had been out continuously from the previous night through the entire following day (we saw her at 4:30 on Friday), yet she did not have enough cash on hand to buy a hoagie for dinner. She implied that she had smoked most of what she had earned.

A group of African-American men in the hotel area fulfilled a variety of roles. Some of the men rented rooms in the hotels and worked there informally as bouncers, were boyfriends whom the women might "help out" with small amounts of cash, were proprietors of small prostitution hotels or sellers of condoms, or were suppliers of drugs. Often, the men fulfilled multiple roles at once, especially at the prostitution hotels. One man, for example, lived at one of the hotels, where he also worked as a bouncer, and had on separate occasions been the boyfriend of at least two prostitutes. Another man who owned the house out of which several of the women work received small, sporadic amounts of cash from the women who slept or worked there as general payment for rent and other services such as drugs. However, the women were not forced to relinquish their earnings to the men without receiving something in exchange, and the money clearly belonged to the women who earned it. For instance, some of the women lived in a row house owned by one of the men:

> Kim told us that Mike and his brother Tyrone own the house. Tyrone is inside selling drugs. The house is nasty; there's no running water or plumbing. Mike gets the water in a bucket. The girls get paid directly by their dates and don't pay regular rent but pay what they can and give the guys some of their drugs occasionally. "We give Tyrone some drugs or money but that's from our heart." Kim says the johns pay the guys $7.00 a room for 1/2 hour, $10.00 for an hour.... Tyrone and Mike make their profits from drug sales, money paid by the johns, and from the sale of condoms to the girls and their dates.

Although the women in the hotel area were also subjected to violence, from their self-reports the violence was not only from clients but often from fights with one another, since they were protected to some degree by bouncers in the hotels and were less likely to be dependent on male managers who could physically abuse them.

The prostitutes in the hotel area were working in a circumscribed area on their own, and they all knew one another. Since they were not dependent on pimps, they were able to both trade information about and access services more easily.

African-American women in the hotel area were at high risk for HIV/AIDS infection. They frequently performed vaginal sex, a higher risk practice than oral sex. They were usually visibly high on crack when they were soliciting business, which may have discouraged condom use.

Similarities in Street Prostitution

Most of the women with whom we worked, regardless of race, drug, or location, were at high risk of violence and HIV infection, and they lacked essential services. All of these women were in need of drug rehabilitation, especially programs that can accommodate women with children. Both African-American and white street prostitutes were also in need of housing services. Although African-American sex workers were more likely than white prostitutes to be living with relatives, their housing conditions were often far from adequate. Many of the relatives subsisted on scarce resources. The white prostitutes generally did not have relatives with whom they were in contact, and thus they and their male partners seemed to have even more acute housing needs. Most of the prostitutes were also in need of financial assistance. African-American prostitutes had generally been on welfare more recently than white prostitutes, but many had had their benefits discontinued. At the time of the research, Pennsylvania's General Assistance program for single low-income individuals lasted only three months, after which able-bodied individuals were cut from the program. At least some of the turbulence in these women's lives stemmed from the fact that many who had begun to stabilize their lives with regular housing became homeless when their benefits were discontinued. Without job skills or other resources needed to find and keep a job, and with a drug addiction to satisfy, many of the women resumed prostitution. In addition, difficulties involved with applying for benefits may have deterred women who were eligible from reapplying once their benefits were canceled. Drug dependency, violence, and a shortage of available services, characterized the lives of most of these street sex workers in our sample, findings also observed in other cities.[27]

Differences in Street Prostitution By Race

The white prostitutes worked primarily in cars. Although they appeared to be generally sicker and in worse physical condition than the African-American prostitutes, this probably is a result of their long histories of heroin injection, although it may also have been related to their lesser degree of access to medical services. The white prostitutes were much less connected to or even aware of social and medical services than the African-American street prostitutes in general, including those African-American prostitutes in the park who also worked out of cars. For instance, many African-American sex workers used the local district health centers, but most white prostitutes did not even know where the centers were located. We observed a similar difference with respect to African-American and white sex workers enrolled in the major local drug detoxification program. Both groups of African-American women were more likely than white women to enter the program in this area, even though this particular one-week residential program was closer to the white stroll area. In part, this may be due to differences in awareness of this service, in part to the white women's reluctance or inability to leave their male partners, and in part to the fact that the white women were less likely to have medical insurance cards. The white sex workers were somewhat less likely to come from Philadelphia, were less likely to have children with whom they were in contact, and even if they came from Philadelphia, were less likely to have family networks on whom to rely for housing needs or links to welfare services. They tended to work to maintain their own drug habits or those of their male partners, and the primary relationship of many of them was with these men, not with other women. However, the relationship with males appeared to be altering somewhat with the growth of crack use among these white women.

African-American prostitutes were more likely to use crack as their primary drug than were the white women and were less likely to be injection drug users. They were also more likely to be aware of services, and they networked with kin more than the white prostitutes did. Although some of the racial differences we saw (especially differences in health or appearance) were related to the type of drug the women primarily used, the greater networking with kin and social services may be an effect of race, especially since African-American and white prostitutes differed in these aspects irrespective of their geographical location. A number of the white prostitutes we saw come from the large white ethnic Catholic community in Philadelphia. They may have been more ostracized by their families and isolated than the African-American prostitutes because of the hostility of this white community to what is perceived as deviant behavior. We frequently observed extreme resistance and open hostility toward AIDS educators in predominantly white welfare and job placement offices, which may indicate a denial of drug addiction and HIV infection in white, working-class ethnic communities. These factors discourage contact with family members who are drug addicted or work as prostitutes. African-American sex workers, however, appeared to be less rejected by their families, a finding suggested by other researchers.[28] Although prostitution and drug use are condemned in

African-American communities, there is also greater tolerance for deviance in low-income African-American communities. Although residents' preferences may be mainstream cultural preferences, deviance may be more tolerated due to structural barriers faced by these populations in achieving mainstream goals. Thus, someone who deviates may be less likely to be totally excluded from her family. Also, extensive networks of real and fictive kin in the African-American community have ensured survival in the face of poverty.[29] Thus, compared to white prostitutes, African-American prostitutes may have multiple family roles as mothers, daughters, or sisters rather than more isolated roles as sex workers or addicts. In addition, kinship networks and contact with their children may ensure the women greater access to or information about community services (see Table 7.1).

Differences in Street Prostitution by Location

Street prostitution varied not only by race but also by locale. The African-American women who worked in the hotel area had more services and support networks than the African-American car prostitutes in the park area and the white prostitutes underneath the El. The African-American women in the hotel area all seemed to be connected to services or at least knew where to get them. This may be because the hotel prostitutes had a closer network, protected each other, and were, as one of the male bouncers said, "like a family." Because they were in regular contact with one another (the same prostitutes tended to use the same hotels, even if they did not live in them), information regarding services passed quickly through the street network. Although the African-American women in the park area were less knowledgeable about services than the African-American women who worked in the hotel area, they were more knowledgeable than the white prostitutes who also worked out of cars and worked for men, perhaps because of the networking with kin in the African-American community.

Violence is commonplace in street prostitution. Although these women were exposed to violence on a daily basis, both white and African-American women who worked out of cars worked in more dangerous and less protected locales and were often exposed to violence not only from their clients but from the men for whom they worked.

POLICY IMPLICATIONS

It is important to understand the context and structure of street prostitution in order to better access street prostitutes, identify their needs, and link them

TABLE 7.1 CHARACTERISTICS OF STREET PROSTITUTION BY LOCALE

	WHITE PROSTITUTES	BLACK PARK PROSTITUTES	BLACK HOTEL PROSTITUTES
Primary drug	heroin (injection)	crack cocaine	crack cocaine
Primary work site	cars	cars	hotels
Primary type of sex	oral	oral	vaginal
Typical relation to males	male partner (1 man, 1 woman)	male pimps (1 man, several women)	work by themselves
Family networks	no	yes	yes
Connection to social services	no	yes, somewhat connected	yes, highly connected
AIDS prevention outreach strategy	needle exchange sites	mobile vans	individual outreach teams

to AIDS prevention and education services. Our ethnographic data suggest that strategies for AIDS prevention and service delivery for street prostitutes must be differentiated by context including race, type of drug use, and ecological location in North Philadelphia.

Delivery of services must be neighborhood-based. Street outreach is an important strategy, because outreach workers know the characteristics of their constituencies, provide personal relationships, and bring information about accessible services directly to the women, as well as bringing them condoms and bleach to prevent HIV infection. Outreach workers are often the primary conduit to essential medical, drug treatment, and legal services for street prostitutes, since these women have a wide variety of needs beyond HIV/AIDS prevention. Poverty, lack of marketable skills, and drug addiction help to push women into prostitution and put them at risk for HIV infection.

The social structure of prostitution in any given area must be identified to specifically design AIDS prevention outreach strategies for the population involved (see last row of Table 7.1). The white prostitutes in our sample were at the greatest risk of HIV infection because of their injection drug use. They were the most isolated from the services and from networks that could help them access services they desperately needed. Also, many were watched by their male partners or lookouts, which made it harder for them to talk with outreach workers. Few community-based organizations do HIV/AIDS prevention and education in low-income white communities, so these women were often cut off from information on how to protect themselves. Providing services in the stroll area, either through the use of a multiservice van or through a program such as needle exchange, is a viable way to reach these women. The needle exchange program that started during our research was located outdoors on a street corner in the stroll area. Prostitutes began using the program soon after it started. They received information about AIDS and medical and social services at the site when they came to exchange needles, and over time they began to trust the volunteers. They frequently brought their male partners, who were often willing to talk to us, so it was possible to get information to both the woman and her partner.

Because the African-American prostitutes were more connected to both social service and family and friendship networks, AIDS presentations and distribution of condoms in welfare offices, city-funded health clinics, and drug detoxification units are effective ways of reaching them. In some cases the information might come to them indirectly, through providing information to their families, who often take the information and pass it on. Reaching the African-American car prostitutes in the park directly was difficult because they were watched by pimps. But workers can approach the women through their pimps with the information; unlike the male partners of the white women, the African-American pimps frequently sat in cars in an open park area where the women were soliciting. A mobile van providing condoms, AIDS information, and information on services for crack users may be another way of reaching these women and their pimps. Weiner has described a similar van-based strategy to reach sex workers in New York City.[30]

In the hotel area, a team of outreach workers who walk the streets can be extremely effective. The prostitutes worked on their own, had more freedom to interact, and also were a more consistent population than in the car stroll areas, and so they came to know and trust outreach workers more easily. Using the men in these hotels as gatekeepers was an important strategy in reaching this population. Street networks are particularly important in African-American neighborhoods, where they are strong and effective at disseminating information. We were assisted, for example, by men at the hotels in the distribution of fliers we created which listed various services the women might need. The male gatekeepers were not always cooperative. In one of the hotels the male manager sold the condoms we gave him and tried to keep the women away from us so we could not give them condoms for free.

Because the African-American prostitutes often mentioned their children and expressed concerns for them, addressing the needs of their children or providing drug rehabilitation services that include children may be an important strategy for behavior change in this population.

We do not know whether our findings can be generalized to other locales in Philadelphia or to other cities. However, even if specific contextual patterns differ, our research in Philadelphia suggests that street prostitution is not uniform and that different services must target different groups of prostitutes. Street prostitution is often in flux. Police raids on drugs and prostitution may prompt the women to disperse to other areas, as happened in the hotel area after the research was completed. Thus, strategies for reaching these women must be flexible and sensitive to the constraints of the locale in which they are working. A large portion of the epidemiological research on street prostitutes is dependent on a survey research methodology, where questionnaire or interview data are collected from individual sex workers, and does not deal with the social context in which they operate or possible variations in that context. Sensitivity to social context not only adds to our understanding of street prostitution but also can enable the effective delivery of HIV-related education and other services to these women.

CHAPTER

8

VICTIMIZATION AND THE SOCIAL ORGANIZATION OF PROSTITUTION IN ENGLAND AND SPAIN

Maggie O'Neill and Rosemary Barberet

Little cross-cultural research exists on sex work. Such research is particularly useful in order for social policy debates to be informed by an international perspective.[1] Researchers often assume that the particular problems of sex workers are local idiosyncrasies. The cross-cultural dimension documents similarities and also helps to shed light on why certain differences exist among countries.

Our project adds to the existing literature by trying to understand in two different contexts the routes into prostitution, experiences of victimization and violence, and prostitutes' survival strategies. We document both similarities and differences between England and Spain, but the most striking findings were the similarities in the women's experiences of victimization and their strategies to minimize male violence against them.

In Spain our major sites were Madrid (urban) and Albacete (rural). In England our sites were Nottingham (urban) and Stoke-on-Trent in Staffordshire (semirural). In-depth interviews and life histories were conducted with twenty female prostitutes, five in each site. About half worked indoors, and half worked on the street. The women were initially contacted at the service organizations described below. Interviews were tape-recorded and took place in the women's homes and at the offices of the outreach projects. The women welcomed the opportunity to tell their stories. We also met with agency staff who work with sex workers. In Madrid, the agencies were the Association for Prevention, Reinsertion, and Attention to Women Prostitutes (APRAMP) and the Institute for the Promotion of Specialized Social Services (IPSSE); in England, Prostitute Outreach Workers (POW) in Nottingham and the Sex Worker Project in Stoke-on-Trent.[2] APRAMP, a nonprofit organization, operates a mobile unit for street outreach and condom distribution; a center offering job training, support groups, and counseling; a shelter for drug-addicted prostitutes; and a program for the social reintegration of former prostitutes. APRAMP has also created a private business devoted to recycling and crafts that employs former sex workers.

We also explored the relationship between the needs of prostitutes and the services available to them in order to suggest interventionary strategies, particularly those in which unrelated agencies work together to assist prostitutes (police, social services, grass-roots agencies, youth agencies, probation service).[3]

PROSTITUTION LAWS IN ENGLAND AND SPAIN

Prostituting oneself in Spain is not criminalized (there is no mention of this behavior in the penal code), nor is it legalized (it is not legally recognized and regulated). Pimping is criminalized. Until 1995, the following behaviors were "crimes related to prostitution" in Article 452 bis (a) of the penal code, for which offenders could earn a prison sentence of four to six years, and a fine of $700 to $3,500:

1. "cooperating in, protecting, or recruiting the prostitution of one or more persons, within the country or abroad,"
2. "obliging one to satisfy the sexual desires of another by means of deceit, violence, threat, abuse of authority, or any other kind of coercion," and
3. "retaining a person against his or her consent, in prostitution or any other kind of immoral trade."

The penal code was revised in 1995, making sentences lighter for some crimes related to prostitution. Prostituting oneself is still not penalized. The language for pimping has been softened: Pimping is now defined as "obliging, coactively, by deceit or taking advantage of a situation of need or superiority, a person over eighteen years of age to engage or remain in prostitution." For adults, pimping is criminalized only if it occurs with coercion. The pimping of minors via coercion is now punished more severely than the pimping of adults. "Noncoercive" pimping of minors is still criminalized ("he or she who induces, promotes, favors, or facilitates the prostitution of minors or invalids"). Until recently, pimping included brothel keeping and was criminally punishable. This part of the law has also now been softened; it has to be demonstrated that a club owner is using coercion, which is hard to prove. If a parlor/club is free of drugs and underage prostitutes, then the police tend to leave it alone. If a club is suspected of underage prostitution and/or drug activity, police will investigate. Police statistics reveal only 98 arrests for pimping in 1995.[4]

Currently prostitution itself is not illegal in Britain, but soliciting, running a brothel, living on "immoral earnings," procuring, and curb crawling (cruising in cars to pick up a streetwalker) are illegal. Prostitution is legal so long as (1) one does not engage in soliciting or loitering on the streets, (2) one does not cohabit with another person, and (3) one does not share one's home with another sex worker. The second condition could provide grounds for living off immoral earnings; the third condition could constitute grounds for the operation of a brothel. But these two prohibitions mean that sex workers are effectively denied the basic right of living with a partner or spouse.

Prison sentences for prostitution were abolished in 1983, but women are still being imprisoned indirectly for prostitution, sentenced for the offense of defaulting on fines. Some of the women we interviewed had accumulated fines as high as £2000. In 1985 the Street Offenses Act criminalized curb crawling. The English Collective of Prostitutes opposed this since it made it harder for prostitutes to screen out suspicious clients. Since a man had to be seen as a "persistent" curb crawler to be prosecuted, the initial transaction became more rushed to prevent either sex worker or client from being arrested. As a result, the women lost valuable time which they needed to negotiate safe sex and avoid dangerous clients. This loss of time left them further at risk with regard to their physical safety and health.

Home Office figures show that in England and Wales between 1989 and 1996, 4,495 females under eighteen years of age were convicted or cautioned (formally warned) for offenses related to soliciting. Following campaigns by the Children's Society,[5] the Association of Directors of Social Services and the Association of Chief Police Officers issued statements that child prostitution should be dealt with as a child protection issue, not as a criminal offense. Although child prostitution remains a crime, there is a growing sense that young people should be treated as "victims not villains" and directed to Social Services, and that the men who buy sex from young people should be targeted by vice officers. The Sexual Offenders Act of 1997 requires pedophiles and other sex offenders to report their addresses and movements to the police for a number of years. The law includes offenses of "causing or encouraging" prostitution and having intercourse with girls under sixteen.

SOCIAL ORGANIZATION OF PROSTITUTION

In Spain, street prostitution occurs mostly in urban areas, and Madrid's Casa de Campo park is a major prostitution area. Rural sex work also flourishes in Spain, still one of the most rural countries of Europe, where brightly lit brothels ("puti-clubs") dot the highways and the outskirts of towns. These clubs are set up as bars or hotels but are fronts for sex work. Workers can reside in the clubs; some are there semipermanently and others work three-week stints. Some of the women arrange the situation themselves, but others are there as a result of deals struck between club owners and pimps, some of whom are involved in an organized pimping network. In some cases the club owners travel to Madrid or other cities to recruit the women. Rarely are the women who work in the clubs from the local town; they are almost always from other parts of Spain or from other areas of the world (South America, Africa). Often the women are "tried out" by both the manager and the customers for a few days to see if they perform well enough; if not, they are dismissed.

In these clubs the women encourage the men to buy sexual services. When they manage to get a man to "go upstairs," part of the money goes to the owner for "renting" the room. In this way the owner gets around the penal code because he appears to be simply running a hotel and bar. Unofficially there is undoubtedly more money exchanged, because the women at these clubs often receive full room and board and medical checkups.

In England the majority of prostitution takes place in urban settings and ports. Prostitution in rural areas tends to be invisible and accessed via magazines advertising services by individual women working from home. Our research in England focused on both street prostitution and saunas and massage parlors. Most of this takes place in urban areas, but we did find evidence of saunas in a semirural area of Staffordshire. North Staffordshire has streetwalkers in Stoke-on-Trent, but the majority of prostitution takes place in saunas and massage parlors. Most of these parlors are managed by women, but few are owned by women. In the urban area, Nottingham, there is considerable street prostitution and also numerous saunas/massage parlors.

Whereas in Spain immigrant sex workers from Africa and Latin America are quite visible, we found no evidence in Nottingham and Staffordshire of prostitutes from Third World countries. However, some of the women working in the sex industry in large cities are immigrants. Recent reports in the British media describe women from Thailand and Eastern Europe being trafficked into Britain by organized crime groups.

The major difference between the countries is that England has a much stronger grass-roots movement of current or former prostitutes who try to assist other working prostitutes (e.g., the English Collective of Prostitutes, POW, EXIT, ScotPep, and the Centenary Project). Such groups are rare in Spain, where the tradition in social services is more of a "top-down" ministering to those in need of services. The recipients of their services (the women) are rarely asked for input or to participate in the design of the program. However, APRAMP does work with its clients to develop their own initiatives and programs.

Entering Prostitution

Routes into prostitution vary. Economic pressures play major roles in most cases, especially in street prostitution, but studies in several countries (including the United States and Canada) show that these economic pressures often result from familial abuse and neglect. Economic need is a result of being runaways, single mothers, or unskilled workers. Other influences include coercion from pimps, frequently masked in "love" relations, and the need to support a drug habit. Women sometimes enter prostitution through association with friends who are prostitutes. Teresa, working in Madrid, left home because her older brother molested her:

> When I was thirteen I started to run away because my brother had sexually abused me. My parents would find me, but I couldn't stand to look at him. Maybe we would be all having dinner and just looking at him was unbearable, so disgusting! I would have to get up and go to the bathroom to cry, it was so disgusting. So because of all of this I started to run away. I never told my mother. I guess I was afraid, and also, if I had a daughter and she told me that, I would feel horrible, and I kept thinking about that, my mother's suffering.... I think that all of that has had a lot to do with the life I am leading.

Carmen, working in Madrid, is another case in point. As a result of a relationship with a boyfriend with whom she claims "nothing happened," her mother kicked her out, saying that she did not want "a whore" in her house. Carmen went to live with her boyfriend's family, but after they forced her out, she started sleeping on the street, met a girl from a neighborhood where prostitution was common, and was soon pimped, at age fifteen:

> The first time I had sex it was with this young man. When I met him he was like a friend. He had led me to believe that we were going out. What did I know? I was a kid. He made us do all kinds of things, and would beat us, too.

Beatriz, in Albacete, described several events that led her into prostitution:

> I was pregnant, and my boyfriend wanted nothing to do with me. So my family put me in a religious boarding school.... Those nuns, they were very good people and all, but they don't help you. From the moment you are put there, it seems like a prison. It makes more sense to talk to people, to help them understand themselves, and be less rigid.... I didn't like that place and that is when I started in prostitution in Madrid. I started to work at a cheap hotel where all the guests were girls working in bars. I couldn't feed my daughter on my wages. So one day when I was crying, a girl said, "Why don't you come out with me tonight?" So of course I did, and I earned a fair amount of money, and I was able to buy my daughter clothing, everything.

Young people can become involved in prostitution through emotional neediness and vulnerability as well as homelessness and poverty. In England, girls are particularly vulnerable to entering prostitution after leaving local authority care (state-run institutions for girls in need).[6] Many of these girls are ill-equipped for independent living, and many have had little continuity of care, being moved from foster care to residential care or between residential homes numerous times. Some girls in local authority care stop attending school, which reinforces their "outsider" status. Low self-confidence and self-esteem can lead them into a peer group offering a sense of belonging and mutual support. All of this may make them vulnerable to a life on the streets.

Janey's mother worked as a prostitute. She was cared for mostly by her father, who also sexually abused her. Her parents' relationship was marked by violence. Janey came into care (in Nottingham) when she was eight or nine. She recounted how she got involved in prostitution "not for the money" but through another girl in care, because she "wanted to belong."

Louise, also from Nottingham, was adopted as a young child, and she started to harm herself (cutting her arms and legs) when she was eight years old. At twelve she was put into the care of the local authority. Louise describes her entrance into prostitution:

> So I got in with the wrong crowd here and I got introduced.... I was told that prostitution was the in thing, [but] I never could see myself as a prostitute; I thought it was dirty. And then I just started doing it with my friend.... It was dead-easy money, £250 a time or sometimes you got more. So I started working, and I have never been assaulted or anything.... Then I started taking crack, and ended up selling my body for rock.

Competition

Prostitution can be socially divisive between women. One source of conflict is price-busting on the part of new, young, drug-addicted, immigrant, or desperate workers, which infuriates other prostutitutes because it lowers the prevailing price for sex. Moira, in Nottingham, states:

> I had to chase two little girls away recently.... I have never been horrible to other prostitutes, but all they are doing is giving the money to a ponce [pimp], and it really pissed me off to see them coming where our group stands.... And I said, "Why are you two doing doubles [two girls with one customer] when we find it so hard to do them?"... One is fourteen and one is sixteen.... I only come out Saturdays and Sundays so I have to defend it. ... You feel gutted. [I'm] out there for an hour, and [I] see them in and out of cars.

The young girls were resented for getting more business because of their youth.

In Staffordshire, Rhiannon described the competitiveness among the workers in massage parlors: "You get the same problem at all of [the parlors].... If a girl gets popular, they [other prostitutes] get bitchy.... [It's] dog eat dog. They stab you in the back. Twice they took my door key, my purse. Nowadays you can't trust anyone." Teresa spoke of being marginalized by the other street prostitutes in Madrid:

> They say that I take away their clients. Maybe a man has gone with them two or three times, and then he saw me, and chose to go with me. I tell them that it's not my fault, that I am here working just like them. What am I supposed to ... say to the client, "No, go away!"?

Victimization

Female prostitutes are particularly vulnerable to victimization due to their occupational lifestyle: working at night in public places, carrying cash, being socially isolated, and often being in abusive relationships with pimps. Victimization also reflects women's lack of power to demand safe working conditions and police protection.[7] One might expect that in Spain, where prostitution is not criminalized, it might be somewhat safer. Yet prostitution continues to be highly stigmatized and marginalized, resulting in a lack of protection against victimization.

Prostitutes can be victimized by pimps and customers. Generally, victimization is more frequent when customers are unknown, as opposed to "regulars," and when sex work occurs in unsupervised areas (lacking the presense of police or outreach workers), where women are particularly vulnerable. Olga, in Madrid, made this general observation about customers:

> You have to be very careful, because in these days men think that since prostitutes are totally unprotected, everything is easier with them: easier to hit them, easier to rape them, easier to abuse them.

For some of our respondents, the violence was unpredictable and sometimes resembled kidnappings. Rapes and assaults were committed by both customers and third parties (e.g., taxi drivers), sometimes in places unfamiliar to the women, sometimes while the woman was high or drunk. Another form of violence is being forced by clients to have sex without a condom. Teresa, a heroin addict in Madrid, has been repeatedly victimized:

> Many times in hotel rooms, the man has paid me and does it with such aggression that I tell him that he is hurting me, but according to him, it has to be that way, it excites him, that is why he pays me. If he pays me he can do anything he wants with me.... One guy, we went to a hotel, he paid me, and then took out a knife. I was so scared! I thought he was going to kill me. But no! This excited him. He put it to my neck, around my breasts, everywhere. He even cut me, this excited him.... I had to go to the doctor to get the cuts disinfected.

And Sandra, in Madrid, stated:

> Once, on my way home from a discotheque where I had been drinking . . . I caught a taxi.... I was half asleep in the taxi and I told him where to go and when I woke up, we were in the park, and I said, "What are you doing?" And he said, "Come on, just touch me, it's not a big deal."...We started to fight, and he ended up raping me.... He raped me and left me there in the park and kept the money for the taxi ride. So I had to go find another taxi and finally I arrived home with my coat all ripped and muddy and my bra torn.

Cathy described one customer: "He was ramming it in and I said, 'You're being too rough....' He said, 'I'll be as rough as I want.' So I just finished with him, got him out.... I thought he was gonna kill me.... It was horrible ... piercing eyes.... He looks at you and wants to rip your head off."

Robberies and thefts were also common, either by strangers or customers who, once having paid for services, took their money back. It is not unusual for men to give excuses for not paying at all, for them to want to pay less when they cannot perform, and for them to demand different services than those originally negotiated. Some men use weapons to get their money back:

> Many times, I've had to give back the money because they have threatened me with a knife. I've been threatened often with knives. I've seen myself in a life-or-death situation. So I've had to give the money back. (Adela, Madrid)

A robbery incident was described by Kim from Staffordshire:

> He started off, and he's covered in sweat and shaking, and I thought, something is not right.... So I said, "Can you stop the car, please? I want to get out, I don't feel right." I don't know what made me say it. I thought he was gonna do me in or something. He turns up this street and slammed on his brakes and said, "Give me your money." I said, "I've got no money.".... He had this knife.... He's got it up to my neck [and said], "You fucking liar, I've seen you get into cars; now give me you're money or I'm gonna slash you're throat." So I just gave it to him and got out.... I had a pen in my bag, and I wrote [the car registration number] on my hand and I gave it to the police.... But I didn't dare go to court and give evidence or anything. I didn't dare, in case he saw me out on the street again.

Another form of victimization mentioned in the Spanish interviews was trafficking in women and children. Trafficking occurs with women who are already part of the underworld, and also with foreigners who are lured to Spain under the guise of domestic employment. It is hard for the women to report this to the authorities because they depend on their traffickers and pimps for survival and are isolated from the rest of society. Much of this trafficking in Spain occurs in rural highway clubs. Virginia, from Albacete, said,

> Prostitution is a mafia, where women are exchanged, where women are sold, children are sold.... I had a coworker who sold her seven children one by one.... These women are given money, sometimes cars, houses, everything.... You can't report [the traffickers] to the police because it is not a specific person; it's many people.

The extent of such trafficking is unknown, but it sometimes results in an arrest and prosecution under the law against pimping.

SURVIVAL STRATEGIES

Downplaying the Prostitute Identity

Prostitutes attempt to divorce their personal selves from their work selves and their emotions from their bodies. Susan Edwards describes this as "selling the body, keeping the soul," and argues that "such boundary defining is essential for survival."[8] Such separation may be very difficult, however, as some of our respondents indicated. In describing the tension between her work and real selves, Moira, in Nottingham, also referred to both the stigma of being a prostitute and its economic benefits:

> I have lost friends; they look at you totally different. It bothered me. I thought, "Fucking hell, I am a prostitute." I am, but I'm not. I have two different lives—work and me…. My boyfriend's friend sat watching the telly and said, "Look at them dirty prostitutes," and I said, "Just remember I am a prostitute and this is my settee paid for by prostitution, and my TV and my carpet," and everybody looked at me horrified.

Isabel, in Albacete, stated:

> Normally it is easy to separate your work from your personal life. Well, it is difficult but easy if you can control your mind. In principle, I don't like to talk about my personal life with clients, not about my son or anything. Although sometimes you have regular clients that you take a liking to and they ask about your family, but even with those, I just say, fine, fine, everyone is fine.

Sometimes, separating the self from the body requires the help of intoxicants. Virginia (Albacete) says that alcohol is the only way that she can stand her work: "One of the things that one does in prostitution is drink a lot of alcohol. If you aren't drunk then many of the things that happen, you can't accept them nor can you do them nor can they pay you to do them."

The women's bodies are their tools, and feelings and emotions are reserved for private moments. At first Sarah (in England) felt "rotten and disgusted with old men on top of me," and she used to hurt physically and emotionally, but not now because she has "cut off her feelings." For many of these women, men came to be seen as commodities, and as a means to an end. Seeing men in this light, combined with previous negative experiences with men, has affected some of their views of and relationships with men outside of work. Jane, in England, said,

Some [men] were better than others, and I kept them separate.... But sooner or later it does begin to affect you ... because you start seeing [men] as prospective clients.... It all became too much for me.

Teresa, of Madrid, has come to regard all sexual relations with loathing:

To have to sleep on the street, to have to sleep with men, how disgusting! Disgusting! I can even tell you that now, having sex with my husband even seems disgusting.

While some manage to divorce their work selves from their private selves with some measure of success, it is clear that, for others, their experiences and identities as prostitutes come to contaminate their private lives.

Strategies for Safety

"Gentling" refers to soothing or calming down an anxious or aggressive customer as a way of preventing an attack. As one woman stated, "You can talk and talk and talk in a calming way about anything—the weather, the lottery." Our respondents talked about smiling at the men constantly, showing warmth, as a method to prevent violence. Prostitutes also make attempts at calming men through caregiving and "counseling." Emotional labor is one aspect of prostitutes' interactions with customers. Emotional energy is directed at "gentling" but also at suppressing and falsifying her feelings and presenting a "self" which manufactures care, concern, consideration, and a listening ear to her clients. For Rhiannon, the caregiving aspect is an important dimension to her role as a prostitute: "A lot of men say, 'You're not what we expect to find. You seem human, warm, friendly. Some of the young girls tend to be cold.... You treat us like people.'" Lola, of Madrid, described this as the "best practice" in order to avoid trouble:

I have never had problems with clients. Other girls see that I never have arguments with the men, and they say, "I don't know how you do it, everything always turns out right for you." I say that it is because I don't speak badly to the clients, I try to understand them.... You are there to listen to him. There are some women who have no patience with the clients.

Women who had not been victimized said it was because they were good at "handling" the customers from the start of the encounter. They tried to be "pleasing" and "polite," and they said that women who were victimized were sometimes "vulgar" and "nasty" to the customers. Indoor workers also learn to use a pleasant demeanor to prevent problems with customers. José, the manager of a club we visited in a rural area of Spain, trained his workers to be polite, not to use swear words, to be "good girls," to work on their presentation of self—thus serving the dual purpose of making his club popular and keeping "trouble" to a minimum.

Our interviewees also attempted to reduce the chances of victimization by controlling the environment. These included working in "safe" places, near other people, with good lighting; avoiding being pimped; controlling drug and alcohol intake; and networking with other sex workers, by asking them to write down license plate numbers of cars, for example; and by wearing "safe" clothes—i.e., clothing that cannot be used against you by a client (such as a scarf or a necklace), or clothing that would impede escape if necessary (such as stiletto heels, tight skirts). In indoor situations, environmental controls included rules against loud music (to hear possible screams in the rooms) and against having glasses in the rooms (which could be used as weapons). Some clubs also employ bouncers. Negotiating payment prior to services being rendered was one way of preventing "broken contracts," but not all workers were able to impose this sort of rule.

Client screening was also considered important, albeit a luxury if work was not forthcoming. "Known" clients were preferred over unknown ones, and consistent with gentling skills, refusal techniques for undesirable clients were practiced, including upping the prices or giving excuses such as "I'm waiting for a friend." Some women, especially those who worked indoors, practiced various search techniques—giving gentle "pat-downs" while negotiating sex, requesting that the men shower before sex, or providing services only in a lighted room.

LEAVING PROSTITUTION

Many of the women we spoke to seemed willing to leave sex work but had found no other option that paid as well for so few hours. In some cases these women are so stigmatized by their work that few other doors are open to them, even if they were to try other means of employment. Rosa, for example, got bored with the street and landed a job as a servant in a wealthy area of Madrid:

> The woman hired me without any references or anything. But after three months she came to me and said, "I'm sorry, but I've found out that you work

the streets, and I am going to have to let you go." I said, "But you've seen me work here for three months, and everything has been all right." But she said that she didn't want the neighbors to know, that they might see me on the street, the whole society thing. I tried to get another job, but everyone asked for references, and I didn't have any.

By contrast, Sam, in Nottingham, believes it would be rather easy to leave prostitution if she wanted to:

> I went into it through choice but I can't see [stopping now] because I am not ready to. I have good clients and I am not prepared to give up them dollars for love or money. I have always known I have high self-esteem because I have other skills and I don't think every prostitute has got low self-esteem because every prostitute hasn't.... Once a woman starts believing in herself she can decide for herself, go back to college, or work in the co-op.... How may women prostitute themselves in relationships they don't want to be in, but stay in a marriage for financial gain? If it wasn't for financial gain how many women would walk out of that relationship?

For some women, leaving prostitution is simply not an option. Some choose prostitution from a subordinate position in which they face few attractive alternatives. For others, coercion or association with other sex workers led to their entry into prostitution, but they remain because of economic need or because they are part of a subculture of similar workers. A sense of belonging to a subcultural network, friends who understand and do not judge, and feeling wanted and needed may be strong incentives for remaining in prostitution.

CONCLUSION: RECOMMENDATIONS FOR CHANGE

The similarities between the countries relate mostly to the prostitutes' experiences with clients and patterns of victimization. The women consider abuse as an occupational hazard, but they also use various strategies to prevent or minimize abuse.

Routes into prostitution are similar in both countries, with the exception of entry from local authority care, which is largely a British route, since very few women are in care in Spain. In both England and Spain, prostitutes had backgrounds as runaways, single mothers, victims of child abuse, and encouragement from partners and pimps.

Our findings suggest some intervention strategies that are free from value judgments on whether sex work is intrinsically harmful and which instead target women's needs; they also reflect specific societal conditions that should be taken into account in formulating policy. In England, the very vulnerable situation of girls exiting care institutions points to the need for better follow-up and for services to promote their independence and prevent their unwilling entry into sex work. Multiagency work has proved to be successful in this regard in the Midlands and other parts of Britain.[9] Little of this is being done in Spain. While multiagency work is not a panacea, it can be instrumental in providing more coordinated and effective assistance than a single organization can on its own. Bringing together government and voluntary agencies is one way to improve services to women and young people in the areas of support, prevention, and safety.

English outreach programs run by current or former sex workers may serve as a model for Spain. A major outcome of our project was an exchange of information between the organizations we were involved with: POW and the Sex Worker Project in England; APRAMP and IPPSE in Spain. Meetings between members of the Sex Worker Project and APRAMP were particularly useful in that the English group shared health and safety advice and presented examples of Ugly Mug Sheets and Tips of the Trade leaflets, which give women warnings about specific violent and aggressive customers.

APRAMP targets immediate needs as well as long-term needs such as shelter, education, counselling, and therapy. Many of the women who have entered APRAMP's program have become outreach workers themselves, using their skills and experiences as well as the training offered to them by APRAMP to help women currently working in prostitution. In the last year APRAMP has conducted grass-roots outreach work in some of the most dangerous locations in Madrid.

The Sex Worker Project in Stoke-on-Trent offers a model of the ways in which paid workers and volunteers can address the sexual health needs of women working both on and off the street. The workers provide outreach work on the street and a drop-in center where women can call in.

POW in Nottingham is a truly unique project in that most of the paid staff and volunteers are working or former prostitutes. POW began in response to the sexual health needs of female prostitutes but has developed into a service that addresses wider social and welfare needs as well. It now provides outreach work on and off the street, a safe-house network, and advice and information on educational/vocational courses. Supported by a multi-agency management committee, POW is involved in interagency responses to juvenile prostitution, working alongside the police and social service agencies.

The Women's Institute in Spain is a model for other nations. Created in 1983 under the Ministry of Labor and Social Affairs, the institute sponsors research, intervention programs, and legal initiatives designed to advance women's rights.

A much broader debate needs to occur regarding public policies and services to prostitutes in both countries. As a first step, a broader understanding of prostitution from the perspectives of prostitutes themselves can help us to better understand the issues involved and to develop and deliver needed services.

FROM VICTIMS TO SURVIVORS: WORKING WITH RECOVERING STREET PROSTITUTES

Nanette J. Davis

As a survivor [of prostitution], my recovery has been a reclamation ... a gathering time of all that I am and all I'm meant to be ... the empowering to choose life and live it in its fullest sense.
—A former prostitute

Among contemporary feminists, there are two main positions on prostitution: the civil rights emphasis on the right to free sexual expression, and the radical feminist perspective that prostitution is a form of male sexual oppression. In the first case, female equality is enhanced by free choice, including the right to engage in prostitution. In the second position, prostitution enhances sexual, social, and economic inequality.[1]

The "freedom of choice" camp is represented by prostitutes' rights organizations like COYOTE, but is most popularly expressed in terms of the "happy hooker" myth, fictionalized in Hollywood. The "happy hooker" myth is a compilation of beliefs and usually erroneous assumptions that portrays a streetwise, sexy "pretty woman" who freely chooses to enter prostitution. She enjoys her job, until "the right man comes along," and in the meantime, finds sexual gratification from prostitution. A subtext suggests that a few fortunate, and extremely beautiful, women become wealthy in prostitution, or acquire riches by seducing a wealthy man. Prostitution is also depicted as "empowering" women. By reversing the standard gender roles, the prostitute has the edge over a mere "trick," and prostitution offers an avenue for sexual liberation.

Empowerment is inevitable when women choose the "life" over a forty-hour-a-week dull job, for prostitutes are free agents who can work preferred hours in the absence of a time clock and boss. The "happy hooker" myth suggests that prostitution is lucrative, glamorous, and sexy.

The radical feminist perspective is very different. Kathleen Barry insists that prostitution is an extreme form of sexual slavery—no woman can sell her body by choice, but only by male coercion.[2] This perspective views female prostitution as a protracted form of victimization that includes childhood sexual abuse, incest, rape, molestation, and other forms of sexual degradation.[3] Several studies indicate that violence against street prostitutes is widespread.[4] Prostitutes are the victims of violent crime, raped and beaten by clients or pimps and murdered by unknown serial killers.

The radical feminist view further proposes that prostitution represents an extreme case of sexual stratification, in which the commodification of female sexuality contributes to women's devaluation and objectification.[5] Ownership and exchange of female sexuality is the core element of our gender system, but the prostitute, as "common property," acts as a counterpoint to those females whose sexual ownership is "exclusive" to one man. Occupying the lowest order of the sex/gender system, prostitutes are defined by what they are not: sexually non-exclusive, nonrespectable, nonlegitimate, and undeserving of protection.[6]

While studies have been done on prostitutes' rights organizations like COYOTE,[7] there is almost no research on antiprostitution organizations. This study helps to fill that gap by focusing on the Council for Prostitution Alternatives (CPA) in Portland, Oregon, which takes a radical feminist perspective and works to get women out of prostitution. The council receives city and county funding as well as private grants; it is run by paid staff, including social workers, as well as volunteers who are former prostitutes. Board members are involved in fund-raising and public relations work.

This study is based on intensive interviews with the founder of the council and its staff, especially social workers involved in counseling and case management of clients. It is also based on interviews with women in the process of leaving prostitution; as a board member with CPA for more than two years, I had access to clients who visit CPA or who work with staff. I further analyzed CPA statistical data and documents.[8]

PERSPECTIVES AND GOALS

The Council for Prostitution Alternatives reaches out to women who have indicated their willingness to leave prostitution. The emphasis in on "willingness," since relapse behavior is common and expected, although less likely if the woman follows a series of prescribed steps.

Founded in 1985 by Susan Kay Hunter, a community outreach worker, the CPA works to enable adult prostitutes to end the cycle of victimization. A current staff member, Joe Parker, describes this as "assisting women as they create safe and healthy life paths."[9] According to CPA, the causes of prostitution are both societal and individual. Victimization of women and children in the form of rape, incest, battery, child abuse, legal and economic exploitation, racism, sexism, and classism make women vulnerable to recruitment into prostitution. Once involved, psychological and emotional abuse reinforces the victimization, and economic dependency makes escape difficult.[10] CPA's mission statement describes its core ideology:

> Prostitution at all levels is a dehumanizing, abusive, and life-threatening experience. It is violence against women. Prostituted women do not "freely" choose prostitution or abusive relationships; they do not choose prostitution as a form of sexual liberation and/or pleasure; they are not empowered emotionally or financially through prostitution. When provided with help and alternatives, they freely choose to leave prostitution.[11]

To treat the prostitute as either a victim or criminal is a poor stratagem, advocates insist, because such labels are counterproductive. In the first place, "victims" need to be rescued; they are not responsible for themselves; they tend to attract revictimization; and they rarely can pull themselves out of the victim lifestyle. Second, labeling a prostitute a "criminal" leads her to organize her life accordingly. Recidivism in such cases is normal. By contrast, CPA's concept of "survivor"—or one who has confronted her past, but moved on—is the key to releasing women from prostitution. The CPA uses terms like "survivor," "struggle," and "fighting the good fight," to refer to women who attempt to extricate themselves from prostitution,[12] and it cautions against treating prostitutes as either victims or offenders:

> Prostituted women should neither be treated as victims to be rescued nor as criminals to be punished. Rather, they should be empowered to take control of their lives and to have increased options in becoming self-sufficient and gaining a sense of dignity.[13]

The goals are twofold. The organization seeks to change women's lives completely: to turn their lives around, as it were. There is no "halfway" approach to leaving prostitution: It is an all-or-nothing decision. The second goal is to call attention to underlying social problems that generate female prostitution in the first place. These include:

1. male sexual control over women: Men both solicit and punish women who provide sex services;
2. gender inequality and discrimination against women: This is reflected in gender bias in enforcement. Most of the persons arrested for prostitution are women; pimps and customers are rarely prosecuted;
3. class and racial discrimination: A high proportion of street prostitutes are minority and poor women, many of whom lack social and work skills that could provide options.

The CPA eschews legal remedies, such as criminalization, decriminalization, legalization, or zoning ordinances. Since these approaches fail to address the causes of prostitution, they do not remedy the problem. Instead, CPA argues that these "remedies" often perpetuate the victimization by making it difficult for the workers to receive services that would empower them to improve their lives.[14] The so-called remedies are more likely to target prostitutes, and allow male pimps, businessmen, clients, and street criminals to continue their exploitation and abuse.

Stiffer sanctions are favored for these men. Community groups have recently fought prostitution by pushing for greater control of customers—confiscation of cars, fines, public notices (including customers' photographs and addresses), informing wives, and other forms of harassment.[15] Most CPA staff welcome the focus on male customers as the culprits, since it signals intolerance of the men responsible for street prostitution.

CLIENTS

The street prostitutes served by CPA may not be representative of street workers in Portland, since they are not a random sample of the population; these prostitutes seek out CPA's services, and may thus be the most desperate segment of the streetworker population. However, it is clear that CPA's clients—and arguably other street prostitutes as well—suffer from severe social and psychological deficiencies that are difficult to overcome: little education, joblessness, minority status, homelessness, dysfunctional families, chronic childhood sexual and physical abuse, frequent arrests, drug and alcohol addiction, and a host of physical and emotional problems. Table 9.1 provides information from 1991 on clients' family histories, involvement in the

TABLE 9.1 CHARACTERISTICS OF 800 CPA
PARTICIPANTS (1991)

	(PERCENT)
FAMILY STATUS	
Have children	82
Living with children	41
Currently pregnant	1
CRIMINAL JUSTICE INVOLVEMENT	
Convicted of crime	84
Misdemeanor	55
Felony	30
Jail or prison	80
ALCOHOL AND DRUG USE	
Drug/alcohol addiction	88
Alcohol	19
Cocaine	24
Heroin	13
Poly drug/alcohol	43
Injected drugs	43
5 Years or more addicted	68
Treatment (pre-CPA)	57
Treatment (in CPA)	70
Still using drugs (in CPA)	30
VICTIMIZATION	
Homeless	
(average 6.3 years)	90
Raped	71
By pimp	85
By john	78
Reported to police	9
Assaulted	95
By pimp	63
By john	100
Reported to police	5
Kidnapped	53
By pimp	77
By john	91
Reported to police	0

criminal justice system, years spent prostituting, alcohol or drug addiction, and victimization by various parties. A large proportion said they had been raped, assaulted, or kidnapped by a pimp or a john, yet almost no one reported these crimes to the police.

The 1994 cohort of CPA participants reported a number of disadvantages and personal problems. For example, 68 percent were school dropouts; 88 percent supported children; 93 percent were homeless; 71 percent had never held a job; and 51 percent were from communities of color. At the same time, personal coping behavior was very poor: Ninety percent were drug or alcohol addicted; 78 percent had attempted suicide; and more than 75 percent reported they were sexually abused as children. Victimization was again very common: eighty-nine percent have been victims of rape, while 93 percent have been victims of nonsexual assault. CPA emphasizes that these clients require extensive services to change their attitudes and lifestyles.

PROGRAM

Initially, the organization focused on the primary goal of safe housing and a twenty-four-hour in-house commitment to prostitutes exiting the life. This goal proved unmanageable, and within a few years was abandoned because of lack of intensive supervision, high costs, and the type of client (many candidates appeared "overly comfortable" and unwilling to leave the deviant lifestyle once provided with stable shelter and other amenities). Such factors undermined the "total care" provision.[16] Instead, the program shifted to a support network and case-management approach that comprises four phases:

Phase I

Phase I entails emergency intervention focused on intake and drop-in services. A ninety-day treatment program assesses clients' needs and secures support services (assistance with locating housing, food, hygiene items, rental assistance transportation, medical care, and personal needs income) and agency referrals. At any given time approximately eighty women are in the program, with 144 outreach participants. Awareness groups introduce the concepts of sex abuse, sexual exploitation, informed consent, and meaningful choice. A central idea is that prostitution is inherently victimizing, a position that most clients initially fail to comprehend. CPA social workers indicate that because women have been numbed by their experiences, they have poor judgment in assessing their own lives. Consequently, they repeatedly fall back into patterns of prostitution or substance abuse or both.

To offset their victim consciousness, CPA introduces the concept of "healing." First, clients must confront the degradation of prostitution. Then, clients must wrestle with high levels of discomfort when "flooding" occurs—or the sudden release of repressed emotional pain. This takes place when women are exposed to prostitution "myths" (e.g., prostitution as sexual freedom or as heightened individualism), and the need to seek options to a lifestyle that is self-destructive.

Phase II

Whereas the first phase was designed to assure that basic "survival needs" have been met, the second phase begins the "long-term stabilization" away from prostitution. Reorienting clients to a "healthy and viable lifestyle" requires a *devictimization* process. Here the victim mode must be abandoned before self-empowerment and choice-making can occur. This process entails two steps: First, reframe past experience, and second, replace destructive patterns with supportive patterns. In the latter case, this requires developing and engaging in problem identification, choice-making skills, and self-awareness. The MAPS Curriculum, a guided set of language and concepts, promotes the learning of a common language that emphasizes both abuse and recovery. The fairly high intellectual level of the "curriculum" unsettles some women, at least initially. Individual case management, however, personalizes the process, modifying the formal categories to accommodate the woman's experience. The goal here is enhanced self-awareness, which may involve considerable psychological discomfort. CPA also includes a parenting skills program, children's groups, employment, or job-training readiness in tandem with the case management. Approximately forty women are in this phase at any one time.

Phase III

The third phase, reconnecting, aims to rebuild or make ready the transition from the CPA program to a self-maintaining regime, and focuses on "personal recovery of self-reliance, self-will, and determination to change."[17] Participants are asked to abandon old associates and maintain only nondeviant personal relationships. They are also expected to seek and develop resources on their own (with the assistance of appropriate service agencies). Case management is less intensive at this phase. Instead, the effort is to create peer groups for ongoing support in the community. Staff speak of this phase as the "takeoff" stage, which requires "developing self-responsibility for recovery, accessing future resources with agency help, and finding individual and group support" (e.g., Alcoholics Anonymous, group therapy).[18] The women respond in varying ways to this phase, since many have shifted dependencies from deviant street associates to staff persons, and may be unwilling to "take off" on their own according to plan. This phase usually involves about forty women at a time.

Phase IV

A final stage, identified as "mentoring," requires a level of maturity and recovery that demonstrates that the former prostitute is now ready for community outreach. The client is asked to lead a peer support group, not on her own, but with "graduates" of the CPA program. The number involved at this phase depends upon the number of CPA graduates who are willing and able to make a commitment to giving community outreach presentations, or even assisting with community outreach training. The arrangement works for some women who feel empowered by this level of participation, welcome the "insider" status they now enjoy (a kind of elite group), and benefit from the ongoing staff support they receive. The "Program Summary" emphasizes that "in becoming a role model for new participants, mentors can maintain connections with other women with common experiences, as well as celebrate their own accomplishments."[19]

CURRICULUM

The program includes an eight-week series of one-hour educational sessions followed by a one-hour support group each week. The support group strives to promote an atmosphere of openness in which the women can freely exchange ideas and experiences. The organization places great importance on the educational sessions to fulfill a number of goals, including: (1) to identify dysfunctional behaviors, (2) to establish a common recovery and treatment language, (3) to provide an environment and tools for self-awareness, and (4) to integrate new information with experience.

The eight-week curriculum is structured as follows:

Week 1. CPA Program Orientation. Here, clients are oriented to the program and treatment expectations, support group, and program guidelines. This also introduces "devictimization" concepts and definitions of prostitution as sexual slavery and oppression. The organization often draws on literature from WHISPER, a now defunct organization that was dedicated to the same radical feminist antiprostitution ideology as CPA.[20]

Week 2. Empowerment vs. Enablement. This phase introduces concepts of "enablement" or codependency (powerlessness, because of dependency upon persons, substances, or things) and empowerment (or personal power), and provides tools for self-awareness and identification of "power points" within the individual.

Week 3. Terror-bonding. The curriculum then shifts to a theory of "terror-bonding," the idea that dependent and "shell-shocked" individuals actually bond to violent perpetrators. CPA applies this to prostitution, with its distorted personal relationships between prostitutes and pimps. Counselors provide self-awareness exercises and cognitive tools both for identification of these experiences and for coping with the memories.

Week 4. Making choices. At this stage, the women are introduced to concepts of mutual consent, informed consent, meaningful choice, and identifying options. The organization presumes that few prostitutes will have explored the need for options or how to create alternatives. As women are provided with the skills and exercises for making choices, CPA believes that most will seek to leave prostitution.

Week 5. Cycle of Violence. During this week, the women are introduced to the theory of the "cycle of violence," to provide an understanding of how this cycle may have worked in their own lives, beginning in childhood and perpetuated in prostitution. Again, women are given tools for self-awareness exercises and identification of these experiences.

Week 6. Sobriety and Recovery. For this phase, the organization has developed a "model of recovery" that sees the use of street drugs as harmful, addiction as self-abuse, and the "three laws of recovery" (Law #1, Sobriety is the first priority; Law #2, Trust your hesitations; and Law #3, You decide). This is a highly significant phase, inasmuch as it is believed that all prostitutes are seriously addicted to drugs or alcohol.

Week 7. A Model of Prostitution and Sex Abuse. Staff introduce the work of Debra Boyer, a Seattle anthropologist, who created a model of how sex abuse and the culture's double sexual standards foster prostitution.[21] Clients are expected to use the model in exercises to identify the personal experiences that led to their entry into prostitution.

Week 8. Retelling the Story. In this final week, the women are introduced to a theory of "attempted resolution patterns." This involves exercises and tools for resolving what CPA asserts are the inconsistencies of being a prostitute and meaningful survival as women.

Part of CPA's curriculum is a critique of the actors involved in prostitution, particularly the johns and pimps. The johns simply want their needs for power and fantasy met. Some johns are ordinary men, but others are sadists, taking pleasure in another person's fear, pain, or humiliation, and others are child molesters:

> [Johns] like the power involved in buying a human being who can be made to do almost anything [because] the business of prostitution and pornography is the use of real human beings to support the fantasies of others. [Johns play games of] super stud and sex slave.... If they need to support the fantasies with pictures, videotapes, or real people to abuse, the sex trade is ready to supply them.[22]

The pimps target as potential prostitutes people who provide a kind of "victim profile." They focus on young people coming out of families that are abusive, broken, or disorganized. Additionally, homeless, underage youth, including those the social service agencies have ignored or abandoned, provide a ready source for recruitment into the sex industry.[23]

CPA clients are taught about various ways individuals are "broken into" prostitution. Some are kidnapped and held in isolation over a prolonged period, during which they are terrorized, tortured, and gang-raped. Once the victim is convinced that her only hope of survival is to do exactly what she is told, she is "turned out," forced to work as a prostitute. Other girls are pressured into prostitution by a boyfriend, who initially treats them much better than they have ever experienced before, but later pushes her into commercial sex. A third approach is used by older and more sophisticated predators, especially with younger children. These perpetrators become adept at identifying abused, neglected, and depressed children, and befriending them. They develop a "special" relationship, one that isolates the child from others and makes the child feel indebted. Once the child's resistance is broken down, she is coerced into prostitution.

CPA neglects alternative patterns of recruitment. Some CPA clients have a less shocking version of the process of being turned out. Client stories reveal a more pragmatic, if sometimes dismal, story of their entry into street prostitution. Thus, there may be inconsistencies between clients' experiences and CPA ideology. Despite these differences, enough women in each cohort have experienced extreme violence and degradation for CPA to continue to incorporate these ideas in the curriculum.

CLIENT STORIES

Clients are taught by CPA that they need a complete turnaround in their attitudes and everyday behavior. Former companions, work, recreation, leisure, feelings, self-concept, medical care—all must change for the recovery program to take hold. The CPA handbook offers a compilation of stories, advice, sad tales, and reflections to assist prostitutes in making necessary changes toward recovering (all quotations in this section are taken from the handbook). The handbook dedication articulates the organization's belief that prostitution is mortally dangerous to women, since prostitutes are often targets of serial killers. The deaths of these women and children are remembered and mourned:

> *In remembrance of the atrocities at*
> *Mollala and Green Rivers—and all the places yet*
> *unspoken ... in the hope that someday*
> *we will no longer need the sacrifices of women and children.*[24]

Entering Prostitution

How do recovering prostitutes talk about their experiences getting into the life? The handbook, with its summary of client reflections and encounters, provides insights into how the organization interprets the movement into and out of prostitution. Staff and counselors' experiences are also included, inasmuch as they have prostitution histories. In some cases, the experiences are "raw," unmediated by organizational ideology. In other instances, the stories reflect the "new learnings" available through the CPA program. Here is one version of why women enter prostitution:

Somewhere in your life, someone pointed the way to the street. Either it was fast money, you were doing a favor for your boyfriend, or someone turned you out—but a lot had to happen before you turned your first trick … a psychologist who works with post trauma stress syndrome victims suggests that women who are prostituting are "retelling the story" of abuse, neglect, and incest that happened to them. They will tell the story to the world until the pattern is broken or until they are themselves broken.[25]

The CPA would support the idea of a "drift into deviance,"[26] a process that characterizes women who move into prostitution in their early teens with a history of childhood sexual abuse.[27] Because of these early childhood traumas, in which the girl was taught "not to say no to sex as a child," as a teenager she became sexually accessible to boys, and later to men. The sexual double standard plays a key role here. The "slut" role becomes "your true value," the measure of who you "really are." This process is carried into the streets, as sociological studies confirm and as two former prostitutes pointed out:[28]

[Because] your sexual value became that of pleasing men, men became your focus and you sought the only approval from them that you were allowed—sexual approval, allowing men to be sexually healthy at the sacrifice of your own health.

Another cause of prostitution is poverty. Women and children will live in poverty in greater numbers and for longer periods of time than men will. Selling your body for money becomes an alternative to starvation for your children and yourself.[29]

Sexual coercion also contributes to recruitment into prostitution. But it is basically men's sexual needs that drive the market for prostitution:

Whatever leads a woman into prostitution, be it sexual abuse, poverty, or coercion from someone in her life, society must take a hard look at the victims it creates. As long as the current sexual double standard exists, and as long as a man's sexual fulfillment is more important than a woman's, there will be prostitution. We will create a market each day where flesh can be bought, used, and abused to insure male sexual release. As long as we create the market we will have to create the victims that will be sold there.[30]

Getting Out of the Life

The handbook aims to uncover why the women seek to leave prostitution, as well as what they must overcome to have a successful recovery program.

Many women have thought about leaving for years, but somehow continue to stay. Advice for newly recovering prostitutes is to remember what it was like to want to leave:

> You have probably said to yourself in the middle of a trick while some stranger is sweating on you, "I've got to get out of here. I'm going crazy. I hate this trick. I hate myself." You've probably raged inside to yourself when your pimp is beating you again for not going out there for him, "I'll kill this bastard before he kills me." But you go back out, you make the dates, you make your connection, you miss your visitation at CSD [Children's Services Division], and you're hiding out from the last warrant for your arrest. You have some nice things and your lover has his new car that you tricked for him to get. You believe you won't always do this, but for tonight you will. How many nights?[31]

CPA respondents spend an average of nine years or longer in prostitution. This is why a very careful plan is required to change life patterns. The woman has learned how to face danger; how to cope with strangers, rapes, assaults, police officers, the cold, and the courts. An exit plan must specifically address the components that will help to overcome the experiences that led to her sexual exploitation and degradation. She must:

> Find support outside the life, especially with people who have experience helping others leave the life. Reach out to someone outside the life. Obtain emergency shelter, food, and transportation. Get detoxed and into an A/D [alcohol/drug] program, NA [Narcotics Anonymous], or AA [Alcoholics Anonymous] support group. Find a person, case manager, or sponsor who will help you set goals and find out what you need to reach these goals. Let the life go.[32]

One of the most difficult tasks is giving up the old associates—street friends, pimps, drug dealers, and johns. These people tell survivors that they should stay in the life, even though it "leaves you empty, feeling incapable, and that everything you have can be gone in a minute. You trust no one. You don't feel or let anyone see you feeling. In the life you have to fake it to make it."[33] Getting into a recovery program requires, above all, finding alternative sources of support among women:

> Reaching out and forming relationships with other women will be hard. We were in competition with each other for the trick, and it's going to be hard to think of other women as anything but competition.[34]

Another important task is finding a job, because prostitution is "not work," according to CPA:

> Work is the providing of specific and agreed upon services for a specific amount of money, good, or reward, without the oppression, coercion, or manipulation of one person over another. Being a waitress can be a crappy job, hard work, and putting up with rude people. Put on a bunny suit and serve drinks, and it's no longer work, it's sexual exploitation.[35]

Because the life was "fast and abusive," driven by a coercive pimp, money for drugs, or simply self-defeating behavior, it can never be defined as "work." Once in recovery, the woman gets her "real self" back, and then comes to realize that the phrase, "I work the streets," as though it were a job, is really "slavery for sale, incest for sale, mutilation for sale, defecation for sale, beatings for sale...." In the final analysis a legitimate job is one that the worker can leave at any time, unlike prostitution:

> The bottom line for me is this: It's better to have a lousy job you can walk away from and find something else, instead of having to turn tricks because you think you can't do better, or you don't want to be out of pocket and get beat. There's no choice in that life. In the legitimate world you have the freedom to walk away from anything that is harmful to you. You may lose the job, you still have *yourself.* And since you have yourself, you can find the way to getting another job with a better employer.[36]

The women are told that "you have lots of choice and control ... and it's still better than the streets." The final appeal is the opportunity to feel dignity and begin healing:

> In the straight world, you have a chance to feel dignity. Sometimes you have to fight for it, earn it, work at it—but when you have it, it's yours. In the straight world you have a chance to heal and love yourself. You have the chance to see who you really are inside and belong to yourself instead of always belonging to someone else, like the pimp, john, boyfriend, trick, criminal system, or CSD.... It matters what you think—not what the world thinks of you.[37]

A final inducement is that of sending their pimps to jail. CPA participants were successful in helping the police bring several men to trial for pimping (a felony in Portland), some of whom were convicted.

OBSTACLES TO INTERVENTION

Between 1985 and July 1991, 399 prostitutes had signed an agreement to enter one of the CPA-related agencies. Seventy-three graduated and left prostitution; 291 received services but dropped out short of successful completion; and 35 remained in services.

The program is organized around the concept of "cadre commitment," the notion that women who move in tightly knit cohort groups through the phases make a commitment to their cohorts, rather than an individual commitment to the program, as such. This is not an easy program: as women move from the initial phase into reframing experiences, they frequently confront painful memories, including a sense of powerlessness and meaninglessness. Before the program, drugs and alcohol and a crisis-oriented lifestyle kept feelings at bay. Once their security needs are met, some women may be overcome by confronting their former life with "new eyes" that perceive only the "horror" and "indignity" of prostitution.

Staff report that most women who enter the program suffer from physical, emotional, or mental disease; among common maladies are malnutrition, pelvic inflammatory disease, poorly healed fractures, unmet surgical needs, extreme stress, and post-traumatic syndrome (including abnormal sweating, gastrointestinal disorders, nightmares, panic attacks, fear). Confronted with homelessness and constant fear that her pimp will discover her whereabouts, most women's energies are easily depleted. Case managers observe that it takes nearly six months before women are ready to deal with their feelings and confront their own lives. CPA's focus on compassion, staff availability, mutual empowerment, and partnership ease the "clearing process." This entails completing the early phases of meeting "survival needs" (without turning tricks or using drugs) and internalization of program goals. Rebuilding identity, for instance, requires not re-creating the old, dysfunctional childhood patterns, but creating new, viable roles which will sustain the woman in relationships, work, and life.

Many women believe they cannot exit prostitution. According to staff, the longer a woman has been in prostitution prior to entering CPA, the more likely she will drop out. The average length of time in prostitution for program participants who succeed is 4.2 years, about half the average for all the women in the program.

Age is another factor in recruitment and retention. Women under twenty-five years of age continue to be seduced by street life, their pimps, and their drug habits, and are less inclined to enter the program, or to remain, once in it. Many women go in and out of the program repeatedly. They are unable either to leave prostitution or to commit to personal change. Yet each time they come, they can accomplish something, program advocates insist: enhanced awareness, refusal to be victimized, better self-management skills, and above all, hope.

CONCLUSION

CPA rejects the ideas that prostitution is a "victimless crime" and that it is legitimate "work." Instead, this group argues that prostitution is a culturally sanctioned system of oppression that uses women and children as sexual objects. The backgrounds of the women who enter prostitution have significant parallels with domestic violence: family history of neglect and abuse, social isolation, sexual, psychological, and physical abuse, drug and alcohol abuse, and limited alternatives for individuals attempting to escape their abusive situations. Moving out of prostitution is very difficult:

> Even with public assistance or a minimum-wage job, safe, affordable housing is hard to find. Moreover, survivors often must relocate to a neighborhood or other cities where they can feel safe from retribution or recognition from pimps or johns.[38]

Advocacy programs for prostitutes are hardly a new phenomenon. From medieval times, Christian groups have attempted to "save" prostitutes from vice and self-destruction.[39] Today, radical feminist programs, like CPA's, share this view but also argue that prostitution reflects gender inequality and the victimization of women. But a lingering question remains: Is female adult prostitution uniformly degrading, requiring intervention "for the woman's own good"? Shall we conclude from the radical feminist position and CPA ideology that prostitutes as a group are not "free" women able to make their own choices, and thus need to be under the tutelage of private or state agencies? I raise this question because CPA deals primarily with street prostitutes—a group with higher exposure to violent predators than indoor prostitutes in bordellos, message parlors, or escort services—yet CPA has generalized its claims to cover all forms of prostitution.

At its best, radical feminist advocacy serves as a reclamation process for some prostitutes, empowering the disempowered. At its worst, it reinforces stereotypes about prostitutes as unfit and degraded persons. It also encourages alliances with other antiprostitution groups (police, local community groups, moralists), some of which may be less interested in rescuing street women than in eradicating public displays of prostitution. Prostitution historically has been subjected to moral crusades that have scapegoated poor women prostitutes.[40] The link between these earlier events and contemporary gender politics is often lost. The insistence that prostitutes are incapable of making sound decisions, except to leave prostitution, is a subtext among intervention specialists. Despite these problematic assumptions, CPA's efforts in assisting street prostitutes to leave the trade have been remarkable.

3

POLITICS, POLICING, AND THE SEX INDUSTRY

THE POLITICS OF PROSTITUTION IN AMERICA

Ronald Weitzer

Prostitution policies in America have remained fairly stable over the past three decades, but change has occurred in some areas of law and public policy and in citizen intervention on prostitution issues. Although to a lesser extent than in some other societies, prostitution policy has become increasingly contested in the United States. This chapter begins with an overview of current public policy and public opinion on prostitution, and then analyzes the clashing views and activities of organizations in the antiprostitution camp and in the prostitutes' rights movement. The chapter concludes with a brief comparison of the United States with the contrasting case of the Netherlands.

LAW AND PUBLIC POLICY

Criminalization is the reigning paradigm in the American approach to prostitution, which means that solicitation to engage in an act of prostitution is illegal everywhere, except in certain counties in Nevada, where legal brothels exist. Pimping and pandering/procuring are also crimes and, in some states, running or residing in a brothel is a separate offense.

Approximately 90,000 arrests are made in the United States every year for violations of prostitution laws,[1] in addition to an unknown number of arrests of prostitutes under disorderly conduct or loitering statutes. The fiscal costs are substantial. A study of the country's sixteen largest cities found that each spent an average of $7.5 million and a total of $120 million in 1985 enforcing prostitution laws.[2] The average cost of arresting, adjudicating, and sanctioning each suspect was $2,000. Data are lacking on the cost of prostitution control nationwide, but since more than 90 percent of prostitution arrests occur in cities,[3] where the cost per arrest may approximate the above figure, 90,000 arrests would cost about $180 million annually; this estimate does not include arrests of prostitutes for loitering or disorderly conduct.

These expenditures have little noticeable effect on street prostitution. At best, the problem is (1) *contained* within a particular area where prostitutes are occasionally subjected to the revolving door of arrest, fines, brief jail time, and release, or (2) *displaced* into another locale where the same revolving-door dynamic recurs. Containment is the norm throughout the United States;[4] displacement requires sustained police crackdowns, which are rare. Containment may be acceptable to residents of neighborhoods free of street prostitution, but quite aggravating to those living in affected areas (see below).

The United States has not been hospitable to alternatives to criminalization, such as decriminalization or legalization. Decriminalization, in its purest form, would remove all criminal penalties and leave prostitution unregulated. *Decriminalization* could benefit prostitutes insofar as police would shift from arresting to protecting them, and prostitutes would feel less inhibited in reporting victimization to the police. But it would also create new problems. Generally, a laissez-faire approach would give prostitutes advantages unavailable to purveyors of other commercial services. As Skolnick and Dombrink ask, "Why should sexual services be exempted from regulation when other consenting commercial activities are regulated?"[5] Taken to its extreme, decriminalization would allow prostitution in any locale, so long as it did not violate other norms, such as public order or nudity laws.

Proposals for decriminalization run up against a wall of public opposition, and policy makers are almost universally opposed to the idea, making it a nonstarter in any serious discussion of policy alternatives. Advocates sometimes manage to get it placed on the public agenda, however. A recent example illustrates the fate of a decriminalization proposal in perhaps the most tolerant of American cities. A Task Force on Prostitution was formed by the San Francisco Board of Supervisors in 1994 to explore alternatives to existing methods of prostitution control. Members included representatives of community and business groups, the National Lawyer's Guild, National Organization for Women, prostitutes' rights groups, the police department, the district attorney's office, and several other groups. From day one the prostitutes' advocates and their sympathizers set the agenda and dominated the proceedings, which led to chronic infighting. Former Supervisor Terence Hallinan was the driving force in establishing the panel but unsatisfied with the result: "I didn't ride herd on this task force. I would have liked a better balance.... Instead of coming up with good, practical solutions, they spent months fighting about decriminalization and legalization."[6] After a majority of the members voted to recommend a policy of decriminalization in January 1995,[7] the six community and business representatives resigned. One of the community members later told me that the exit of his faction angered the remaining members and shredded the legitimacy of the panel: "They were upset as hell because the task force lost credibility without the citizens' groups participating."[8] While the comment is not made from a disinterested position, the task force report itself expresses regret that consensus was not achieved on its main recommendation.

The panel's endorsement of decriminalization reflected the interests of prostitutes' advocates and their allies and doomed the report's prospect for serious consideration in official circles. The city's Board of Supervisors promptly shelved the report. It is possible, however, that a less radical recommendation would have been received more favorably by city officials; Supervisor Hallinan and even some community leaders had floated the possibility of legalization (zoning in red-light areas) when the task force was first proposed.

Unlike decriminalization, *legalization* implies regulation of some kind: licensing or registration, zoning of street prostitution, legal brothels, mandatory medical exams, special business taxes. Although a segment of the American public favors legalization, this has not crystallized into popular pressure for legal change anywhere in the country, in part because most citizens see it as far removed from their personal interests and because there has been relatively little public debate on prostitution policy.

Advocates of legalization sometimes cite with approval Nevada's legal brothels. Confined to small-scale operations in rural areas of the state (prohibited in Las Vegas and Reno due to opposition from the gaming industry), this model hardly solves the problem of street prostitution in urban areas. Streetwalkers flourish in Las Vegas and Reno, despite the existence of legal brothels in counties adjacent to these cities. What is needed is an urban solution to an essentially urban problem.

Since Nevada legalized brothels in 1971, no other state has seriously considered legalization. Legislators fear being branded as "condoning" prostitution and see no political advantages in any kind of liberalization. On those rare occasions when the idea has been resuscitated, it has had a short life. Bills to permit licensing of prostitutes and brothels were introduced in the California State Assembly in the 1970s, to no avail.[9] In 1992 New York City Council member Julia Harrison offered a resolution for licensing prostitutes, restricting legal brothels to certain parts of the city, and requiring AIDS tests of the workers. Harrison's proposal met with stiff opposition in the city council and quickly died.[10]

Legalization raises several important questions. First, it institutionalizes and seems to condone prostitution, and arguably makes it more difficult for workers to leave the business. Government officials, feminists, and prostitutes' rights advocates alike object to legalization on precisely these grounds. Whether legalization would indeed make it more difficult for workers to leave prostitution than is the case under criminalization would depend in part on whether the workers were officially labeled as prostitutes—via registration, licensing, special commercial taxes, or a registry for mandatory health checks—or whether their identities would remain unknown to the authorities, as might be the case if legalization took the form of zoning.

The second question is whether legalization would lead to a proliferation of prostitution. Would it increase the number of individuals working as prostitutes? The number of prostitutes is partly affected by demand, which might limit the growth of the sex trade, though it is possible that greater supply—especially under conditions of legality—might increase demand. Were legal prostitution limited to one or a few cities, it would undoubtedly attract an influx of prostitutes into that locale. Were it more widespread, each locale would hold less attraction to outside workers, reducing the migration problem.

Third, will prostitutes comply with the law? The decisive factor in the success of any regime of legalization is the willingness of prostitutes to abide by the regulations. Insofar as legalization includes stipulations as to who can and cannot engage in sex work, those ineligible (e.g., underage or HIV-positive prostitutes) would be forced to operate illicitly in the shadows of the regulated system. In addition, every conceivable form of legalization would be rejected by some or many eligible prostitutes, who would see no benefits in abiding by the new restrictions and would resent the infringement on their freedom. It is precisely on these grounds that prostitutes' rights groups denounce licensing/registration, mandatory health checks, and legal brothel systems. A possible exception would be the zoning of street prostitution into a suitable locale: away from residential areas but in places that are safe and unintimidating for prostitutes and customers alike. Some streetwalkers would be satisfied with this kind of arrangement, but others would reject it for personal reasons. Red-light districts in industrial zones have been proposed, for example, but most streetwalkers would shun such areas because they typically lack places of refuge and sustenance, such as restaurants, coffee shops, grocery stores, bars, parks, and cheap hotels—amenities required by most streetwalkers.[11] Even if a generally acceptable locale could be found, there is no guarantee that street prostitution could be confined to that area; possible market saturation in the designated zone is only one reason why some workers would be attracted to other locales. Moreover, while zoning presumably would remove street prostitution from residential areas, it would not necessarily remedy other problems asssociated with street work, such as violence and drug abuse. Indeed, such zones may simply reproduce these problems in a more concentrated manner.

Whatever the possible merits (health, safety, cost-effectiveness, etc.) of any particular model of legalization, is it feasible in a country like the United States? Not very. Advocates face almost impossible odds trying to marshal support from legislators and the public, and proposals for legalization will remain nonstarters in this country for the foreseeable future.

PUBLIC OPINION

How does the American public view prostitution? Is there popular support for changes in existing laws and public policies?

Most Americans see prostitution as immoral. One survey asked respondents whether they thought "men spending an evening with a prostitute" was morally wrong: fully 61 percent considered it morally wrong; 34 percent did not.[12] Citizens' attitudes are mixed regarding public policy. There is no majority support for relaxation of prostitution laws, though a significant minority does support legalization (unfortunately, most polls leave "legalization" undefined, so it remains unclear what respondents have in mind). Men are more likely than women to favor legalization or toleration, as shown in Table 10.1, questions 1, 2, and 5. Question wording makes a difference. When respondents are provided with a scenario presenting potential benefits of legalization (e.g., reducing AIDS, question 2), the percentage favoring legalization is higher than when no benefits are mentioned (question 1). Question 3 allows us to track trends in opinion: Between 1978 and 1990 there was a modest increase in approval of legalization ("regulated by law"), declining support for laissez-faire, pure decriminalization ("left to the individual"), and growing approval of criminalization ("forbidden by law"). Increasing support for criminalization is in line with an earlier trend in public opinion, between the 1970s and 1980s.[13] Question 4 again shows little public support for decriminalization: Only 7 percent of the public thought "there should be no laws against prostitution."

In most surveys the term "prostitution" is not broken down into its different types. In fact, the only American poll that disaggregates prostitution was a 1988 survey of residents of Toledo, Ohio (a blue-collar, working-class city).

163

TABLE 10.1 ATTITUDES ON PROSTITUTION POLICIES

1. "In your opinion, should prostitution involving adults aged 18 years of age and older be legal or illegal?"

	MALES	FEMALES	TOTAL
Legal	32%	21%	26%
Illegal	63%	77%	70%
Don't know/refused	5%	2%	3%
Total	100%	100%	99%
(N)	(497)	(522)	(1,019)

$x^2 = 25.77$, $df = 2$, $p < .001$

Source: Gallup poll, May 28–29, 1996.

2. "Some people feel that in order to help reduce the spread of AIDS, prostitution should be made legal and regulated by the government. Do you agree or disagree?"

	MALES	FEMALES	TOTAL
Agree	46%	34%	40%
Disagree	49%	61%	55%
No opinion	5%	5%	5%
Total	100%	100%	100%
(N)	(604)	(612)	(1,216)

$x^2 = 18.91$, $df = 2$, $p < .001$

Source: Gallup poll, August 29 – September 3, 1991.

3. "I will read you some activities that some people feel are matters of private choice or consent that ought to be left to the individual, that other people feel should be regulated by law, and others feel should be forbidden by law altogether. Please tell me how you feel that activity should be treated: Engaging in prostitution."

	1978	1990
Left to individual	35%	22%
Regulated by law	24%	31%
Forbidden by law	37%	46%
Not sure	4%	1%
Total	100%	100%
(N)	(1,513)	(2,254)

$x^2 = 126.65$, $df = 3$, $p < .001$

Source: Louis Harris polls, November 30 – December 10, 1978; January 11 – February 11, 1990.

TABLE 10.1 (CONTINUED)

4. "Which of the following best describes your feelings about prostitution in the U.S.? It should be illegal; it should be legal under certain restrictions; there should be no laws against prostitution?"

Illegal	43%
Legal under restrictions	46%
No laws	7%
No opinion	4%
Total	100%
(N)	(1,200)

Source: Merit Audits and Surveys, Merit report, October 15–20, 1983.

5. "How much do you agree or disagree with the following statement? There is nothing inherently wrong with prostitution, so long as the health risks can be minimized. If consenting adults agree to exchange money for sex, that is their business."

	MALES	FEMALES	TOTAL
Agree strongly	25%	26%	25%
Agree somewhat	25%	16%	20%
Disagree somewhat	22%	16%	19%
Disagree strongly	25%	40%	33%
Don't know/no answer	3%	3%	3%
Total	100%	101%	100%
(N)	(646)	(798)	(1444)

$x^2 = 46.77, df = 4, p < .001$

Source: General Social Survey, NORC, 1996.

It found that 28 percent supported legal "government-controlled brothels" and 19 percent supported decriminalization of "private call-girl prostitution."[14] (It is unclear why support is lower for the more discreet and invisible call-girl prostitution than for brothels, but it may be related to the general public preference for legalization ["government-controlled"] over decriminalization.) A 1984 Canadian poll found greater support for three types of indoor prostitution. While only 11 percent of Canadians found street prostitution acceptable, there was greater support for designated red-light districts (28 percent), brothels (38 percent), escort and call-girl services (43 percent), and prostitution on private premises (45 percent).[15]

165

American opinion is put into perspective when compared to public attitudes in other nations. Recent polls suggest that the British, French, and Canadians are more willing to endorse legalization: 61 percent in Britain approved of the idea of legalizing and licensing brothels,[16] while 65 percent of Canadians thought prostitution should be "legal and tightly regulated"; and 6 percent said it should be "completely legal," which appears to mean unregulated.[17] A similar proportion (68 percent) of the French population want legalized brothels: 71 percent thought legal brothels would reduce the spread of sexually transmitted diseases, and similar majorities thought legal brothels would make it easier to control prostitution and that the change would not lead to an increase in the French sex trade.[18] Americans, as we have seen, are less inclined to endorse legalization.

NEIGHBORHOOD ANTIPROSTITUTION CAMPAIGNS

While there is almost no public debate on prostitution at the national level, citizen activism at the local level has been growing. In the 1980s and 1990s neighborhood antiprostitution groups have flourished in many American cities.

I examined patterns in the grievances and practices of these groups, based on newspaper reports on a dozen cities and interviews in two cities. Analysis of the complaints of these groups shows that they are concerned largely with the tangible *environmental effects* of the skin trade on the streets, more than moral concerns per se; with *overt street behavior,* not the status offense of being a prostitute; with the immediate and long-term *consequences* of prostitution for host communities, not the social and economic causes of prostitution.[19] For community activists, street prostitution is perceived as threatening the quality of life in a neighborhood as well as its image and reputation. It both symbolizes and contributes to neighborhood decay and a sense that law and order is eroding. It also affects residents' own behavior—making them anxious over the future of their neighborhood, wary of venturing outside their homes, and fearful of altercations with marginal people on the street.

Each of the following themes appears frequently in the litany of grievances I uncovered:

Disorderly Conduct. Judging from activists' claims, prostitutes do not ply their trade unobtrusively. Quite the contrary. They often cause commotion, flagging down customers' cars, arguing and fighting with people on the street, partying, and performing sex acts in public (in cars, alleys, bus stops, and on residents' property). Complaints about offensive and disorderly conduct were pronounced in each of the cities studied.

Nasty Paraphernalia. One by-product of street prostitution that is not widely known, but which is a source of frequent complaints in affected neighborhoods, is the problem of discarded paraphernalia. Residents often complain that prostitutes leave used condoms and syringes in alleys, sidewalks, and other public places. This paraphernalia is viewed not simply as unsightly trash but also as a public health hazard, vehicles for the possible transmission of AIDS.

Public Health Risks. The spread of AIDS was a concern in its own right. As a San Francisco activist remarked, "These women are very sick, emaciated. I know they are spreading diseases whether or not they're using condoms."[20]

Harm to Children. Residents who live in prostitution zones have complained that it is difficult to shield children from the vice in their midst. In several cities activists claimed that prostitutes sell and perform sexual favors in close proximity to schools. Moreover, children are sometimes propositioned. In Manchester, New Hampshire, a resident of one neighborhood reported:

> My children go to Catholic school, and there are women working the corner where they wait for the bus. They are always high as a kite. A prostitute approached the son of one of my neighbors while he was on his way to school and asked him if he wanted to turn a trick.... What did she want? His lunch money?[21]

Residents tell horror stories of having observed children playing with used condoms and syringes in the street, fueling fears of AIDS transmission.

Harassment of Women. A common theme in these accounts is that nonprostitute women and teenage girls are often verbally accosted and propositioned by prospective customers. This is not only annoying but has the cumulative effect of impeding women's routine outdoor activities, as illustrated in these remarks: "I can't sit in the park because the gentlemen in the cars slow down and start waving dollar bills at me";[22] "A normal person cannot stand at the bus stop because they think you're a hooker";[23] "My daughter can't even go to the store without being approached by men who are asking her for sex."[24] Customers' remarks can be offensive, vulgar, and degrading. As one person recounted, "You walk down the street, the men say such disgusting things to you; suddenly you feel dirty, like you should go home and take a bath."[25]

Costs to Merchants. In prostitution strolls where local businesses exist, many merchants claim they lose business because of the very presence, noise, and brazen demeanor of prostitutes and pimps on the street. These merchants are likely to reap no benefits from prostitution, as opposed to those owners of cafés, liquor stores, and cheap hotels who profit from it. Owners of higher priced hotels complain that streetwalkers drive away some customers, although at least some hotel owners are not bothered by the prostitutes working in hotel bars, and may even welcome them.[26] A line is drawn between discreet, indoor liaisons and the more obtrusive, outdoor sex trade.

Neighborhood Decline. Coupled with other signs of street disorder and decay, prostitution is seen as contributing to the decline of a locale's quality of life. Property values erode. Prostitution and other street deviance may hinder economic development in a commercial district, deterring entrepreneurs from moving in. This may coincide with a gradual exodus of upstanding residents, further fraying the fabric of public order on the streets. None of this is lost on merchants and residents, who complain about longitudinal deterioration: "Nobody has a right to deteriorate a whole neighborhood. We could see the whole street change";[27] "We're tired of standing around watching our neighborhood decay";[28] "Now we're starting to lose very good parts of San Francisco. There's been a complete breakdown in this area."[29]

The effect of street prostitution on a neighborhood is measured not only by its tangible effects on everyday life, but also by its larger impact on a neighborhood's image. Communities may be stigmatized if a critical mass of disreputable people frequent the street. The former president of the Logan Circle Community Association in Washington, D.C., lamented, "The image of our neighborhood is one of pimps and prostitutes. We have trick pads and shooting galleries."[30] The current president adds, "It's not a very edifying sight. People don't want to come into the community."[31] (Logan Circle has long been a mecca of street prostitution in Washington.) Neighborhood stigma contributes to a community's decline over time, as more disreputable elements are attracted to the area and "upstanding" residents flee.[32]

Invasion by Outsiders. Community anticrime groups often believe their neighborhoods are under siege by outsiders, a perception shared by antiprostitution groups. Residents claim that prostitutes, pimps, and johns have invaded the community, which residents seek to "take back." In fact, it does appear that in most cities the majority of customers reside outside these areas, whereas varying numbers of prostitutes are local residents, depending on the locale.[33]

Johns. Several other patterns are found in these accounts, foremost of which is the scorn directed at *customers* as well as prostitutes; in fact, some residents reserve their harshest criticism for the men, who are seen as the root cause of the entire prostitution problem, without whom it would not exist. Customers stand accused of a number of obnoxious behaviors: causing traffic congestion in their ritual cruising and transactions with steetwalkers, verbally molesting women whom they apparently mistake for prostitutes, and engaging in sex acts in public.

For residents and merchants, therefore, street prostitution is anything but a mere nuisance or "victimless crime." From their perspective, it is a "quality-of-life crime" that victimizes the community by contributing to street disorder and neighborhood decay.

To what extent are the grievances reflections of *moral* concerns? If defined narrowly, it appears that morality is the least of their concerns. Only rarely were complaints made about the degradation of selling one's body, the exploitation of women, or the sinfulness of prostitution. One San Francisco activist remarked, "This is not a moral issue. Prostitutes are spreading disease and disrupting our neighborhood," and another was similarly unequivocal:

> Morals don't even come into play when peoples' lives are turned upside down [by street prostitution].... The moral issue here is not even in question. I don't care what people do behind closed doors, and I have talked to residents who feel the same way.[34]

This does not mean that moral concerns were completely absent from this discourse. Some activists were alarmed by the performance of sex acts in public, which might be construed as a moral position; others used a discourse that seemed to pit "good" against "evil," such as the need to force "shady" and "low-life" elements out of the community so that it could be restored to its "family-oriented" character; and others said that the sight of prostitutes on the street was an affront to public decency and especially troubling when children were present. In Hartford, Connecticut, for example, a member of a coalition against prostitution stated, "Children are growing up thinking it's okay because it's so open. They see it on a whole row of streets. Our kids are saying, 'Is it O.K.? Is it legal?' They could buy one of these women."[35] While the *conduct* of streetwalkers and customers, more than their mere presence, aroused the strongest condemnation, at least some of this behavior was defined as a threat to conventional *values* as well.

It is possible that many activists harbor strong moral objections but are careful not to express them out of fear of hurting their cause. Moral arguments might seem puritanistic; complaints about tangible social problems are more likely to get a sympathetic reception. Obviously, this question cannot be definitively resolved here, except to reiterate that activists emphasized the specific environmental problems sketched above. It should also be noted that relatively little concern was expressed over off-street, indoor prostitution. Opposition to this variety of prostitution might suggest a broader moral objection to prostitution in general. In both the interview and newspaper data, activists claimed that they did not object to escort agencies, massage parlors, or even isolated brothels. Commercial sex in private appears to be acceptable, so long as it has no spillover effects in the public arena. In San Francisco, a leader of Save Our Streets told me that most residents of his community would not be bothered by indoor prostitution: "My gut feeling is, yes, that would be OK. No one has voiced concern over massage parlors," several of which exist in the neighborhood.[36]

Of course, it is not unheard of for community groups to wage battles against indoor vice establishments. Efforts to shut down adult video stores, massage parlors, and strip clubs have been mounted in various cities, just as there have been broader efforts to "clean up" entire districts, such as Times Square in New York City. But community groups rarely organize specifically against indoor prostitution, especially if it remains discreet. For the reasons cited above, it is street prostitution that arouses the greatest opposition at the local level.

What actions have been taken by these groups to combat street prostitution? Frustrated by the typically haphazard and ineffective responses of the authorities to local prostitution problems, residents of many cities have begun to take direct action. Public humiliation of prostitutes and johns is the favored approach. Common tactics include:

- citizen patrols: groups that follow prostitutes and johns along sidewalks for purposes of surveillance and harassment, sometimes videotaping the action or carrying posters declaring, "You're Hooking, We're Looking" or "Prostitution-Free Zone"; the patrols usually have a temporary effect in scattering sex traders, who reappear once the patrol ends;
- recording customers' license plate numbers, which are then traced to their addresses, to which a warning letter is sent;
- public shaming, such as publishing the names of alleged johns in local newspapers or on television.

Customers have been increasingly targeted, since they are seen as more vulnerable to embarrassment and more easily deterred than prostitutes. As a member of one civic association put it, "These guys are the weak link in this chain. He's the one with the most to lose; that's why he's got to be kept out."[37] The third tactic—public shaming—is all the rage. Kansas City is now experimenting with "John TV"—a weekly cable TV show displaying the names, addresses, and pictures of men arrested for attempting to solicit a prostitute. The city council designed the program to humiliate arrested, rather than convicted, men since so few suspects are ultimately convicted (most plea-bargained down to a lesser offense).[38] Radio and TV stations in some other cities (Aurora, Colorado; Tulsa, Oklahoma) have also stigmatized the johns in this way; some newspapers have also published clients' names, but others have refused on the grounds that it is not newsworthy or that publication might bring lawsuits for defamation. The Pennsylvania state legislature, however, took the unprecedented step of passing legislation (in 1995) requiring courts to publish in the local newspaper the name and sentence of anyone convicted a second time of patronizing a prostitute, in addition to a fine of $300 to $2,500 and a minimum of seventy-five hours of community service.[39]

Other inventive shaming tactics have been used against customers, in addition to those described above. In New Haven, Connecticut, in 1992, posters naming a "John of the Week" were stapled to trees and telephone polls in one prostitution stroll. Included on the poster was the name and address of a man observed soliciting a prostitute, with the warning, "Johns! Stay out of our neighborhood or your name will be here next week."[40] In Miami, freeway billboards have been used to announce the names of convicted johns. In Kansas City, activists created a "hooker hotline" in 1993, a recorded list of the names of persons arrested for soliciting a prostitute. The hotline received several hundred calls per month.

There is considerable public support for shaming johns via the mass media. A 1978 national poll found that 47 percent of the public thought it was not an invasion of privacy for newspapers to publish the names of men who had been accused of soliciting prostitutes,[41] and a 1995 poll found that 50 percent of the public endorsed punishing men convicted of soliciting prostitutes by placing their names and pictures in the news.[42]

A few cities have gone beyond sheer shaming of johns to the creation of programs aimed at consciousness-raising and rehabilitation. One particularly innovative program is the "johns' school" for arrested customers. Since 1995, when San Francisco launched its First Offenders Prostitution Program for customers, several other cities have followed suit, including Buffalo, Las Vegas, Nashville, and several cities in Canada and Britain. The brainchild of community activists, San Francisco's school is a joint effort by the district attorney's office, the police department, the public health department, community leaders, and former prostitutes. The men avoid an arrest record and court appearance by paying a $500 fine, attending the school, and not recidivating for one year after the arrest. Every aspect of the eight-hour course is designed to *shame, educate,* and *deter* the men from future contact with prostitutes. The content and tone of the lectures are designed for maximum shock value. During my observations at the San Francisco school, the men were frequently asked how they would feel if their mothers, wives, or daughters were "prostituted," and why they were "using" and "violating" prostitutes by patronizing them. The audience was also exposed to a graphic slide show on the dangers of sexually transmitted diseases, horror stories about the wretched lives of prostitutes and their oppression by pimps, and information about the harmful effects of street prostitution on the host neighborhoods.

Chapter 5 analyzed customers' motivations for patronizing prostitutes, based on questionnaires completed by men arrested in three cities. A survey of 169 men enrolled in the Edmonton, Canada, school revealed several additional things. The men like to keep their encounters secret: Only one-quarter had told anyone else that they had seen a prostitute, and only 2 percent had told their spouses or partners. More than half the men were currently in a relationship with a spouse or partner, and 72 percent of these men reported that they had a satisfying sexual relationship with their partner. What is particularly interesting is that 71 percent said they did not enjoy sex with prostitutes, and two-thirds said that patronizing prostitutes had caused problems in their lives.[43] Yet, this did not prevent them from buying sex on the street.

My review of responses to open-ended questions on a survey completed by the men at the end of the school in San Francisco found that many seem to experience "consciousness-raising" about the negative aspects of street prostitution and pledge to never again contact a prostitute, but others express cynicism or resentment at getting caught, at having to take the class, at being "talked down to" by the lecturers, and being otherwise demeaned. Some men insist that they were innocent victims of police entrapment.[44]

Unlike other shaming sanctions—such as printing customers' names or photos in local newspapers or cable TV shows—where humiliation or "stigmatizing shaming" of the offender is a goal, shaming in the johns' schools occurs in the context of a day of reeducation about the various harms of prostitution.[45] This is closer to the "reintegrative shaming" model which links punishment to rehabilitation, though this ends once the class concludes. A measure of rehabilitation is recidivism: Of the nearly 2,200 graduates of San Francisco's school from March 1995 to February 1999, only eighteen were subsequently rearrested for solicitation. None of the 600 men passing through Toronto's program had been rearrested between the opening of the school in March 1996 and August 1997.[46]

Low recidivism, or "specific deterrence" among the graduates of the johns' schools does not mean that the program is having a larger "general deterrent" effect (on the never-arrested population of prospective johns), since the demand side—the number of johns on the streets—is thus far unabated. Moreover, nonrecidivism may be due to the school experience or to the arrest itself. Official statistics show low recidivism among previously arrested customers generally (including those who had not attended a johns' school), suggesting that the arrest is the decisive deterrent.

OTHER ANTIPROSTITUTION GROUPS

Among the antiprostitution forces active in the United States are local organizations that work to rescue prostitutes from the streets. Notable examples are PRIDE (From Prostitution to Independence, Dignity, and Equality) in Minneapolis,[47] SAGE (Standing Against Global Exploitation) in San Francisco, HIPS (Helping Individual Prostitutes Survive) in Washington, D.C., and the CPA (Council on Prostitution Alternatives) in Portland, Oregon. Some of these groups provide services and do not propound an official ideological position on prostitution, while others (SAGE, CPA) adopt a radical feminist perspective. As Nanette Davis shows in her study of the CPA (Chapter 9), this group defines prostitutes as oppressed by both individual men (johns, pimps) and by the larger system of patriarchy, and works to empower women to reject such domination and to escape from prostitution. This perspective is influenced both by radical feminism and by the experiences of the street prostitutes with whom they have contact—that is, the population most likely to suffer violence and other abuse, in contrast to the majority of sex workers who work off the streets.

For the most part, antiprostitution campaigns in the United States have been local, not national. A few groups, however, have fought a broader war against prostitution. The most notable group was WHISPER (Women Hurt in Systems of Prostitution Engaged in Revolt, founded in 1985). Articulating a radical feminist perspective, WHISPER denied that women freely choose prostitution, that prostitution is a valid career, and that it can ever be organized humanely. Prostitution is based on male domination, women's commodification, and "enforced sexual access and sexual abuse."[48] Hardly victimless, it is universally an act of violence against women. The violence is not restricted to incidents of physical assault, but includes the sexual interaction itself, which is seen as a sexual and emotional violation by its very nature. Those who manage to leave prostitution were referred to as "survivors" who have "escaped." As an abolitionist organization, WHISPER was at loggerheads with the prostitutes' rights movement: It advocated not the rights of prostitutes as workers but the right to escape from prostitution; sought not to normalize but to further stigmatize prostitution; and was committed to universal eradication of the oldest profession. WHISPER ceased operations in 1996.

Antiprostitution groups like these can be criticized for failing the tests I sketched in Chapter 1. By uncritically embracing the radical feminist line on prostitution (seeing it as inherently oppressive and demeaning), these organizations fail to draw important distinctions between different types of prostitutes (most of the individuals they work with are street prostitutes, yet most prostitutes in America work in off-street settings). However, insofar as such organizations provide needed assistance to women who want to leave the streets, their work is obviously laudable. Even their opponents in the prostitutes' rights movement endorse such assistance: The World Charter for Prostitutes' Rights proclaims that "shelters and services for working prostitutes and retraining programs for prostitutes wishing to leave the life should be funded."[49]

THE PROSTITUTES' RIGHTS MOVEMENT

At the opposite end of the spectrum from antiprostitution groups like WHISPER stand prostitutes' rights groups, which insist that prostitution is not inherently evil and that prostitutes have the *right to engage in sex work*. Such groups advocate the decriminalization of prostitution because they view it as *a legitimate and valuable service*. Founded in 1973 by former prostitute Margo St. James, COYOTE (Call Off Your Old Tired Ethics) is the premier prostitutes' rights group in the United States, and is affiliated with kindred organizations in the United States and internationally.[50]

Goals

COYOTE's chief goals are (1) public education about the "myths" and "realities" of prostitution, (2) decriminalization, and (3) normalization. Public education takes the form of challenging a number of common misconceptions: that prostitutes are a significant source of AIDS and other sexually transmitted diseases, that organized crime is heavily involved, that most women are forced into prostitution, and that street prostitution is linked to other street crime. Insofar as any harms are associated with prostitution, they are attributed to criminalization, not to prostitution itself: The very illegality of prostitution increases prostitutes' vulnerability to exploitation and victimization. It follows that decriminalization would ameliorate these problems.

COYOTE favors full decriminalization of consensual adult prostitution, that is, the elimination of all legal restrictions on prostitution. It flatly opposes legalization, whether in the form of registration and licensing, special taxes, zoning, compulsory health examinations, or restrictions on brothels.[51] Regulations are rejected because they would allow the state to "regulate what a woman does with her own body."[52] Decriminalization, by contrast, would allow prostitutes maximum control over their bodies.

COYOTE seeks to destigmatize and *normalize* prostitution. It challenges conventional stereotypes of prostitutes by arguing that they have normal needs and aspirations, and that their work is no more degrading than that of other service providers.[53] Although it is a hard sell, COYOTE argues that prostitutes are not involved in immoral behavior. Instead, it is claimed that "the real undermining of morality results from making illegal conduct engaged in between consenting adults and in which no one is victimized"[54] and that it is nonsense "to suggest that society's moral fiber is undermined by 'sex-for-pay' but not by promiscuous sexual behavior without pay."[55] In any event, the state should not be legislating morality anyway.[56] Decriminalization is expected to promote normalization. As one leader told me, "Once they don't go to jail, they can come out of the closet and become normalized."[57]

Leadership and Support Base

COYOTE has been run by a handful of activists. The dynamic and flamboyant founder, Margo St. James, headed the organization for a dozen years, but she was replaced by Priscilla Alexander in 1985, who was followed by Samantha Miller in the early 1990s, after which Margo St. James returned.

Winning popular support poses such an enormous challenge that it has not been prioritized. While COYOTE claimed to have several thousand members in the 1970s, almost all were simply names on a membership list. Support is also measured by the number of adherents, people who endorse movement goals. Public opinion data presented in Table 10.1 indicate significant support for some form of legalization, but much less for COYOTE's central goal of decriminalization. Attempts to mobilize supporters via specific events (picketing, demonstrations, conventions) have been few and far between. This is a campaign led by entrepreneurs, not a mass movement.

Mobilization of prostitutes has been equally elusive. About 3 percent of COYOTE's members are prostitutes,[58] and most of them have been upscale call girls rather than streetwalkers (it is not clear who makes up the other 97 percent of members). Why such meager involvement of prostitutes? First, COYOTE has not prioritized recruitment: "We don't go looking for constituents," Margo St. James told me, "They come to COYOTE."[59] Given the lack of recruitment efforts, many prostitutes may be unaware of the movement's very existence. Second, open participation in the movement carries risks, such as fear of police harassment, discouragement from pimps, and anticipated repercussions among family and friends.

Customers might be expected to support the movement's goals, and Chapter 5 reported that 72 percent of a sample of arrested customers supported decriminalization. However, such support is virtually impossible to mobilize, given customers' abiding interests in remaining anonymous.

Alliances

Strong alliances with other groups may offset a social movement's lack of internal resources and constituent support. Some influential third parties have formally endorsed decriminalization, but their contribution to the movement has been quite limited. The ACLU is a case in point. It announced its formal support for decriminalization in 1975, and it has occasionally filed suits, lobbied state legislators, and defended individuals prosecuted under prostitution laws. But this is a very low-priority issue for the ACLU. Another example is the National Organization for Women (NOW), which issued a resolution endorsing decriminalization in 1973, a position that remains unchanged today. NOW is in a position to contribute to COYOTE's finances, legitimacy, and membership base, but has offered almost no support of this kind.[60]

Why this lack of third-party support? Prostitution is an unpopular cause, unlikely to yield gains for and more likely to discredit organizations that embrace it in a prominent and sustained fashion. The "contamination" resulting from an individual's association with deviants[61] also may apply to organizations that champion deviant causes. Actively fighting for the decriminalization of prostitution would be a liability for an organization such as NOW, both in terms of its public image and its membership base. Feminists inside and outside NOW are split on prostitution, just as they are on pornography. A libertarian minority sees it as a valid occupational choice, which decriminalization would make safer; an abolitionist majority considers it inherently degrading and advocates the eradication of prostitution. The latter, dominant view prevents most feminists from lending support to COYOTE.

Impact

A social movement's success can be measured by its impact on public opinion, legislation, and the practices of control agents. Trend data presented above show that *the movement has had no positive effect on public attitudes regarding prostitution*. The vast majority of the public want prostitution laws "strictly enforced," and the percentage who think prostitution should be "forbidden by law" increased between 1978 and 1990.

Nor have local or state policy makers been moved by COYOTE's claims. Since the beginning of the movement in the early 1970s, virtually all state and municipal action on prostitution issues has resulted in passage of increasingly *punitive* measures. Consequently, COYOTE complains that "for most legislators [prostitution] remains a joke except when they think they can gain prominence by attacking prostitutes."[62]

COYOTE has not failed in every area. It has attracted some media coverage, won some minor victories, and given prostitutes a "voice" in the public arena. COYOTE's survival for twenty-five years is also noteworthy, and it has built an international reputation as a vanguard in the campaign for prostitutes' rights. But the movement's arguments and demands have largely fallen on deaf ears among elites and the wider public. An exception that proves the rule is COYOTE's recent involvement in San Francisco's Task Force on Prostitution, mentioned earlier in the chapter. Even when COYOTE was included in official discussions of the issue, and persuaded the Task Force to endorse decriminalization, the recommendation was dismissed by local officials.

As former COYOTE director Samantha Miller told me in 1993, "For twenty years, nothing has changed" in American public policy; indeed, she considered it time to "move away from the hard-line COYOTE position on decriminalization" and instead press for the "more realistic" goal of legalization.[63] COYOTE's official position, however, remains the more radical goal of decriminalization, not legalization—which helps to keep it marginalized.

*   *   *   *   *

A brief comparison to another society will demonstrate that there are alternatives to the American approach to prostitution, and that the failure of prostitutes' rights groups like COYOTE is not preordained everywhere. Prostitution in the Netherlands is not against the law, but third-party involvement in prostitution (such as running a brothel) remains a crime, although the law is not enforced (and in February 1999 one house of the Dutch legislature voted to legalize third-party involvement in prostitution). Dutch tolerance for prostitution does not seem to have encouraged widespread consumption.

Only 22 percent of Dutch men report that they have patronized a prostitute during their lifetime,[64] compared to 16 to 18 percent of American men (see Chapter 1).

Dutch views on prostitution differ radically from those of most Americans. A 1997 poll found that 74 percent of the Dutch public regarded prostitution as an acceptable job and 73 percent favored the legalization of brothels.[65] And in 1999, 78 percent said prostitution was a job like any other, so long as there was no coercion involved.[66] As a Dutch woman told me when asked about prostitution in her country, "It doesn't even cross my mind that it should be illegal!"

The American and Dutch scenes also differ strikingly in terms of the role and influence of interest groups. Organizations with a stake in prostitution policy have much more legitimacy and influence over policy makers in Holland than in the United States. They do not have to fight for acceptance and they enjoy more freedom to organize publicly. Unlike the United States, Holland has a state-funded organization that conducts research and develops policy proposals on prostitution, the Mr. A. de Graaf Foundation. This organization takes the view that prostitution is a profession that should be dealt with pragmatically by the government. The foundation neither condemns nor promotes prostitution, but is committed to improving the conditions for workers in the industry as well as building a consensus on policy among all interested parties—all of which meet monthly at the foundation's offices.

Another key player is COYOTE's Dutch counterpart, the Red Thread, a prostitutes' rights organization created in 1985. In a 1997 interview, the then-director, Sietske Altink, was asked to identify the major opponents of the Red Thread. She responded, "That doesn't really exist in the Netherlands. It's hard to think of any enemies of Red Thread."[67] There is, of course, some opposition from some church leaders and right-wing politicians, but Red Thread is not locked in conflict with the government or dismissed as irrelevant, as is COYOTE. Instead, says Altink, "We are important for them to correct their policies." In fact, the Dutch government helps *fund* Red Thread, and the group also participates in the training of police officers with regard to prostitution issues.

Of course, organizations involved with prostitution experience a degree of stigmatization even in Holland. The head of the Brothel Owners Association noted that some people denounce the organization, but people are also curious about its aims:

You have the possibility to explain, to tell something about the business. If I'm in an ordinary group of people and they've heard what I'm doing, it doesn't take ten minutes and they start talking with me; they want to know everything. And that is my chance to change their minds, but I have to open them.[68]

Unlike brothels, which employ several women and entertain customers in a club atmosphere, "window prostitution" takes place in small rooms rented by independent prostitutes in red-light districts. (Amsterdam has 420 window units and 70 brothels; about 30 percent of Holland's prostitutes work in window units, 40 percent work in brothels, and the remainder work as escorts or on the streets.)[69] A Window Owners Association formed fifteen years ago, and 90 percent of the window owners are members. The goals of the association are more limited than those of the brothel owners' association, since they have much less involvement with the workers, essentially serving as landlords who rent premises and make occasional visits to see that workers are complying with regulations. As the secretary of the organization stated, "The organization exists only to deal with the rules [imposed by the local government, e.g., the prohibition on workers under eighteen, the limit of only one worker per unit], and only when it is necessary to raise our voice with local authorities."[70] The organization is pressing for licensing, in order to increase the legitimacy of window prostitution. The secretary also made the point of insisting that he and his organization were in no way "shamed" by their association with prostitution and that his members were ordinary businesspeople, not really involved in "managing" prostitutes. They shun the "pimp" label and want to be called "entrepreneurs in the relaxation industry."[71]

The Dutch climate is even conducive to the existence of a clients' rights organization, perhaps unique in the world! Created in 1986, the Foundation of Men and Prostitution has the goal of promoting the "legal and moral emancipation of prostitution and all those directly or indirectly involved in the prostitution industry," as stated in the group's brochure. The organization holds meetings for clients during which problems and interests are discussed; it represents clients' interests to the media, government, and other groups interested in prostitution; and it attempts to clarify the rights and obligations of clients. In an interview, the head of the clients' organization elaborated on its raison d'être:

> There is no reason why they shouldn't have a consumer organization. They have rights to good service, not to be maltreated, just like any other consumer. The fact that clients are a big silent group is no reason not to fight for rights, and they should. We feel there is every reason to enlighten the general population about clients' involvement in prostitution. As I feel prosti-

tution is a valuable asset, I think there's a need for society to be informed of this. The value of prostitution is that men who are in need, or even urgent need, can find relief.... People are justified to seek outlets for, in many cases, a very burdensome frustration. Of course, a lot of prostitution is fun and entertainment, not just due to man's frustration.

But there is also some vagueness in the organization's goals:

The fact of the matter is we don't know what we want. For the clients, I don't have much hope that they can be reached, and if they can be reached I don't know what to say to them! I'm way out ahead of the rank and file. They couldn't care less about codes of conduct, migrant women, club owners who take advantage of workers, et cetera.... Some clients we meet find prostitution fascinating and want to learn more or feel a need to unburden themselves from their lonely life or feelings of guilt.[72]

The organization not only works to advance the interests of clients but also exhorts clients to follow a code of conduct in their encounters with prostitutes. The code instructs customers to be polite, clean, sober, and to use condoms. Other commandments include:

- "Make clear agreements" with the prostitute.
- "Take into account that the prostitute has her own limits" on the services to be provided.
- "A contact can be less than successful, often through unfamiliarity with each other. Take this into account and don't be disappointed."
- "Remain resasonable in a situation where conflict arises and leave it for what it is. Absolutely do not demand your money back."
- "Create as little inconvenience as possible for the surroundings. Neighbors appreciate their sleep and are really not interested in your sexual experiences."

In the Netherlands, in short, there is a vibrant and active network of organizations working on behalf of the interests of different sectors of the sex industry and enjoying a significant measure of success in their efforts. The Dutch government regularly meets with leaders of such organizations and takes their views into account in formulating prostitution-related policies. It seeks to incorporate and balance the views of organizations that have at least somewhat different interests or policy preferences. This state of affairs could not contrast more sharply with the American scene, where prostitutes' advocacy groups are fully marginalized and where criminalization reigns supreme.

POWER AND CONTROL
IN THE COMMERCIAL SEX TRADE

Wendy Chapkis

One of the most profound misunderstandings about sex work is that it involves the purchase of a prostitute's body for indiscriminate sexual use.[1] In fact, workers' control over the terms and conditions of the sexual exchange is a central concern within the trade. Sex workers' ability to exercise control over the labor process, however, varies widely. Some sex workers appear able to determine most aspects of the transaction, while others are severely limited in their ability to do so.

In-depth interviews conducted between 1987 and 1995 with forty-seven sex workers, activists, and law enforcement officers in the United States and the Netherlands confirmed that there is no one consistent experience of sex work.[2] Indeed, sex workers' experiences differ substantially according to their location in the trade.[3] These differences of location heavily determine the extent to which they can exercise control over their work process.[4] This chapter will examine some of the structural factors that can undermine or enhance a worker's power and control.[5] These include legal status, customer demands, drug use, isolation, competition, management rules and regulations, and workplace organizing.

WORKER'S LEGAL STATUS

Legal status has a profound effect on a worker's power relative to clients and to employers. In the United States, like many other countries, certain aspects of sexual commerce are largely criminalized (most notably prostitution), while others are legal or quasi-legal (like pornographic performance, exotic dancing, lap dancing, and phone sex). Workers will often surrender some measure of control over their labor in order to work in legal or quasi-legal environments. In the United States, only one state, Nevada, has a limited form of legalized prostitution: state-licensed brothels. Terry, who worked for six years in the legal brothels of Nevada, reports:

> Like everyone else, I was just there to make money. A lot of the women had traveled quite a distance to work there because it was legal; they'd had enough of being arrested. Looking back on it now, I really do think that sometimes working for someone else like that can serve a useful function. But it's a matter of having alternatives available, too. And in Nevada there were no other legal alternatives. The fewer options you have, the more control you lose. [6]

In other parts of the United States, workers can shield themselves somewhat from arrest by working for quasi-legal third-party businesses like escort agencies or by working with agents or "madams." Rita entered the trade through a madam who referred clients to her:

> I started getting my clientele from a madam, so the guys were all thoroughly screened and had seen other women before. That meant that the odds of them being vice cops were essentially nil. But I finally decided to run my own ad and start working for myself because the madam took 40 percent of every call I did for the first five calls with any particular client. I thought that was exorbitant. For her cut she was supposed to tell me what his name was, what he liked, and the easiest way to get him off. She was also supposed to provide some sense of security. Well, forget it; when I'd call she often wasn't even there. If I'd felt like my ass was being covered, that would have made a difference. The only protection was the sense that the client was probably not a cop.[7]

Rita soon decided that the risk of arrest for call girls was not so pronounced that it offset the loss of income to the referral service:

> From what I've heard, vice doesn't bother to bust call girls that much. The only time they really go after us is when neighbors or boyfriends narc. Of course, they'll bust street walkers like there's no tomorrow, but they don't bother with call girls so much. So it's not that big of a concern to me anymore.[8]

As Rita suggests, the location of the worker within the trade—indoors or on the streets—largely determines the level of risk she runs of being arrested. In most major U.S. cities, indoor prostitution represents as much as 80 percent of the trade, but street prostitutes make up the vast majority of arrests.[9]

In prohibitionist countries like the United States, the legal harassment of street workers by the police drives prostitutes into the "protection" of pimps and undermines the worker's ability to protect herself from dangerous clients by making speedy negotiations necessary to avoid detection and arrest. Police become a further obstacle to the worker's attempt to establish authority and control with clients as well as depriving her of police protection in a particularly dangerous segment of the sex trade.

Even in countries like the Netherlands with a substantially decriminalized sex trade, some forms of sex work and some categories of sex workers remain illegal. The most important legal division within the Dutch sex trade is that which divides Dutch nationals (and European Community members) from migrant workers employed without proper work and immigration permits. This is a particularly serious problem because migrant prostitutes make up the majority of sex workers in the large cities of the Netherlands.[10]

Legal status has a profound effect on a worker's power vis-à-vis clients and employers. Licia Brussa of the Amsterdam migrant prostitutes' project, TAMPEP, notes that migrant prostitutes working illegally in the trade are less able to demand condom use:

> There is so much that they can't control in their lives here. And that is a critical difference between Dutch and migrant prostitutes. Everything is in a precarious balance for them. Their priorities are different: first it's daily survival, then sending money home, then protecting yourself from the police who could deport you, and then maybe only after all these other things comes safe sex. In a good situation, safe sex might be the first priority for migrant women, too. In our interviews everyone says that it's super important. But when things aren't so steady, then other problems might look much larger. So we have to help them sort out those other problems before we can even get to safe sex. It's about survival; they are trying to make the best of a difficult situation.[11]

The challenges facing illegal migrant sex workers in the Netherlands are only likely to intensify over the next few years. Currently, all third-party involvement in prostitution (escort, club, brothel work, and pimp-controlled street prostitution) is formally illegal—though the indoor trade is tolerated and even informally regulated. This means that both foreign and domestic workers in the third-party-controlled trade have illegal relationships with third parties. But the Dutch government is moving closer to formally decriminalizing third-party involvement in prostitution in order to more closely regulate prostitution businesses. Municipalities will be responsible for issuing licenses and controlling businesses for hygiene and worker safety.[12]

The de Graaf Foundation, which does research and policy work on prostitution, notes that the proposed change in the law will have a particularly detrimental effect on migrant prostitutes:

> Even if they have a tourist visa, they do not have a work permit. The consequence is that they have no legal status…. Many Dutch cities will include in their licenses the condition that the owners cannot employ illegal prostitutes. Therefore we can conclude that illegal migrant prostitutes will not benefit from the new legalization.[13]

Recent developments in the city of Amsterdam suggest that a two-tier system will indeed develop under the new policy. In 1996, that city began to regulate prostitution businesses through a system of licensing and, as the de Graaf Foundation reports, "Already some brothels have had to close down because they could not conform to the requirements for a license, especially not to the condition that prostitutes who work there be legal."[14] The likely result, then, will be the move underground of a large portion of the prostitution sector that employs foreign workers. This likely will further undermine migrant prostitutes' power relative to clients and employers as well as making them less accessible to public health and social workers attempting to assist them.

MANAGEMENT REGULATIONS

All workers, legal and illegal, who are employed in third-party-controlled sex work face special challenges in their efforts to exercise control over their work. Often employers institute formal rules designed to regulate worker/management relations as well as worker/client contact. In many strip clubs, for example, exotic dancers earn the bulk of their income performing individual "lap dances" with customers. Lap dancing is situated in a legal gray area in the United States between prostitution, which is illegal, and performance, which is protected. Club owners may face charges of pandering if workers or clients cross the legal line. For this reason, some clubs institute formal in-house regulations specifying what parts of the worker's body a customer may touch during a lap dance.

The intent of these rules, where they exist, is less to protect the worker from unwanted and excessive groping than to protect management from legal action. This is made clear by the fact that management rarely communicates the rules to customers. Instead dancers are left with the full responsibility of maintaining the boundaries (see also Chapter 12). Teri, who performs at an upscale San Francisco club, The Mitchell Brothers' O'Farrell Theater, notes:

> In lap dancing, we're not allowed to say a dollar amount; I guess that would be too much like prostitution. Instead you have to say, "Do you have a present for me?" You can't tell them they have to tip you to get you to sit on their dicks. You have to say, "The girls don't get paid to work here, we just work for tips." It's not like management tells them that. Plus there are all these rules about where they are allowed to touch you. But management doesn't do anything to help you out, like telling them when they come in what the rules are. So these guys will be trying to grab you, and who gets blamed for it? You do. That's how I got fired.[15]

Some sex trade businesses under third-party management do institute policies that assist sex workers in establishing authority over clients. Policies at one San Francisco peep show, the Lusty Lady, work to enhance dancers' control. Luna explains:

> According to management rules, the men aren't even supposed to direct you; so if someone says, "Come here" or "Turn around," you can say, "I'm sorry, we don't take directions. Be patient." That makes all the difference; you have the power to do your own show, and you aren't just waiting on them.[16]

One key difference between a peep show, like the Lusty Lady, and a strip club that offers lap dancing is the amount of contact between performer and client. At the Lusty Lady, the physical barrier of glass separating dancers from the audience helps to establish worker control. Susie explains:

> Dancing was certainly my first sexual interaction with men where I felt in control. Because of the thick glass and the music, I could ignore them if I wanted to. It didn't matter that they were watching because I could control how much contact I had with them. That felt very powerful.[17]

Workers' power relative to clients, however, is carefully monitored by management. As one dancer at the Lusty Lady explained, in a situation where dancers work for a set wage and no tips, dancers have a low incentive to put out extra energy for clients. Management, therefore, operates a tight system of surveillance including video monitoring of dancers: "If you don't smile on stage, they won't give you a raise. Because they watch you."[18] Similarly, a colleague reports:

> You really felt management looking over your shoulder watching to see if you were sexy, attractive, popular with clients. Every time you'd walk past the office, you'd feel the manager evaluating your body. She was always dressed of course, but you'd be walking around naked all the time. That always irritated me, talking with the management when I'm sitting there naked and she's not. It was like being nonconsensually topped [dominated] on an emotional level.[19]

DISCIPLINING THE BODY

Sex workers not only are required to maintain a proper attitude but also to produce an appropriate body type and personal style. For workers employed by third-party-controlled businesses, there are often explicit rules of appearance inspired by a competitive marketplace. One exotic dancer reports:

> One of the reasons I had decided to work at the Lusty was that they hired a wide variety of women to dance. Of course, there were your typical nineteen- and twenty-year-olds who looked like they stepped right out of the pages of a teen beauty magazine, but there were also older women, and big women, and women with body hair. But by the late 1980s, as management became more concerned about making more money, little by little they started firing women whose bodies weren't quite "right." It was amazing to me that they could do that, just say, "Something's wrong with your body, and we're getting rid of you."[20]

Because workers at the Lusty are employed for a straight wage with no possibility of tips, management assumes the primary responsibility of disciplining the workforce to comply with perceived market demands:

> Since at the Lusty we work for a wage instead of tips, management has to watch our appearance because, you know, we don't care. We don't make any more if someone likes us or doesn't. So they have a whole long list of things we can and cannot do. For example, they don't allow short hair, so almost everybody wears a wig. And management is always trying to get us to adorn things with sequins and glitter even though it's basically a nude show.[21]

Company policies on appearance can be quite detailed, including recommendations and rules on weight, body hair, hairstyles, piercings and tattoos, and costumes. Jane reports, "When I first started working at Mitchell Brothers, I asked if they had a policy on shaving. The woman told me, 'You aren't required to shave your pubic hair, but we strongly recommend it.' And I was thinking about armpit hair!"[22]

While appearance rules are generally clearly defined and vigorously enforced by management, even self-employed workers and independent contractors are under pressure to discipline their bodies to conform to what they perceive to be customer preferences. As one dancer reports, "If you've got bigger tits, it's worth a couple of hundred more at least. I'm telling you, there's a reason why so many of those women have tit jobs."[23]

Sex workers both recognize and chafe under these market constraints, as Karen explains:

> I have very close to the stereotypically ideal body: I'm tall and thin, and I have good-sized breasts. One time I did a double with a woman who was fairly large. She definitely didn't fit the stereotype of an attractive body. And I remember she didn't shave anywhere either. I had such respect for her; when she was out there she was fully in her sexuality, fully confident. But we were doing the show together, and when I came out the men went wild. During her second set, they got kind of quiet and then started yelling, "Send the other one out, send the other one out." That was a kind of a wake-up call for me; it made me want to leave the business.[24]

Another type of appearance rule is skin color. Among both clients and managers in the sex industry there is a bias in favor of white women and there are often informal quotas on the number of women of color hired. This policy was evident at both the Lusty Lady and the Mitchell Brothers. Because of this sort of racism on the part of management and clients, women of color are disproportionately clustered in the least well-paid and most stigmatized sectors of the sex industry such as street prostitution.

DRUG USE

One of the most commonplace associations with prostitution is the image of the sex worker as drug addict. In fact, drug dependency varies widely within the sex trade, as it does in other professions. Still, drug and alcohol use can have significant effects on workplace relations in the sex industry. For some workers, limited drug or alcohol use can enhance a worker's sense of power and control by "building confidence" and easing the shift in character from the sex worker's "ordinary self" to a "professional persona." Karen, who sometimes danced at private "bachelor parties," described the role of alcohol in her first performance:

> I was really, incredibly nervous and excited, and I remember I had to have a drink before going out. I drank down a beer and that made me a little less nervous. I also remember thinking, "If I continue to do this, I can't make myself drink beforehand every time. But this time, I'm going to."[25]

Alcohol and drug use in some areas of the sex trade is not simply a personal decision but an integral part of the work culture or even a workplace requirement. Women working as exotic dancers or club prostitutes, for example, are sometimes required to solicit drinks from the customers, as exotic dancer Terez reports:

> A big part of the money you make is on drinks. You get the guys to buy you a $20 drink; the bar gets fifteen of that, the bartender gets one, and the girls get four. In this one club, the waitress comes over and asks the guy, "Would you like to buy the lady a drink?" And if the man says okay, you are then required to say, "I would like champagne." You have to say it loud enough for everyone to hear. The waitress comes back with a full bottle of "champagne." It costs the guy $40 "plus a $20 tip for the lady." Sometimes the guys refuse; after all, no one told them how much it was going to cost. Then the waitress comes back with a half-bottle for $25 and a $10 tip. And if he still says no to that too, she'll try to barter him down to a large glass, which is $15 and a $5 tip. The very bottom is a drink for $2 plus a dollar tip. So there you are, reduced from $60 to $3 right in front of your face. And you only have a certain amount of time to drink whatever it is that they buy you. Even if it's a whole bottle of champagne, you have to drink it within three songs. Then the waitress is back starting the whole routine all over again. A lot of the guys feel forced into buying the bottle, and they really resent you for it. And it makes you feel sleazy; you don't even make a dime on the drink. You only get the tip. In fact, you only get half the tip. You have to split it with the waitress.[26]

In some forms of sex work, for example street prostitution, drug use may be the motivating factor for involvement in the trade when a worker turns tricks in exchange for drugs or to support a drug habit. Sometime drug dependency is encouraged by a pimp to tie a sex worker more closely to him, especially if the pimp is also the drug supplier. Barbara, who worked as a teenage street prostitute in San Francisco, describes the relationship to her pimp:

At first, I just had to give him a 25 percent cut of every trick. For that, I got a place to live, someone to teach me the ropes, someone to look out for me on the streets, someone to post bail when I got picked up. And, in the beginning, I also got free smack. Pretty soon, though, he stopped giving it to me for free, and I had to buy it. That meant that the 25 percent cut was only the start. I had to keep giving more and more of what I was making just to pay for the smack. Pretty soon, I was working only for the smack. That—and the high—took away most of my motivation to work. Of course, if you really became worthless, you might just end up dead of an overdose. That's the way the pimps got rid of the girls they had no more use for, the ones who had lost their motivation.[27]

Clearly, addiction can undermine a worker's control and her ability to discriminate among clients and services. Gloria Lockett, a former San Francisco street prostitute, explains:

Things are a lot different now than what they used to be, and I think it's because of drugs. I mean, heroin has always been around, but it used to be that even heroin addicts had to carry themselves nice because they had to compete with the other women on the streets. The worst addiction most women had was to alcohol, and if you were going to get drunk, you waited until after you finished working that night. You wanted to be in control so you wouldn't be taken advantage of. But crack has made such a difference, it's not funny. With crack, you just can't keep it together, so things have gotten really bad.[28]

As Lockett suggests, one effect of intensified drug use within a segment of street prostitution has been a division between "drug prostitutes" and "professionals." Women working in exchange for drugs (or primarily to support a drug habit) are seen as undercutting the market by working below the going rate and offering unsafe sexual services (sex without condoms, for example.)

Of course, drug use among prostitutes is not limited to street prostitution. Jo, a former brothel worker in the Netherlands, argues that some brothels may make more money on drugs than on the sexual services being performed:

There is an incredible amount of drug use in the clubs. It's the big hidden drug problem in prostitution. Everyone thinks of drug-addicted prostitutes as heroin-addicted street workers. But there are many more coke-addicted women working in clubs than heroin-addicted women working on the streets of Amsterdam. I am actually convinced that a lot of clubs are covers for coke dealing from behind the bar.[29]

Drug and alcohol use by clients also shapes workplace relations of power and control. Jo explains:

> The work itself was typical for a club. You hang out at the bar, and clients come in and drink something with you. At this particular place, you didn't get any money for drinking, which was actually quite good because you didn't feel like, "God, I have to get drunk to be able to earn any money." You just sit with the guys while they drink and chat with them and chat with them and chat with them.... And eventually, hopefully, they go into one of the rooms with you. The hook is that, for the entry price, the guy is promised whatever he wants. The women can't charge extra for anything. So there you are with a drunk guy in your room, trying to establish boundaries nonverbally.[30]

Workers in other parts of the sex industry rely on a variety of strategies to deal with difficult clients perceived to be drunk or high. Julia describes interactions with cocaine-using phone sex clients:

> The service I worked for paid a flat rate: $5 a call, or $6 if they requested you. So it was in your interest to get them off as quickly as possible. Usually that took about five minutes, but the guys who wanted sensual SM [sado masochism] and were high on coke could go on for twenty minutes. You were supposed to stay on the line until they came, but you could hang up and hope they didn't call the company and complain.[31]

As Julia suggests, in third-party-organized sex work, worker's ability to control intoxicated clients may be undermined by employer attitudes or rules. Terry, who briefly worked in a brothel club in Manhattan before becoming an independent call girl, found that management encouraged client drug use:

> I went to work in a brothel in midtown Manhattan, but I only stayed a week. The money was good, but the madam was selling coke. The men were so high they couldn't get hard, and they were difficult clients. They didn't want to wear condoms for oral sex, for instance, and she didn't do anything to encourage them to do so—quite the opposite in fact. Under those conditions, you might make good money, but at what price?[32]

Teri, who worked as a stripper for bachelor parties, varied her performance rules according to the state of intoxication of her audience. If the clients appeared drunk or high, she offered a much more restrained and guarded performance that provided little opportunity for client/worker contact:

It was my job to control the room, so I would start off by very clearly introducing myself and telling them what was, and wasn't, going to happen. It was
easy to read the energy in the room; if they'd been drinking or doing a bunch
of coke, you could tell. I'd totally change the rules of my tipping games
depending on how I was reading the crowd. I mean, sometimes I wouldn't
even take my G-string off.[33]

RATE OF EXPLOITATION

Drug use, management regulation, client and management discrimination, and
harassment by police officers can all serve to undermine sex workers' power in
the trade. Yet, despite these tremendous obstacles, the sex industry still offers
workers greater flexibility and control than many other forms of available
employment. Most significantly, in some sectors of the sex industry, workers
exercise substantial control over scheduling and rates of exploitation. Jane
explains:

> There are two shows per day, and during each shift there are between eigh-
> teen and twenty-four dancers scheduled. You can make your own schedule;
> everything is up to you. You are in business for yourself. You can call in sick,
> and it's not going to be the end of the world. Nobody needs to cover for your
> shift per se, because on the main stage it's just a constant rotation of dancers.
> You can also call in in the morning and say, "I want to come to work," and
> usually they can fit you in.[34]

Clearly the greatest degree of control over scheduling is enjoyed by workers operating as independent contractors, call girls, or street prostitutes working without pimps. For these workers, the financial demands of supporting
themselves and their families (or, in some instances, a costly drug habit), are
the key determinants of the pace of work—not management-imposed work
rates. But even in such circumstances, pressure to increase the rate of exploitation may not be entirely eliminated, just internalized. Teri, who works as an
independent contractor at a San Francisco strip club, notes that, in a situation
where income is entirely dependent on tips, she feels pressure to constantly
work the lap dancing room when she is not performing on stage:

> I just can't handle working at the Mitchell Brothers more than once every
> couple of weeks. It's too intense. First of all, you have to be there for nine
> hours, immersed in that environment. After you dance, you go downstairs
> and have pretty intense contact [lap dancing] with the men. You can defi-

nitely make some money, and it's all cash. But you can't leave. Of course, as long as you're on stage when you're supposed to be, you could sit upstairs in the dressing room the whole rest of the time if you want. But you've constantly got the feeling of "Why am I sitting up here? I should be downstairs making money." You can get totally manic behind it.[35]

Similarly, a Dutch window prostitute, Margot, notes:

At first I was satisfied with just making enough money to cover the basics. After a while, though, I decided I wanted to earn more—and that meant learning how to pimp myself, really pushing myself: "Put down that book, open those curtains, make contact with that client." It meant that I could earn my money quickly and spend the rest of the week doing what I wanted and found important—working for the Red Thread [the Dutch prostitutes' rights group].[36]

As Margot notes, independence, flexibility in scheduling, and a relatively high rate of remuneration in the sex industry allow some participants to engage in more personally significant activities such as political or cultural work, education, or parenting. Dawn, an exotic dancer in San Francisco, reports:

I was working for an agency that provides services for battered women and, of course, I was totally broke. I wanted to continue to do the work, but I needed to make more money, so I decided to start working in the sex industry. Dancing was a very vital economic choice for me, which allowed me to support myself and have the kind of schedule I needed to do that other kind of work that really matters to me.[37]

Luna began dancing to earn money for education:

I started graduate school, and I was desperate for money. I knew that a forty-hour workweek was out of the question, but there weren't that many jobs out there that paid enough to just work part time. Even though I'm college educated with a bachelor's degree and five years of activist experience, there weren't a lot of options. Plus I didn't want to do serious work and go to school at the same time; it's just too stressful. So the choices for me were waitressing, computer processing, or dancing. I only schedule myself to work eight to ten hours a week now, and I'm doing okay with that.[38]

Worker control over scheduling, however, varies enormously within the trade. One Amsterdam worker reports:

192

The first brothel I worked in wasn't really strict about working hours. There were two shifts, one in the afternoon and one at night, and you could work one or both. They were also pretty easy with how many days you wanted to work. But the next place I worked you had to work five days a week, and it was really hard to get any time off.[39]

In the most heavily controlled environments, for example the legal brothel system of Nevada, workers are scheduled for shifts that last several weeks and provide little or no flexibility. One longtime Nevada brothel worker explains:

When I first started at the Mustang Ranch, they expected you to work for three weeks and then take a week off. If you really needed to, you could have a day or two off in between. After a while, they started getting a little looser, so you could more or less set your own schedule, which is the way it should be if you're considered an "independent contractor."[40]

CONTROLLING SPACE AND THE EXERCISE OF AUTHORITY

Sex workers not only struggle with management (if any) over control over the labor process and rate of exploitation, they must also work to establish control over their clients. Especially for workers in independent outcall prostitution and private-party exotic dancing, establishing authority on the client's turf requires carefully executed strategies of control. Teri said of her work as a stripper at private parties:

I was scared at first. I mean, you go into people's homes, people you don't know at all. So you're putting a lot of faith in the universe that they're not going to be psychotic or what have you. I'd start off by telling them, "Do not grab me, or I'll leave." Plus I'm pretty strong, so if they started to get out of hand, I would usually just throw them somewhere and take back control that way. Actually, I did leave a few times.[41]

Karen developed a softer but no less effective strategy for reestablishing control with difficult audiences at private parties:

At some parties the men really tried to put me in my place with hostile comments or by touching me. When they got out of line, I just relied on what was familiar to me: being sweet and coy, smiling my way out of the problem. I was very much on my toes but, for whatever reason, I didn't feel at liberty

to be more tough in setting my boundaries. I was amazed when I did a double with this other woman who started things off by saying: "You touch my
tits, you touch my ass, I kick you in the balls. Now enjoy, gentlemen." Everyone has their own style.[42]

For women working out of their own homes as call girls, familiarity with
the work environment can enhance their sense of authority over clients.
Vision, who worked as a "sacred prostitute"[43] out of a private home, explains
the advantage of home-based work from her perspective: "It really helps that
they are coming into my environment, so the [energy] is set up by me. They
are walking into my game. I'm the priestess, and it's my temple. I like it that
they have to come to my space, and I get to say what happens."[44]

Working at home, though, does involve some risk, as clients know where
a sex worker lives, diminishing her autonomy and erasing one important
boundary between work and private life. In addition, in places where prostitution is illegal, the sex worker risks eviction from her home if it is discovered
that she is operating a sex business on the premises. Nonetheless, according to
some sex workers, the benefits outweigh the risks. Carol explains:

> I do worry about clients having obsessional relationships with me, which is
> one reason I live in a security building. But I like working out of my apart-
> ment because I think it's good that they can come in and see that a whole per-
> son lives here. They sit here and see a bookcase full of books from ten years
> of school; they see all these feminist and lesbian titles. I think it challenges
> their ideas of who a prostitute is.[45]

COMPETITION AND ISOLATION

Sex workers' attempts to establish authority and control in their dealings
with clients and management can be significantly affected by their relations
with other workers. In the sex trade, as in other professions, worker relations
vary from collegiality to fierce competition. Workers in third-party-controlled
sex businesses are often intentionally pitted against one another to improve performance, atomize the workforce, and discourage organizing. One exotic
dancer describes the competitive dynamic created by management:

> When someone was fired, it created this incredible tension, with everyone
> worried "Am I going to be next?" There I was in my early thirties, watching
> women even younger getting fired because they were "too old." One effect

was that it made you see the new women coming in as competition. You'd look at them and think, "I'm not that young. I'm not that beautiful. My breasts aren't as large." I really hated that because the best part of the job was the interaction with the other women.[46]

Similarly, former porn star and stripper Candye Kane describes hostility among workers on the professional stripping circuit between locals working for tips and "stars" brought in on contract:

When I did live strip shows, the other girls could be just fucked. I got the feeling that they thought it wasn't fair that I was way fatter than them, but I was the celebrity who had been flown in and was making a lot more money. They were completely right to feel like they should be making more money; they were beautiful girls, like Playboy bunnies. But I had successfully marketed myself and became a celebrity instead of just a house stripper.[47]

Competition among workers is also intensified when managers hire too many dancers to work a limited number of clients. This is typically a problem in strip clubs where management collects a "stage fee" or "commission payment" from each dancer rather than a portion of her tips. In such a situation, management has an interest in adding additional dancers both to increase the amount collected up front from dancers and to increase the variety for customers who have paid a substantial admission fee. Teri argues that this creates a direct conflict between management and workers' interests:

At work meetings they would get on us about how whorish we were behaving by being too direct about asking for tips. But it's like, "I ain't here for my health, motherfucker." Still they'd tell us, "Don't hustle so hard for money; there's a recession on and the men don't have as much money in their wallets when they come in. Be nice to the men." In other words, don't insist on what you deserve. But meanwhile they book way too many women to work each shift.[48]

Women working as independents also compete for client dollars, but may also experience a sense of shared risk that can lead to practical alliance and bonding. Street workers, for example, often develop networks of protection. Sandy, a former teenage street prostitute, reports: "Once I had done the first couple of tricks, I started talking to the other girls a little bit. We all would keep an eye on each other.... It was good to have other people around."[49]

Barbara, who also worked as a teenage prostitute, describes both the solidarity among street workers and its limits:

We'd really keep an eye out for each other on the streets, pass on the word about bad johns and who was with vice, refer guys to each other if we didn't have time or they wanted something we didn't do. There was no backstabbing or petty competition. None of that stuff. But there was a line you just didn't cross, and that was something hard for me to learn. In fact, I think I never really could learn it or accept it, which is why I eventually had to leave the streets. You don't mess with the relation between a bitch and her pimp. Solidarity and morality on the streets just can't cross that line.[50]

For some workers, an informal alliance may be a means of ensuring price-fixing for a basic standard of service. Samantha, a California call girl and activist, organized a support group for call girls: "We called it the 'union,' and we used union meetings to try to convince women to charge more money; if someone wasn't charging $200 an hour, we'd invite her to the meetings and assure her that she was good enough to ask for more."[51] However, not all sex workers are equally positioned to demand top dollar for their services. Licia Brussa of the Dutch migrant prostitutes' project argues that foreign workers are often seen as unfair competition undercutting the market:

Colombian women will admit that they might work under the price a bit, or do more for the money, but they won't work without condoms. Dominican women admit that sometimes they won't demand a condom if there's not enough money to be made otherwise. But all the women do have a stake in encouraging each other to work safely and not to work under the going price.[52]

Still, in a largely unorganized industry where prices have remained stagnant, the temptation exists to blame other workers for problems in the trade. Jo Doezema, a sex worker and prostitutes' rights activist in Amsterdam, argues:

The problem with prostitution is the way it's organized as a business. Women don't have enough control over their work, and prices aren't keeping up with inflation. The disturbing thing is, you hear from so many whores that it's the fault of the foreign women that prices are down. And I just don't believe it. It's such a simplistic analysis to look at two things and see a causal relationship, especially when it's "blame the foreigner."[53]

Related to the problem of competition within the workforce is the issue of worker isolation. While self-employed and home-based workers in all trades risk some measure of isolation, for those in the sex industry the problem is often exacerbated by the effects of social stigma and criminal status.

Samantha, an independent call girl in San Francisco, reports: "It's really isolating if you work for yourself. You wait for the phone to ring, talk to some jerk and hope he shows up. There is so much silence and secrecy involved that you need to talk to someone."[54]

Similarly, Licia Brussa describes isolation as one of the biggest problems facing migrant prostitutes working as independents in Amsterdam's window prostitution district: "What they complain most about is the isolation, which they describe as inhuman, not the work. Their lives become a closed circuit. They spend twenty-four hours a day in a ghetto always available to clients. That really affects them."[55]

For some sex workers, involvement in third-party-controlled prostitution, like brothel and club work, can actually mitigate some of the problems of isolation and competition. Terry, who worked for six years in the legal brothels of Nevada, explains: "There were some advantages to working within the brothel system. You weren't isolated. You had other women around who were in the same business, so there was a lot of camaraderie."[56] One woman who worked in an illegal brothel in California, agrees: "The best thing about it was having a group of people around all the time, so you get this incredible camaraderie going."[57]

MOVING FROM CAMARADERIE TO WORKPLACE ORGANIZING

Alliances among workers that go beyond simple camaraderie to more politicized and organized solidarity are still relatively rare in the sex industry. The independent and transitory nature of many workers' involvement in the trade makes organizing especially difficult. In both the United States and in Europe, prostitutes' rights organizations have managed to mobilize only a small fraction of working prostitutes.[58] In the Netherlands, Yvette, an organizer with the prostitutes' rights organization the Red Thread, explains the low number of organized workers as follows: "Many women see themselves as independents and don't want to join anything. Many choose this profession precisely because it's independent."[59]

Terry, a San Francisco sex worker and activist, agrees: "Many of us are sort of petit bourgeois. We're self-employed free spirits, so we're a difficult population to organize. Most prostitutes, I think, would like to see their status change, but you really do have to get out there and show them that change is possible."[60]

A further complication is that many sex workers do not identify as members of a profession, seeing their involvement in the sex trade as a temporary activity, not a professional identity. Nonetheless, in those areas of the sex trade where participants do identify as workers, some movement in the direction of organizing and unionizing is taking place. Not surprisingly, the most successful attempts at workplace organizing have occurred in those venues within the sex industry where workers are legally employed. At the Lusty Lady in San Francisco, dancers' status as employees made it possible for workers to unionize and to become the first sex club in the country to win a contract.[61] In the absence of tipping, and in a situation in which seniority determined pay scale, competition among workers was at a minimum, and they were easier to mobilize.

Paradoxically, another reason the Lusty Lady may have been such a likely site for organizing was management rhetoric about how much better the Lusty was to its workers than other San Francisco sex clubs. Susie explains:

> The management had this attitude that the Lusty was such a great place to work. They'd tell us, "We're encouraging you to love your bodies, we're not discriminating against different body types, we want you to have fun." So people really did have a different vision of where they were working. And when it turned out to be bullshit, they got mad. So some of us met on our own and discussed our complaints; and then we met with the management. When it looked like they weren't taking us seriously, a lot of women just walked out. It was kind of exciting. I think some of them thought, "Fine, I might as well go somewhere else where I can make more money and the management just says straight out, 'We're hiring good bodies', instead of pretending it's some kind of special place."[62]

For workers at the Lusty Lady who stayed, organizing was risky business, as another dancer explains: "We all knew we needed a union, but everyone was really afraid, afraid we'd just get fired. It happened all the time; they'd pick somebody out and fire her, and everybody else would get real paranoid."[63]

In 1997, dancers at the Lusty Lady successfully organized to be represented by the Service Employees International Union (AFL-CIO) and won a contract guaranteeing work shifts, protection against arbitrary discipline and termination, automatic wage increases, sick days, and a contracted procedure for pursuing grievances with management. They recently negotiated a second contract expanding those benefits.[64] Dancers in several other cities (Anchorage, Philadelphia, Pittsburgh, San Diego, North Hollywood), have been engaged in similar organizing efforts.[65]

However, most exotic dancers, like other workers in the third-party-controlled sex industry, are not legally defined as workers. In order to collectively bargain, sex workers must first obtain recognition as *workers* not *independent contractors*. But, in the absence of real worker solidarity and effective shop-floor organizing, this change of status can, at least in the short run, actually reduce worker power and control, as the following description of recent developments in other San Francisco sex clubs suggests.

In the early 1990s, dancers in all clubs but the Lusty Lady were classified as independent contractors who received no wages and made their incomes entirely from tips. Management made its income from customer admission fees. But in 1992, club owners began charging workers for the right to perform by imposing a "stage fee" of about $10 a shift. Within a year, those fees had doubled. In response, dancers organized the Exotic Dancers Alliance and filed a complaint with the California State Labor commission. The Commission ruled that the dancers were indeed employees and that it was illegal to charge for the right to work.[66]

This success, however, has also presented unforeseen challenges for dancers. While clubs have been forced to abolish stage fees and to acknowledge that dancers are employees (and pay them a minimum wage), they have also replaced the stage fee with a much more costly (to dancers) "commission" system. Under the new system, dancers are required to pay management a commission on every dance they "sell" to customers on the grounds that the clubs own the dancers' product.[67] Since it is impossible to keep track of each dance, dancers are required to pay a daily minimum commission of between $150 and $250 dollars at the end of each eight-hour shift, regardless of how much they earn in tips.[68] Since the imposition of commission quotas, some dancers now pay out more than they earn on any given shift. As a result, the pressure to perform "extra" services to make higher tips has increased. One dancer reports, "Girls get desperate, so they're pulling tricks. It's right out in the open."[69]

Management has thus effectively both reduced workers' earnings and their ability to determine which practices they will perform.[70] Furthermore, the reclassification of dancers as workers, coupled with the commission system, has led to serious divisions among dancers. San Francisco clubs are now divided between those who support the Exotic Dancers Alliance and those who hold organizers responsible for loss of independence on the job and high commission fees. The case of San Francisco demonstrates that while obtaining the status of worker is necessary for unionization, it is by no means a sufficient condition to ensure worker rights. In order to benefit from a change of status from independent contractor to employee, workers must collectively confront management's workplace regulations and exploitive wage system. In the absence of such organizing, workers may find themselves with even less power than they enjoyed as nominal independents.

OPTIONS AND OPPORTUNITIES

Decriminalization of prostitution, collective bargining, and workers' increased independence from managers are crucial to enhancing the power of those who work in the sex industry. But for sex workers to be best positioned to control their work they must also be able to leave should conditions become unsatisfactory. Unfortunately, many sex workers have few options beyond the trade. Sex workers' lives, like most women's lives, are rarely models of "free choice." In the mid-1990s, more than 12 million American women worked full time at jobs that paid wages below the federal poverty line, and many more women than men were part of the working poor.[71] Women are clustered in low-paying, low-status jobs: In the United States, women account for 98.5 percent of secretaries and 96.8 percent of child-care workers.[72]

Sex workers, like all women performing low-status work, would find their bargaining power enhanced by greater employment opportunities. To achieve this would require a profound shift of national priorities away from criminalization and toward education, job training, and higher wages for "women's work." In the absence of such a change in priorities, workers' ability to exercise power and control within the sex industry will continue to vary widely according not only to location within the trade but beyond it. As sex worker and writer Carol Queen points out, while not every sex worker can choose to work part time or to transition out of sex work into equally lucrative employment, for those who can, the experience of sexual labor is significantly improved:

> Women who are call girls could turn around and be executive secretaries if not CEOs in two minutes if they could find somebody to hire them with the gap in their résumés. A lot of women in my circle are graduate students, law students, or women who have "straight" jobs that they supplement with work as prostitutes. I don't know too many women who are working full time at our level. And one of the reasons that is true is we don't have to work full time to make ends meet.[73]

Options are crucial in increasing a worker's power over both clients and third parties in the trade, and in their ability to leave it. While feminists have been deeply divided for more than twenty years on whether prostitution should be conceived of as sexual violence or sex work, the women interviewed in this study suggest that all who are concerned with women's rights and well-being might unite around proposals to enhance women's power within the trade and to increase their options beyond it. As these workers report, sex workers' power is reinforced when police are a resource, not a risk; when workers—not management—control rules of behavior and rates of exploitation; and when desperation is not the driving force behind participation in the trade. This suggests that a broad-based feminist politics would demand decriminalization of consensual adult sexual activities, mass organizing and collective bargaining for sex workers, and increased employment options and higher wages for women in the sex trade and beyond.

CONTROLLING LAP DANCING: LAW, MORALITY, AND SEX WORK

Jacqueline Lewis

Since its beginnings as burlesque entertainment, exotic dancing has been the subject of public scrutiny. Since the early 1990s public attention has focused on one particular form of strip club activity, lap dancing. During a typical lap dance a dancer sits either between her customer's legs or directly on his lap with her tailbone pressed up against his genitals, moving her body against the customer's in order to arouse him.[1] The nature of the physical contact that occurs during lap dances has resulted in a blurring of the boundaries between stripping and prostitution.[2] This blurring of boundaries has been used in the defining of lap dancing as a social problem. Lap dancing prohibitionists argue that due to the sexual contact involved in lap dancing, this form of exotic dance is harmful and should be banned.

The media coverage and legal decisions concerning lap dancing in Ontario, Canada, between 1994 and 1997 helped frame lap dancing as a social problem in need of attention. Two discourses regarding lap dancing dominated media reports. Some public officials and members of public interest groups (e.g., Women's Christian Temperance Union) viewed lap dancing as harmful to the moral order of society and preservation of the family. Others, including the Association of Burlesque Entertainers, argued that lap dancing was harmful to the health and well-being of the individual dancer and possibly other members of society. Regardless of the particular framing of the problem (i.e., lap dancing as a threat to public morality and the family or to the health and well-being of dancers), the positions presented in the media coalesced into one dominant discourse: Lap dancing was harmful and should be prohibited. This discourse elevated latent public fears and concerns regarding the threat posed by sex workers to public morality, health, and safety, and it increased public support for the lap dancing ban.

The problem with making policy decisions based on this discourse is that alternative discourses of harm were not taken into consideration. For example, some dancers reported having few problems with lap dancing and viewed the ban as an infringement on their lives, both economically and in terms of their freedom of choice. In addition, a critical feminist discourse warns of some potential dangers in the state's control of sex work. While recognizing the potential harm individuals may face while engaging in sex work, this discourse draws our attention to the potential harmful consequences of governmental restrictions, particularly for those individuals whose activities are being controlled.[3]

This chapter examines the contemporary lap dancing debate in Ontario, the legal decisions concerning lap dancing, the implications of both lap dancing and its subsequent ban on exotic dancers' lives,[4] and the relevance of social constructionist theory to this analysis. Using the everyday experiences of exotic dancers, this chapter also illustrates the difficulties associated with attempts to regulate or ban sex work and the potential contradictions inherent in the protectionist ideology that typically frames such policies.[5]

EXOTIC DANCING LITERATURE

Since the late 1960s exotic dancing and the experiences of exotic dancers have been the focus of academic inquiry. The relevance of the available literature to the present study is limited, however, by the focus of the research and the fact that many of the studies were conducted prior to the introduction of lap dancing. Most of the literature has focused on three broad areas of inquiry: factors influencing entry into exotic dancing, and job-related socialization;[6] the stigma associated with the occupation and the means by which dancers engage in stigma management;[7] and patterns of interaction between dancers and customers.[8] Little attention has been paid to the regulation of strip club activities, the experience of dancing, or the impact of dancing on dancers' lives.

Several studies of strip clubs have described their rules aimed at controlling physical interaction between dancers and customers.[9] Some researchers found the existence of strip club norms prohibiting all forms of touch.[10] Others reported less rigid rules that specified which parts of the dancer's body customers were and were not allowed to touch (e.g., breasts and genitalia).[11]

Although most of the available literature has focused on rules regarding customers' behavior, some researchers also mentioned the existence of norms aimed at controlling the dancers.[12] Usually dancers could casually touch customers as they moved around the club trying to "drum up" business, but they were prohibited from touching customers once they had begun a dance. The literature indicates that, in practice, these norms were often violated.[13]

Absent from the literature is a discussion of the impact of the legal prohibition of certain strip club activities, or the charging of dancers with criminal offenses by law enforcement officials. The only researchers to briefly comment on these issues are Prus and Irini and Boles and Garbin [14] Prus and Irini found that the dancers in their study never knew when their acts would be judged too explicit and they would be arrested by police. Boles and Garbin noted that dancers were frequently arrested for "violating local statutes prohibiting 'lewd and obscene dancing'" or for soliciting.[15]

In terms of the experience of dancing and the impact of dancing on dancers' lives, Ronai's study[16] is the only one that provides an insider's perspective (as a dancer herself) on what dancing and being sexually propositioned and touched in the context of dancing is actually like. "This [being kissed and touched] is gross to be going through. Why am I doing it? I keep getting angrier and angrier."[17] Her work also illustrates the things dancers do to limit physical contact between themselves and their customers, such as scolding customers through actions or words (e.g., slapping or grabbing their hands, giving them nasty looks, verbally scolding them, etc.); appealing to customers' concerns for their own health and safety (e.g., "imagine if I kissed every guy in the bar like that before I kissed you");[18] altering the tempo of the dance in order to avoid wandering hands (e.g., dancing faster; swaying quickly side to side); and appealing to club rules and the dancers' fear of getting in trouble with management.

Ronai's research is also important in that she provides details on the nature of the physical contact that occurs within clubs offering table dances.[19] Interactions during table dances, as she describes them, resemble those that occur during lap dances. The most frequent form of physical contact between dancers and customers involved "the customer sliding down to the end of his seat, spreading his legs, and pulling the dancer close to him where she could then use her knees discreetly to rub his genitals while she danced."[20] The main differences between such contact and that reported by women who have participated in lap dancing had to do with customer expectations, genital proximity, and the degree of control dancers have while working. Control included both the degree of choice dancers felt they had to refuse to engage in sexual contact with customers and the availability of rationales for such refusals. As discussed below, when sexual touching, or the expectation that dancers would provide sexual services to customers during private dances, became the norm, dancers had more difficulty controlling their customers and more negative experiences on the job. When dancers could no longer cite club "no-touch rules" or "fear of getting in trouble with management" as reasons for abstaining from such activities, some dancers felt they lost some degree of agency while working and that they became more vulnerable to sexual pressure and exploitation.

METHODS

Between June 1995 and February 1998, observations at ten strip clubs in southern Ontario and in-depth interviews with thirty female strippers and eight other strip club employees (e.g., disc jockey, waitress, bouncer, shooter girl, doorman) were conducted. Bars were selected to maximize the diversity of the sample: in cities of all sizes, in clubs ranging from those that cater to professionals and celebrities to bars whose clientele were primarily factory workers or farm laborers.

Participants were recruited by key informants,[21] members of the research team during field trips to the clubs, or dancers who referred other respondents to us. Each interview was taped and took place in a location chosen by the respondent. Interviews lasted from one to four hours, with the majority lasting approximately one and one-half hours. Questions explored how each woman got involved in dancing, how long she expected to work as a dancer, types of interaction with clients, experiences of lap dancing, personal control over the work situation, relationships among employees, and other issues. Field observations were conducted primarily to supplement interview data and to illuminate the strip club environment, including the physical setting and atmosphere of different clubs and the interactions between dancers and clients.[22]

At the time of the interviews, two-thirds of the women were working as dancers. The women began dancing between 1979 and 1997 and had been dancing anywhere from less than one year to seventeen years, with the median time on the job being four and a half years. Age ranged from eighteen to thirty-eight years, with the median age being twenty-six. Approximately half of the women either had completed some high school or had received their high school diploma. The other half had at least some postsecondary training. One quarter of the women interviewed were attending school. Half were single or divorced, and half had partners. Of those with partners, less than half were living with their partner. Approximately one-third of the women interviewed had children. More than half of the dancers with children were either single mothers or lived separately from their partners.

LAP DANCING AND THE LAW

In 1991, the Metropolitan Toronto Police received a complaint alleging that indecent acts were occurring at Cheaters, a strip club in Toronto. A two-month undercover investigation revealed that physical contact and sexual activity were occurring between dancers and patrons during lap dances at the club. According to the police, during their investigation officers observed dancers:

a. being nude except for wearing an open shirt or blouse;
b. fondling their own breasts, buttocks, and genitals while close to the customer;
c. sitting on a customer's lap and grinding their bare buttocks' into his lap;
d. sitting on a customer's lap, reaching into his crotch and apparently masturbating him;
e. permitting the customer to touch and fondle their breasts, buttocks, thighs, and genitals;
f. permitting the customer to kiss, lick, and suck their breasts;
g. permitting what appeared to be cunnilingus.[23]

Following the undercover investigation, club owner Patrick Mara and manager Allan East were charged under Section 167(1) of the *Criminal Code of Canada*[24] for permitting indecent performances in their club.

In February 1994, Judge Hachborn of the Ontario Court, Provincial Division, ruled in *R. v. Mara* (1994)[25] that lap dancing did not exceed "community standards of tolerance," the Canadian test for obscenity and indecency.[26] Hachborn's decision was overturned two years later by the Ontario Court of Appeal.[27] However, in the interim between the two court decisions, lap dancing began to appear in clubs across Ontario; Hachborn's decision had been interpreted by club owners, managers, and dancers as permitting physical contact between dancers and customers, including lap dancing. In response, some municipalities starting implementing bylaws designed to control activities in strip clubs.[28] In some cities, such as Mississauga and Toronto,[29] the new bylaws banned both physical contact between dancers and customers and private booths within the clubs (referred to as Champagne or VIP Rooms).

These changes were reinforced by providing for heavy fines for bylaw violations.[30] For example, according to City of Mississauga Bylaw 572–79, strip club owners, operators, or entertainers who violated the bylaw could be fined up to $25,000 or imprisoned for up to one year, or both. In addition, the clubs could be fined up to $50,000.

The decision of the Ontario Court of Appeal in *R. v. Mara* (1996)[31] was upheld by the Supreme Court of Canada on March 12, 1997. Applying the legal test of obscenity/indecency established in *R v. Butler* (1992),[32] the Supreme Court found lap dancing to exceed "community standards of tolerance in contemporary Canadian society."[33] According to the Supreme Court ruling, lap dancing violates Section 167 (1) of the *Criminal Code of Canada* because "it degrades and dehumanizes women, it desensitizes sexuality, it is incompatible with the dignity and equality of each human being, and it predisposes persons to act in an antisocial manner."[34]

Since all Canadians are regulated by *Criminal Code* statutes, the Supreme Court's decision in *Mara* (1997) applied to Canada as a whole. Municipalities then had the choice of either relying on the *Criminal Code* and its enforcement as a means to control lap dancing, or taking the extra step of introducing municipal bylaws targeting such activities. As a result, exotic dancing has not been treated consistently across Canadian municipalities. Even in those jurisdictions where municipal bylaws exist to regulate exotic dancing, many bylaws do not contain a separate lap dancing provision. Instead, it is up to the discretion of each individual municipality to decide if it needs a bylaw and, if so, what will be included in it. If exotic dancing or lap dancing are not deemed to be problems in their communities, then control of strip club activities is left to the discretion of the police, through the use of the *Criminal Code* (i.e., sections 210 and 167(1)).

LAP DANCING AS A SOCIAL PROBLEM

Social constructionist theory is a useful tool for analyzing the framing of lap dancing as a social problem. According to Kitsuse and Spector, whether a given condition becomes a social problem is contingent upon some concerned group or individuals recognizing it as problem and asserting the need to eradicate, ameliorate, or otherwise change the condition.[35] Participation in the definitional process can be based on a desire to serve or protect one's own interests (e.g., social, political, economic, etc.), or to eliminate something that is perceived as offensive, wrong, or immoral (e.g., lap dancing). In either case, participants engage in claims-making activities designed to convince their audiences that a particular social problem exists and that something needs to be done about it.[36]

The framing of lap dancing as a social problem began with the criminal charges laid against Mara and East, for allowing lap dancing to occur in their club. A number of claims makers responded to the charges and began speaking out against lap dancing. These efforts intensified during the two years between the Hachborn ruling and that of the Ontario Court of Appeal. Media coverage of the charges, legal decisions, and the claims makers' accounts helped arouse public concern for this issue. As dancers and other members of the public increased the pressure on government officials to label lap dancing as a community health and safety risk, municipal government officials began voicing their opposition to lap dancing and introducing bylaws to regulate strip club activities.[37]

Media reports and the views of many of the women interviewed revealed that the objections to lap dancing and the efforts to define it as a social problem were based on a discourse of harm. The perceived credibility of this discourse was enhanced by the diversity of individuals supporting the lap dancing ban (i.e., special interest groups ranging from the extremely conservative Women's Christian Temperance Union to the more left-wing Association of Burlesque Entertainers [which consists of two members], and from conservative municipal officials such as Hazel McCallion to liberal officials such as Jack Layton). According to these claims makers, lap dancing is harmful because it is offensive and threatening to moral order and stability in Canadian society. As Erika Kubassek, superintendent of legislation for the temperance union, said, "Stripping, lap dancing, and prostitution are signs of a degenerated society.... Canada is now in an advanced state of moral decline."[38] The imputed immorality of lap dancing was echoed by a number of Toronto city councilors and Mississauga city officials. McCallion, the mayor of Mississauga, said, "It's time we restored some standards to our community.... There is already enough of a breakdown in society and in the family."[39]

In addition to claims makers who relied on a morality-based discourse of harm, other claims makers pointed to the harmful effects of lap dancing on the health and well-being of dancers and possibly other individuals. Toronto councilors Olivia Chow, Jack Layton, and Judy Sgro repeatedly emphasized the coercion and victimization involved in lap dancing.[40] The Association of Burlesque Entertainers (ABE) released an information packet in 1995 titled *Why Lap Dancing Is a Health Danger and Must be Banned—Exotic Dancers (and Others) Speaking Out,* which detailed the health risks associated with lap dancing for dancers, club employees, customers, and their families, and the adverse effect lap dancing had had on dancers' lives (e.g., their relationships and self-esteem).[41] In a section of the packet titled "What people don't know about lap dancing could be deadly to their health," Katherine Goldberg, one of the founding members of the association wrote:

> Everyone is at risk. I'm not saying all exotic dancing is bad, but lap dancing and prostitution in the bars and clubs is [sic] bad.... I don't think lap dancing can be controlled, so I urge that we get rid of it. I ask everyone to help get lap dancing out. Lap dancing hurts everyone. It hurts other women. For instance, a man fingers a girl, and he has a cut finger. It's dark in these rooms. We can't see what they have. So he fingers a woman and he gives her AIDS, or venereal diseases, or hepatitis, or maybe another contagious disease. She goes home, gives it to her husband, and so on. Or another customer who tries something gets it.... And how about our kids when they become of age, and they start going in these places. Most women don't know their husbands come here. Yet those women wash their hands of the problem. Remember that this is not a stripper thing. Lots of people's lives are at risk. It's an unhealthy thing. It's a deadly thing.[42]

The dancers who participated in this study who opposed lap dancing echoed Goldberg's concerns. Specifically at issue was contact with customers' ejaculate. Such contact could occur when ejaculate penetrated the men's clothing during lap dances.[43] As one dancer stated: "So halfway through the song, like no warning, you're sitting on their lap, and all of a sudden you're wet." Another area of concern was dancers' genital contact with other dancers' vaginal secretions, left on customers' clothing.

In addition to physical health issues, these women also talked about the harmful effects of feeling pressured to lap dance by club owners, managers, and customers, or being threatened with job loss if they refused to engage in such performances.[44] These women reported feeling disempowered and victimized while dancing and being repeatedly asked or pressured to engage in sexual activities with customers. As two dancers complained,

> I remember the very first night we lap danced, when we came home. We were driving home from the club, and we were crying our eyes out. We both felt like this is not what we were brought up to do. These strangers' fingers all over you—it was really nasty.

> I had enough of men saying to me, "I'll give you fifty bucks for a blow job," or "I'll give you a hundred dollars if you suck me off." I hated the way it made me feel. So I'm actually enjoying dancing more since the ban [on lap dancing].

The women who supported the lap dancing ban reported that lap dancing affected how they felt about themselves. Although some exotic dancers in general have always engaged in prostitution,[45] most of the women we spoke with reported that they only worked as exotic dancers[46] and therefore identified themselves as entertainers or dancers. As predicted by McCaghy and Skipper, as exotic dancing evolved from theatrical performances to sexual acts (lap dancing), dancers increasingly disliked their jobs.[47] Eliminating the no-touch rule removed the barrier between dancer and customer that many dancers relied upon to maintain their self-image as dancers or entertainers.[48] The result was a change in the women's feelings about themselves; they felt akin to prostitutes, for example, or contaminated by the men.

Although the majority of women in this study held a position similar to that of Katherine Goldberg and the ABE regarding lap dancing, a few of the dancers did not.[49] The main difference between these dancers and those who wanted to stop lap dancing was the degree of agency and control they felt while on the job. The women who did not feel compelled to quit lap dancing felt a sense of control over their work and were confident that they could do their job in a manner they found personally acceptable:

> All it was, really, was just riding on somebody's lap. And the thing is, if some girls were fucking in different booths or whatever, that was their choice. If they wanted to risk getting sick or they wanted to catch AIDS or whatever, hey, that's up to you. If that's how you want to make your money, fine. But, for me, I had a set of standard rules for myself, and I applied that to every customer, good-looking or ugly. It was just a straight set of rules. If they didn't like the rules, and they didn't like what I was offering them, they could leave.

> I tell them what they can do up front. "This is what you can touch, this is what you can't touch, this is how you can touch me, and this how you can't touch me, and if you go over that line the dance is over, I get up and leave." I'm not gonna let some guy do something to me that I don't want.

Some dancers thus felt confident they could regulate their own and their clients' behavior through self-imposed standards and therefore had little problem with the continuation of lap dancing. In contrast, women who felt they had few choices open to them while on the job, in terms of what they could do and with whom they could do it, and those who reported feeling victimized by the whole lap dancing experience, supported the lap dancing ban.

Although only a few dancers who participated in this study were opposed to the ban, the amount of such opposition within the larger dancer community in unknown. A review of newspaper reports between 1994 and 1998 provides some evidence that the dancer community is divided on the lap dancing issue. One newspaper columnist said, "One is hard pressed to find outraged lap dancers [who were outraged over having to lap dance] in the clubs."[50] And another report stated, "Toni Thomas-Johns, speaking on behalf of about twenty other lap dancers ... said 'reports of sexual activity have been exaggerated and dancers don't take health risks.... Dancers know how to handle clientele. They aren't scared that they're going to be raped or assaulted.'"[51] Another dancer, Victoria, was quoted as saying that she was part of the "silent majority" who "resented the implication that they had been victimized while dancing and were being forced into prostitution."[52]

Dancers were not alone in voicing their opposition to the ban. Several municipal officials and local newspaper columnists also publicly criticized the ban and the efforts of the lap dancing prohibitionists. Toronto Councilor Mario Silva said that he thought lap dancing is a "valid trade" and that women should be "totally entitled" to lap dance as part of their job "without municipal politicians imposing their values."[53] And Councilor Dan Leckie, too, critiqued the "moralistic tone that has crept into the discussion."[54] These sentiments were elaborated upon by Rosie DiManno, a columnist for the *Toronto Star*, who noted that the lap dancing controversy "has provided local politicians with a stage from which to shimmy and gyrate in oratorical excess ... and ... thrust their morality on to a legitimate, if rather cheesy, industry."[55] In addition, questions have been raised about the legitimacy and accuracy of other claims makers' accounts. As Colin Leslie reported, "the forty page report of the Metropolitan Toronto Licensing Commission concerning lap dancing [upon which the bylaws were based], shows very little evidence of touching and sexual activity within the clubs."[56] But, despite some opposition to the ban, the claims of the lap dancing prohibitionists dominated the public debate.

PROBLEMS WITH THE BAN

Both dancers and other club staff reported that, despite the Supreme Court decision in *Mara* (1997) and the existence of bylaws in some municipalities banning such activities, lap dancing was still available in some Ontario clubs. As one dancer noted, "It still goes on. Girls are getting felt up, and guys are doing what they want." Recent newspaper reports from Toronto substantiate these claims.[57] In some of the study sites, lap dancing and VIP rooms disappeared after the ban, only to be later reintroduced with a new name (towel dancing,[58] taboo dancing, etc.) or with different dancers (e.g., women brought in from countries such as Thailand or the Philippines,[59] where exotic dancing may involve greater sexual contact between dancer and customer).[60] In other sites, lap dancing was not affected by the Supreme Court's decision or the presence of municipal laws prohibiting such activities.[61]

From the perspective of the lap dancing prohibitionists, the Supreme Court's ruling in the case of *Mara* was problematic because the court was limited to addressing only the issue of whether lap dancing in a public place is an indecent act. An important issue not addressed by the ruling is the distinction between what constitutes a "public" and a "private" place. On the one hand, it can be argued that "private booths" are "private" and therefore what goes on inside them is not covered by the ruling. On the other hand, it can be argued that "private booths" in a "public club" are not genuinely "private," thereby making sexual contact or lap dancing within them illegal. The former interpretation of the Supreme Court's ruling opened the door for lap dancing to continue in strip clubs, as long as it did not occur on the main floor of the clubs.[62] Both the municipalities and the police, however, had other social control policies to fall back on in their efforts to eradicate lap dancing. Municipalities can curb lap dancing by adopting and enforcing bylaws to control such activities. The police also have the power to charge dancers, customers, and club owners and managers with violations of Section 210 of the *Criminal Code*, the section pertaining to bawdy-house offenses.[63]

Another problem with the 1997 *Mara* decision is that it illustrates the contradictory nature of legal sanctions. The ruling implies that women have limited agency, "are unsafe and can only be made safe through the protectionist activities of the state."[64] Similar to the *Butler* (1992) decision, both the Supreme Court's and various interest groups' use of a discourse of harm to justify controlling commercial sexual activities is linked to a conservative sexual morality.[65] While lap dancing may indeed pose certain risks for participants, it is important to acknowledge the harm to dancers and other women that can emerge from legislating morality. Although the supposed objective of the Supreme Court ruling in *Butler* (1992) (and its application in *Mara* [1997]) was "the prevention of harm, particularly harm towards women," and "promoting the equality and dignity of women,"[66] state discourses that rely on an image of "women as silent and passive victims of male violence and idealize the state as protector" (e.g., the moral purity discourses of the last century; contemporary state discourses on pornography)[67] may actually have unintended, adverse effects on women's lives.

In setting legal precedents that present women as weak and in need of protection, the courts may in effect reduce women's sense of agency, create a "fearful, protected feminine object,"[68] and perpetuate patriarchal notions of the subordinate status of women relative to men, thus restricting women's equal participation in our society. State control of commercial sex (e.g., banning lap dancing) can have the effect of reinforcing divisions between "good girls" and "bad girls," so that the "good girls" are the ones who are protected and the "bad girls" (i.e., the dancers) are the ones who are punished. Although many dancers supported the ban on lap dancing, it appears that they were unaware of (and to some degree surprised by) the implications that the ban could have on their lives. Rather than enhancing the limited sense of agency some dancers experienced while on the job, the ban further reduced it, at least for some dancers. Policies based on protectionist discourses may result in the reduction of harm to dancers in some respects, but may increase harm in other areas. For example, municipal laws and police enforcement actions have reduced business in the clubs and therefore the amount of money that dancers and club staff can earn.[69] Although the ban provided dancers with a new rationale for refusing sexual contact with customers (i.e., "It is illegal"), they also lost income. The reduction in income resulted in some dancers' risking lap dancing–related charges or moving into prostitution in order to earn the money they felt they needed to survive. Some women, even those who supported the ban, talked about the problems with it:

> It all went to shit when lap dancing got banned. Guys wouldn't pay ten dollars or fifteen dollars for a dance on the floor if they couldn't touch.

> I like it, and I don't like it. I like it because they can't touch you, and you don't have to grind on them. But I don't like it because those were twenty-dollar dances, and guys buy more lap dances than anything else. You made so much more money when lap dancing was around.

To the extent that banning lap dancing restricts women's abilities to maximize the financial rewards of the job, the ban may be viewed as reducing their agency.

In addition to the ban's impact on income, dancers were also worried about the potential financial implications of being charged. For example, prior to the ban dancers could casually touch their customers while dancing. Now, however, they may lose their licenses[70] or be subjected to heavy fines (up to $25,000) if they come into physical contact with a customer while dancing for them. A number of the women felt the new restrictions were too extreme. "I don't think it [lap dancing] is something that the government or somebody else should be clamping down on," one woman said. "Personal decisions shouldn't be regulated that way. I think it is up to the individual to decide what they will or will not do." In addition to dancers being charged for touching their customers, even if the touch was not sexual in nature, they can also be charged if customers touch their bodies, even if they did not consent to being touched.[71] Fines, revocations of licences, criminal charges, and lawyer's fees can be seen as harms to dancers resulting from the ban.

The lap dancing ban therefore has done little to enhance the overall sense of agency dancers feel while working and has made it difficult for dancers to do their jobs in a manner that they find personally acceptable, that maximizes their pay, and that protects them from legal charges and from physical violation by customers.

CONCLUSION

The Supreme Court's ruling in *Mara* (1997) suggests that it was arrived at, at least in part, from a desire to provide women, including exotic dancers, with protection from the "degradation and exploitation" associated with lap dancing. There are, however, several problems associated with using a protectionist discourse to justify state restrictions on sex work. The first is the assumption that women, including female sex workers, are victims of male violence and are in need of protection from the state. This assumption is problematic because it can serve to further reduce women's sense of agency. The second problem with the protectionist discourse has to do with who ultimately falls under the "protected status" category. Although dancers were supposed to be included in this "protected status" category, judicial decisions, such as *Butler* (1992) and *Mara* (1997), essentially drew a line between the "good girl" and the "bad girl," with the "good girl" being the one who is viewed as deserving of protection. The third problem with using a discourse of harm to justify state control of sex work is that it perpetuates a particular moral order through the regulation of certain forms of sexual behavior, rather than the protection of some specific group of individuals.

The Supreme Court's decision in *Mara* (1997) is also problematic because in making its decision the Court was restricted to addressing only the issue contained in the original charge—whether lap dancing in a public place was indecent.[72] As a result, club owners and managers have interpreted the Supreme Court's decision as pertaining only to exotic dances performed in public areas of strip clubs. Control of private dances has therefore fallen to municipal governments and the police.[73] One problem with the municipal bylaws, as they are currently structured, is that they apply only to people working within the clubs, not the customers. The alternative is for the police to charge customers with an offense under Section 210 of the *Criminal Code* pertaining to bawdy houses, which applies to anyone found in such a place. Banning lap dancing targets the dancers' more than customers' behavior and puts dancers in a disadvantaged position in their interactions with customers, increasing their risks and reducing their control while on the job. This law is thus part of a patriarchal system of justice that generally protects male interests.

Although the ban on lap dancing has been couched in a protectionist discourse, in many respects it has worked to the disadvantage of the dancers. The problem is that little attention has been paid to the effects of various forms of control on exotic dancers' lives. While the ban may advance some of the interests of dancers (e.g., no longer feeling forced to lap dance) it does so at the cost of other interests, such as their income and risk of being charged. Social control policies can be fashioned that benefit dancers, meeting more of their needs, including the prevention of harm. An alternative to the current policy would be to treat exotic dancing as a form of work and provide dancers with the same protections as other workers. Such policy change would shift the emphasis to regulating the exotic dancing industry, rather than the dancers themselves—using employment standards, human rights, occupational health and safety, and workers compensation laws to help improve work conditions and protect rights.[74] These changes would provide more meaningful protection for exotic dancers than the policies currently being used.

INSIDE NEVADA'S BROTHEL INDUSTRY

*Kathryn Hausbeck
and Barbara G. Brents*

In Nevada's dusty desert, in a small gambling town, a lone traveler might turn off main street and find himself on a dirt road, facing a row of screen doors and front porches illuminated by the neon words Penny's Cozy Corner, My Place, or the Pussy Cat. These rural brothels are remnants of a bygone era of itinerant miners, small-town saloons, powerful sheriffs, and women who survived by selling one of the rarest and most sought-after commodities in many Old West towns: sex.

While these images project a mythic version of the old Wild West, the ten counties in Nevada that license brothels exist within a modern political and economic culture. The Old West cowboy culture of ranching and mining is increasingly being transformed into a New West consumer culture built on a service-and-information economy, tourism, and modern bureaucratic politics.[1] Where the Old West was predominantly frontier, with small towns growing up around railroad, agricultural, or mining hubs, the New West is marked by the growth of urban centers surrounded by sprawling suburbs. The New West strives to attract tourists to new tourist attractions, focusing on the appeal of sports (mountain biking, skiing, snowboarding, rock climbing), dude ranches, music festivals, and gambling casinos. The result is a bifurcated sensibility in which the historical legacy of libertarian ideals, frontier individualism, mining, agriculture, and ranching now coexist with the cosmopolitan New West.

Despite the uniqueness of Nevada's legal brothels, few studies of the industry exist.[2] In this chapter we examine how legal brothel prostitution is situated between its origins as part of a rural, cowboy Old West culture and a

FIGURE 1

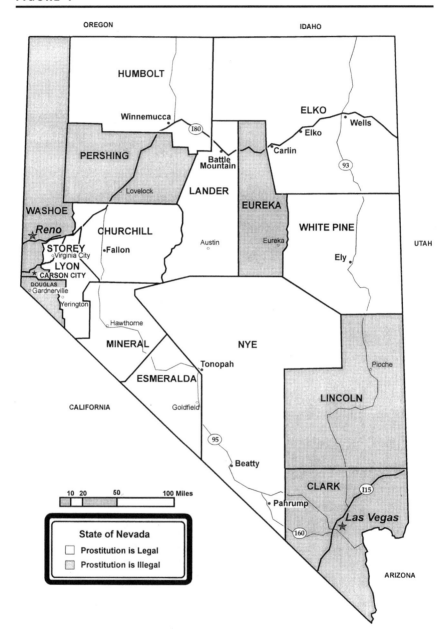

growing New West economy and culture. One might ask: Why does legal brothel prostitution persist in Nevada, and what is the likelihood of its continued existence given the changes associated with the transition from the Old West to the New West? To answer this, we examine: (1) the contemporary structure of the Nevada brothel industry, (2) the relationship between the brothels and the government, (3) brothel owners' relations to one another, and (4) the relation of the brothel industry to the larger postindustrial service economy in Nevada.

DATA AND METHODS

This study is based on several data sources. We examined newspaper articles and archival data for the historical and sociopolitical context in which brothel prostitution was legalized in Nevada and to identify existing regulations governing the industry; we observed and collected documents from nine brothels in northern and eastern Nevada during 1997 and 1998; we conducted twenty-five semistructured, open-ended interviews with owners, managers, and working women; and we conducted interviews with government officials, lobbyists, businesspeople, brothel industry regulators, former industry employees, and the head of the Nevada Brothel Association. We were interested in how these individuals characterized the contemporary brothel system, how they justified their association with the industry, and what they identified as problems and challenges of legal prostitution.

THE OLD WEST, THE NEW WEST, AND THE BROTHEL INDUSTRY

The few studies that have addressed the anomalous existence of Nevada's brothels attribute it to some combination of economics and political culture. Most historical studies argue that prostitution arose from the mining economy of the Old West and survived thanks to an Old West libertarianism that persisted in Nevada more than in other Western states.[3] Others have argued that the economic needs of declining rural economies allowed prostitution to outlive its Old West past.[4] Drawing from these, we argue that the culture and political economy of the West had three dimensions that help explain the existence of the brothels: first, a migrant economy; second, a particular set of sexual values and politics; and third, a "cowboy" libertarian, antiurban, antifederal culture.

The economics of the gold rush and silver mining in Nevada drew large numbers of single men to a harsh desert environment. Mining economies were often marked by dramatic, unpredictable cycles of boom and bust. This kind of economy bred a migrant labor force. With the discovery of silver or gold, a mining camp could grow to ten times its size in a matter of months. In good times, residents splurged, living like royalty, only to lose their wealth later when a vein went dry. This instability made it difficult to bring families in to settle. In these communities of men, prostitution thrived.

This migrant mining economy was also associated with a particular set of sexual values and politics. Prostitution, if not prostitutes themselves, became an accepted part of the community from the perspective of working men. Women were considered far from equal to their male counterparts. "Good girls" on the frontier needed protection; "bad girls" were sexually available and provided necessary services to frontiersmen. Patriarchal gender roles reflected and reinforced the idea that male (hetero)sexuality was driven by natural biological needs which require frequent tending. Lonely, isolated men toiling in the harsh climate of the Old West and in a boom-and-bust economy constituted an excellent customer base for working women. Prostitution became an integral part of many of these early frontier communities.

The key to the rise and persistence of brothel prostitution rests on this sexual culture: Where the values of the citizenry were open to a particular definition of gender roles and sexuality, the sale of sex in brothels became acceptable. A rhetoric of legal brothel prostitution is based on a discourse that maintains (1) that the sale of sex is one of the world's oldest professions and is unlikely to suddenly disappear, (2) that government-regulated prostitution is superior to illegal prostitution insofar as it allows for limitations on what is sold, on the terms and conditions of sales, and on brothel on ownership and employment practices, (3) that such businesses are revenue generating, (4) that legal prostitution provides a valuable service to certain individuals who have desires that cannot be easily fulfilled otherwise, and (5) that limiting such activities to particular licensed venues curtails related criminal activities (drugs, pimping, physical violence) while offering the safest way for sex to be sold (limiting risks of violence, controlling the spread of disease through testing and Health Department regulations).

Central to these five beliefs is the notion that humans are sexual beings and that it is inevitable that some women will resist traditional feminine roles and norms to engage in whoring and that men will want to have sex available on demand. As one local politician explained to us over a beer at a frontier brothel, "Prostitution isn't going anywhere. There will always be guys passing through town, trucking or working, and guys who can't get a woman themselves. This is a community service to meet natural needs. If we got rid of brothels it would still happen at the truck stops, on streets, and that just isn't good. There will be drugs, violence; it looks bad in the community, bad for families."

The form of legalized prostitution that emerged in Nevada places limitations on what kind of sex is sold, between whom, under what circumstances, and where the exchange occurs. This social control reflects the dominant discourses of gender and sex as well: In Nevada only women have ever been recognized as legitimate prostitutes whose services can be sold; prostitution is valued only as women's work. The norm of heterosexuality permeates brothel regulations. The idea that women are sexual objects whose services can be purchased while men are sexual subjects who are consumers is replete in brothel rhetoric. These are largely unquestioned assumptions in discourses that legitimate regulated prostitution. An owner of a small-town brothel explained, "It's safer for the girls here than anywhere else, because they will do it anyway. We take care of them here; the girls need that. It's safer for the men, too, from a health perspective. Guys are afraid of getting something from the street girls; you know, you never know what they have. But guys will be guys no matter where they get it."

Together, the traditional migrant economy and the corresponding conservative and paternalistic sexual values that persist today kept prostitution alive as mining camps grew into small towns and economies diversified in the first half of the twentieth century. From the 1880s to the early 1900s, newly incorporated cities and growing counties began to pass ordinances regulating places where brothels could operate, segregating them from family-oriented businesses and homes.[5] In 1871, during a huge mining boom in Nevada, the state almost legalized brothel prostitution statewide.[6] Storey County, home of the great silver Comstock Lode, officially designated a brothel district for booming Virginia City in 1878.[7] Other towns followed suit. Such regulation reflected a spirit of receptivity toward some forms of prostitution, and Nevada's brothels survived the Progressive Era reform movement that closed many urban brothels in the East.

As the century wore on, a libertarian, antifederal political culture that allowed the development of Nevada's brothels as part of the Old West economy came up against an increasingly powerful federal government. During World War I, and again more strongly in World War II, the Federal Security Agency pressured county governments throughout the West to pass ordinances to close down prostitution to prevent "the spread of venereal disease to the detriment of members of the armed forces of the United States sojourning in said city or in the neighborhood."[8] Many counties strongly resisted federal intrusion, but many brothels closed despite the opposition. Virginia City closed its historic brothels; Tonopah closed twelve of its thirteen brothels.[9]

Rural and frontier counties reopened their brothels as soon as World War II ended. But federal military spending and works projects had already begun to transform the cowboy culture in urban areas, and these forces slowly chipped away at the brothel businesses in Reno and Las Vegas. In Las Vegas, city managers had enthusiastically promised to close down the brothels so that the federal government would build Nellis Air Force Base there. In 1949, the Nevada Supreme Court ruled that brothels were a public nuisance. In the context of a profitable gaming industry, Reno, Las Vegas, and their county governments had a strong desire to legitimate themselves. They began to crack down hard on the "vice" of prostitution, closing remaining brothels in and near the two cities. Meanwhile, the rural and frontier counties, still dependent on their traditional economies and resenting urban interference, passed ordinances to avoid the nuisance charges.[10]

Nowhere is the cowboy, antigovernment culture more evident than in the popular story of the passage of the statewide legislation in 1971 that allowed brothel licensing. A brash individual, Joe Conforte, opened a brothel in the 1950s and for years battled Washoe County District Attorney Bill Raggio (now the Nevada State Senate majority leader). Conforte claimed that the best way to deal with orders to close down was to ignore them.[11] At one point, Conforte and Sally Burgess (his prostitute/madam business partner and wife) located their brothel in a mobile trailer at the border of three counties, allowing them to move the trailer into whichever county was most hospitable at the time. After spending time in jail in the 1960s, Joe took over the famous Mustang Ranch in Storey County. A district judge ordered Conforte to close the brothel and repay Storey County $5,000 in monthly installments of $1,000 to offset patrol costs. Conforte kept paying each month, and kept the brothel open. Three years later, a county attorney advised Storey commissioners that they needed an ordinance to make the money coming in legal. On December 5, 1970, commissioners passed the first brothel-licensing ordinance in the nation.[12]

Meanwhile, rumors spread that Conforte planned to open a brothel in Clark County. State legislators representing Clark County, still fighting to make gambling look legitimate, scrambled to introduce a statewide bill banning prostitution. State representatives from rural counties would hear none of this. Finally in 1971, Clark County was able to push through a bill making prostitution illegal in counties with populations of more than 200,000, which at that time meant only Clark County. The Nevada Supreme Court ruled in 1978 that this explicit mention of brothel prostitution tacitly allowed the sixteen counties not mentioned to license brothels. In the following years both Conforte and local brothel owners individually lobbied county commissioners to pass brothel licensing ordinances in the majority of counties.[13] Each county created its own unique ordinance that essentially legislated its existing practices.

Nevada's brothels were born of a boom-and-bust mining economy and became a stabilizing force in the frontier. They existed in a sexual culture that saw a legitimate function for prostitution by meeting the biological "needs" of a migrant labor force, while offering a means of survival and a viable lifestyle for some women. As towns developed, this legitimation of prostitution became institutionalized in brothels, which could be regulated in ways reflecting local sex and gender norms and kept separate from local families. A libertarian, antigovernment, antiurban, "cowboy" political culture framed the eventual legalization of brothels. The mythology of Joe Conforte as a brash renegade and charismatic leader of brothel legalization is a signifier of this Old West cowboy politics—both the libertarian value system and the normalization of old-boy back-room deal making. Brothels remained in the rural areas despite the growing urban dependence on tourism and a gaming industry that sought to legitimate itself by its opposition to prostitution. And that, in a nutshell, is how the Old West cultivated a culture of brothel prostitution that persists in the New West.

STRUCTURE OF THE BROTHEL INDUSTRY

Today Nevada is home to thirty-five licensed brothels in ten counties. The brothels bring in a total of $40 million a year, according to the Nevada Brothel Association. The economic and legal contexts in which brothels are organized vary significantly by county and proximity to metropolitan areas. Table 13.1 summarizes, by county, the regulations regarding brothel prostitution in Nevada, and Figure 1 is a map showing counties in which legal prostitution exists. Only Clark County is prohibited by state law from licensing brothels; the 1971 law that excludes counties with populations of more than 200,000 is regularly amended with population growth, and now is at 400,000. A few counties currently have ordinances prohibiting prostitution, including Washoe, which contains Reno.

As shown in Table 13.1, brothels are currently licensed in the unincorporated areas of Churchill, Esmeralda, Lander, Lyon, Mineral, Nye, and Storey counties, which means the county is the licensing and regulating body. Four counties—Elko, Humboldt, Pershing, and White Pine—prohibit brothel

TABLE 13.1 BROTHELS IN NEVADA (1997)

COUNTIES	CURENTLY OPERATING BROTHELS	WITHIN 1-HOUR DRIVE OF MAJOR METRO AREA	POPULATION PER SQUARE MILE
Carson City	prohibited by county law	yes	337.0
Clark	prohibited by state law	yes	139.8
Douglas	prohibited by county law	yes	50.8
Washoe	prohibited by county law	yes	48.2
Lincoln	prohibited by county law	no	.4
Pershing	prohibited by county law	no	.9
Eureka	no written ordinance	no	.4
Churchill	2 outside Fallon	yes	4.6
Elko	1 in Carlin	no	2.6
	4 in Elko	no	
	2 in Wells	no	
Esmeralda	1 at Lida Jct	no	.3
Humboldt	5 in Winnemucca	no	1.8
Lander	2 in Battle Mtn[2]	no	1.3
Lyon	4 outside Carson City	yes	14.5
Mineral	1 at Mina	no	1.5
Nye	6 near Pahrump	yes	1.5
	1 near Beatty	no	
Storey	3 in Mustang	yes	11.4
White Pine	3 in Ely	no	1.2

[1]Income from prostitutes' work cards are estimated as the county issues the same work cards as for other workers.
[2]License fees are paid on two brothels though only one is currently operating.
[3]Income from prostitutes' work cards is estimated because the work-card program in Ely is brand-new.

COUNTY LAW PROHIBITS IN UNINCORPORATED AREAS	TOWNS WITH LICENSING ORDINANCES	TOTAL YEARLY INCOME FROM LICENSE FEES, ROOM AND LIQUOR TAXES	TOTAL YEARLY INCOME FROM WORK CARDS
yes			
yes			
yes			
yes			
yes			
yes			
		$12,720	$7,500[1]
yes	Carlin	$1,500	$500
	Elko	$12, 960	$6,000
	Wells	$4,600	$2,600[1]
		$2,260	$100
yes	Winnemucca	$30,750	$2,600[1]
		$840	$500[1]
		$207,175	$6,000
		$580	$644
		$122,000	$50,000
		$124,150	$9,325
yes	Ely	$2,788	$2,280[3]

prostitution in the unincorporated areas of each county but allow it by municipal option; the cities of Elko, Wells, Winnemucca, and Ely license brothels.

The geography of the state of Nevada has a significant impact on the structure of the industry. Nevada is one of the most rural states in the country, with only two metropolitan areas, Reno and Las Vegas. Most of the state's population is in one of these two areas, and two-thirds live in Clark County. The average distance between towns is 100 miles, between 180 and 200 miles in the more isolated counties. According to the Nevada State Department of Taxation, eleven of Nevada's seventeen counties are classified as frontier (with fewer than six people per square mile), four are rural, and two urban.[14] Of the eleven frontier counties, eight have legalized prostitution. Of the four rural counties, two (Lyon and Storey) have legalized prostitution, and neither of the urban counties has legalized prostitution. One frontier county, Nye, has five brothels just forty-five minutes from Las Vegas. One of the most significant splits within the brothel industry is between brothels in the frontier counties and those in the rural counties closest to urban areas.

Financially, the largest and most profitable brothels are in the rural counties closest to Reno and Las Vegas—Storey, Lyon, and Nye. The brothel industry statewide grosses approximately $35 million a year, according to the Nevada Brothel Association. But the fourteen brothels in these rural counties bring in 80 percent of the state's brothel income. The largest is the Mustang Ranch outside of Reno, which employs up to eighty women at a time. The remaining twenty-one or so frontier county brothels bring in less than $2 million in total income for each county, and most employ two to ten women at a time.[15]

The cost of investing in a brothel also differs significantly between these frontier and rural counties. Prices vary from more than $4 million to less than $150,000. For example, Bobbie's Buckeye in Tonopah, in northwestern Nye County, sold for $135,000.[16]

The economy of both the frontier and rural brothels remains based on a migrant economy, just as it was in the Old West. But the nature of that migrant economy is changing. While the small and isolated towns in northern and eastern Nevada have grown since the 1870s to become primarily dependent on service jobs in gambling and tourism, their economies are still far more dependent than urban areas on mining's boom and bust. Pershing, Lander, and Esmeralda counties, for instance, had 35 percent or more of their economies concentrated in traditional Old West industries of mining, logging, farming, or ranching in 1994.[17] But in addition to their economic dependence on the young men who have temporarily left home to earn big paychecks in the mines, these counties are increasingly dependent on several new migrant groups—construction workers, the military, truckers, and tourists.

The brothel owners and workers that we interviewed in these small towns consistently report similar kinds of migrant customers as the Old West brothels—miners and ranchers—but also truckers, construction workers, and other newer migrants. Depending on where each brothel is located, they may rely heavily on customers from one or more of these groups. Prostitutes at some brothels on Interstate 80, the major east-west interstate between Salt Lake City and San Francisco, use CB radios to beckon passing truckers into the houses. We heard one of the prostitutes at the Calico Club croon into the CB, "C'mon in for libations, excitations, titillation, conversation; no obligations. C'mon in for free coffee, showers, and to pass the hours." The customers we interviewed in the Calico Club had been working on a construction project in Montana.

But there is also a new tourist demanding more "cultured" entertainment in the New West.[18] The cowboy poetry festival brings 10,000 people to Elko each winter. The Burning Man festival in the Blackrock desert north of Reno, and even Nevada's "Extraterrestrial Highway" (State Highway 375) bring an alternative tourist to the West. The rugged amenities that surrounded the migrant miner are being replaced by espresso shops and the Ruby Mountain Brewery in Elko and the alternative Meta Tantay community in Carlin. California's rich and elite are increasingly purchasing ranches near popular areas for world-class fly fishing, mountain biking, and rock climbing, driving the cost of living out of reach of many locals.

In some ways, this new breed of tourists who visit the brothels may be no different than the customers in times gone by. However, this new Nevada culture may bring customers to the brothels who are less immersed in the cultural climate of the rugged American West. As one new owner told us, "I bought this brothel because it reminded me of what an Old West brothel ought to look like." Some brothel customers may desire the experience of Wild West cowboy culture as much as their tryst with a prostitute. In the New West, a brothel visit may be just another stop on a local tour and an opportunity to collect a good story along the tourist trail, rather than a way to fulfill sexual needs. A couple who owned two brothels in northern Nevada turned one of them into an Emmigrant [sic] Trail Interpretive Center to meet travelers' new demands for an experience of the Old West that does not involve sex.

Just as in the Old West, it is not just the customers that are part of the migrant economy but the workers as well. Rarely did anyone we interviewed report that local women worked in the brothels. Labor largely comes from outside the town, and often outside Nevada. All but one of the dozen women we interviewed reported that they work in the brothels for several weeks or a few months before returning home to their families, friends, and other jobs elsewhere. Many women also report moving between brothels depending on business. When things are slow in one town or region, it is quite common for the prostitutes to obtain work cards in another county and change brothels. There is a brothel trail along which the working women migrate from region to region, and carry messages and stories from one house to the next.

This migrant brothel labor force, coupled with the fact that owners are not allowed to advertise for workers without facing charges of pandering, means that the industry experiences frequent labor shortages. This is particularly true for the frontier brothels, where locating and retaining women as prostitutes is the single greatest challenge to business survival. Some of these owners report that it is difficult to get workers to stay in a small, isolated town when they could be closer to big cities or working in other parts of the sex industry, perhaps selling nude dances, and sometimes making just as much money. The Nevada Brothel Association sees the availability of work as strippers and escorts in Reno and Las Vegas as the greatest challenge to finding and retaining brothel prostitutes. Competition for workers is often intense, and several of the small brothel owners we interviewed charge the larger brothels with unethically enticing the best workers away. One of the most valuable commodities to owners are "turn outs," girls entering the business for the first time. In an industry where recruiting workers is difficult, attracting new workers is seen as vital to replenishing the work force.

So, the brothel industry exists in and around a changing West. The migrant economy and the isolation of small-town brothels means that in many ways they are part of the Old West. At the same time, changing metropolitan sensibilities are transforming the businesses and customers, as well as the availability of prostitutes.

BROTHELS AND THE STATE

The amount of government oversight and regulation in the brothel industry is one of the least surprising elements of Nevada's system. Given the criminalization of prostitution elsewhere in the United States, one would expect that where it is legal, it is highly regulated. What is interesting, however, is the relative independence that local governments have in regulating brothels. Nevada statutes play a relatively small role in regulating brothels. State law restricts prostitution to counties of a certain size, and prohibits brothels from being closer than 400 yards from a school, a religious building, or on a principal business street. Beyond these regulations, the strictest state intervention in brothel culture comes from the Nevada State Health Department.

Since 1985, the health department has strictly controlled sexually transmitted diseases (STDs) in the brothels by imposing stringent health testing on working women. Every prostitute must have a state health card certifying her safe and healthy prior to applying for work in a brothel; this means testing negative for all STDs, including syphilis, gonorrhea, and HIV. Once hired, a prostitute is required to have weekly exams by a registered doctor to certify that she is not carrying any STDs. If she tests positive, she is unable to work until the treatment cures her and the physician reinstates her health card. Additionally, once a month all prostitutes must allow a registered doctor to take a blood sample to determine if she has contracted HIV or syphilis. According to a report in the *Reno Gazette Journal* on January 15, 1995, not one case of HIV has been contracted by a brothel prostitute since this testing regime was instituted in 1985. Finally, every brothel must post notices at the door and around the brothel informing customers that condom use is mandated by the state. All of the prostitutes we interviewed reported that they are supportive of the condom laws as they offer the best protection available to working women. Contracting any STD is detrimental from a financial standpoint because the women lose work time while recuperating.

Local governments are the most important regulators of brothels and regulate both through formal licensing ordinances and through informal norms that govern the "privilege" component of licensing. Formal laws establish license procedures and fees, restrict locations for brothels, require background checks of potential owners, sometimes set their own health guidelines in addition to the state's, and occasionally establish rules for prostitutes' behavior. Local governments vary widely in the licensing and regulation of brothels. As shown in Table 13.1, since brothels are only licensed in the unincorporated areas of Churchill, Esmeralda, Lander, Lyon, Mineral, Nye, and Storey counties, the county is the licensing body. In the counties of Elko, Humboldt, Pershing, and White Pine, the cities of Elko, Wells, Winnemucca, and Ely license brothels. Counties in the north and eastern parts of the state give licensing rights to the individual cities.

Legal brothels are required to pay various taxes and fees. Counties derive income from annual brothel licenses and new application fees, liquor and other business license fees, room taxes, personal property taxes, and work cards for workers. License fees and structures vary by county. Some have flat business fees for brothels, and others charge on the basis of the number of rooms or workers. Brothel license fees tend to be higher for counties closer to urban areas than for the frontier counties. New application fees are typically costly, often much more than the yearly license fees. Every county has a liquor tax, which applies to the bars inside each brothel, and these are typically the same as those for hotels. Personal property taxes are usually at the same rate as for any other property. Some counties charge room taxes, some do not. Sheriffs' departments issue work cards after a check for prior felony convictions. In most counties the cards issued to prostitutes are the same as those that all casino employees must get. Work cards amount to significant income for some counties, yielding up to $120 per year per worker.

Table 13.1 reports revenue to each county from their brothels. In Storey County, which contains the largest brothel in the state, the Mustang Ranch, annual license, room tax, and work card fees brought in $133,475 in 1997. In Lyon County, which also contains some of the largest brothels, these fees totaled $213,175 in 1997. In some counties, license fees and taxes can account for up to 30 percent of their budgets.[19] However, we found that for the frontier counties in northern and eastern Nevada, the brothels bring in a relatively small percentage of county income.

County and city ordinances have essentially institutionalized existing Old West practices. Many of the ordinances made brothels legal where they already existed and do not permit new brothels. For example, Lander County limits the number of brothels to two, both in Battle Mountain, at locations where brothels have existed since the turn of the century. Ordinances have therefore severely restrained the growth of the industry. The number of brothels in the state has remained fairly stable: thirty-three in 1973 and thirty-five in 1998. It is unclear whether this was an intentional effort by the counties to restrict growth of a distasteful but tolerated business, though Pillard argues that county officials indeed intended to limit growth,[20] and it is also unclear how much the owners themselves have lobbied to restrict competition. In any event, competition is greatly controlled by the licensing process, which makes this unlike other service industries and unlike the nonbrothel sex industry nationwide. Most counties license only two or three brothels and regulate and limit the areas in which brothels can be located. It is all but impossible to get a new license. According to the owners we interviewed, the only way a new business can open is to buy out an existing license. Brothel owners are among the strongest opponents to new licenses.

Old West sexual norms persist. Not only are brothels located away from the good families of the community, but in some counties (Carlin, Winnemucca, and Churchill) men have been explicitly forbidden from working in the brothels.[21] These rules assume that men would either be pimping or getting free sex from the working girls. Only recently have counties changed the rules prohibiting male owners. In addition, informal rules within brothels very clearly reproduce heterosexual norms. Many owners felt that local governments would absolutely not tolerate the sale of homosexual services in the brothels, and that women would never want to purchase sex from straight male prostitutes, especially when, according to one owner, "they can get it free at any bar."

Not only are brothels regulated by a set of formal rules that reinforce Old West sexual norms, there is an informal structure of regulation. Because the brothels are privileged licenses, officials have the power to revoke licenses for any reason and are quite free to impose all sorts of regulations. Pillard analyzed the informal rules and customs imposed on both the workers and the brothels. In Winnemucca, the rules include: The prostitute's family cannot live in the community, the prostitute must be back in the brothel by 5 P.M., a prostitute's vehicle must be registered with the police, and its use is limited such that she can go, for example, to the movies but not to a bar. Any violation may result in the revocation of her work card. Rules also dictate that no men other than customers are allowed on premises except repairmen, and they must leave before 5 P.M. Only prostitutes and customers are allowed in the brothels, and owners are not allowed to seek publicity. In Ely, prostitutes can go to the movies but not to a bar, and if she goes to a restaurant with a bar, it must have a side entrance. And she may not have a male escort.[22] An owner in Ely told us that these rules have now been abolished, but we found similar rules in other counties. Appendix 1 shows a set of rules from Carlin as an example.

Regardless of whether these rules are codified, they do two things. First, they impose an almost feudalistic set of restrictions that working women have little power to resist. Whether the town has a set of rules or not, owners often impose their own house rules. Appendix 2 presents an example of house rules in one frontier brothel, although rules vary greatly.

The most controversial of these rules dictates the visibility and mobility of working women. In some brothels, contracts with prostitutes generally require them to work for a certain number of weeks (usually three) with one week off. During the week off, the worker is expected to either stay in the house or leave town. The rules regarding mobility during the weeks on duty vary greatly from house to house, but most clearly restrict the movement of women in town. These ranged from not being allowed to leave the brothel at all without being health tested again, to just reporting when you leave, where you are going, for how long, and for what purpose. The closer the brothel is to an urban area, the stricter the policy. A manager of one of the urban brothels justified these strict rules for health reasons, "Because you never know what she [the prostitute] will do out there." Others justified the rules based on a tradition of unwritten local norms or because "it is just good business practice."

It is these kinds of rules and informal norms that have led critics of legal brothels to charge that they are total institutions that violate the women's human rights. Legal prostitutes, who are restricted in their movement due solely to the nature of their work, are clearly being treated differently than any other category of service workers. However, of the women we spoke to in brothels in frontier counties, none reported feeling constrained. A few who worked in the larger brothels did feel more constrained, but most voiced acceptance of the rules. Most often, we heard such comments as, "It's like living in a dormitory or a sorority."

House rules governing when workers could leave the brothel premises were not always strictly enforced. For many of the rural brothel owners, the exigencies of today's labor market make it difficult to attract workers to a remote brothel, let alone to confine them to their quarters. The rules about staying on premises are especially difficult to enforce if the owner wants to maintain good morale. As a result, the best workers can sometimes write their own rules. The brothel with the loosest practice was in a frontier town that had only one worker. This prostitute went to a local home each night at the end of her shift. She had worked on and off for about three years and the owners justified the relationship by saying she had "never gotten into trouble in town." Notably, though, these owners also had a very good relationship with the community, which made this liberal attitude acceptable among the locals.

The second point about these informal rules is that they reflect their Old West roots. The informal relationship to the community is crucial in brothel culture. The owners walk a fine line between doing their business and pleasing local government and community leaders. As one owner said, if you go outside of proper channels, local politicians can make things tough for you. A former county district attorney told us that "the secret to doing this is good relations with law enforcement." The rule of the Old West seems to prevail, and the law is whatever the community sees fit. In short, the politics of brothels is very local, very delicate, and very informal.

Communities can get away with imposing legally questionable regulations out of fear of making waves. There is a ban on advertising brothels that is undoubtedly unconstitutional, but, as one owner said, "I'm not sure I would want to get involved and bring criticism." And, although many of the regulations seem to violate the prostitutes' civil liberties, neither the workers nor the owners want to upset the delicate balance of running a prostitution business in a traditional community.

Brothel owners also strive to maintain a good image in the community by donating scholarships to high schools, buying jackets for fire departments, participating in local parades, carnivals, and holiday festivities, and planning and running town events. By supplying the Little League with uniforms, organizing the Fourth of July parade, and making regular donations to the local Rotary Club, some brothel owners have become respectable members of their community who are rewarded with trust and support from local residents.

THE NEVADA BROTHEL ASSOCIATION

One way to analyze the present state of the Nevada brothel industry and its likely future is to consider the ways in which individual brothel businesses and their owners interact with one another. This relatively small and unique industry has formed a lobbying coalition to protect its collective interests from conservatives, gaming interests, and others who oppose legal prostitution.

The Nevada Brothel Association (NBA) was formed in 1984, largely on the initiative of Joe Conforte, in order to lobby for owners' collective interests and to educate policy makers. The association's lobbyist is George Flint, undeniably the most visible advocate of brothel prostitution in Nevada despite the fact that he is not a brothel owner or manager; he is a full-time justice of the peace at his own wedding chapel in Reno. The association brings together the largest and most powerful brothels in the state, as well as some of the smaller rural and frontier brothels. The NBA reflects and reproduces the relative power among brothels. The executive committee consists of the owners of the largest brothels, and several smaller brothels report that they feel that their unique interests are overlooked by the NBA. In terms of internal organizational dynamics, around 55 percent of the money for the Nevada Brothel Association's operations come from the Mustang Ranch, and the nine largest brothels are the primary supporters, according to Flint. Of the twenty smallest brothels, only six are members.

There are no regular NBA meetings, and most of the brothel owners participate only sporadically in organizational planning and decision making. The last meeting of the association, in 1989, drew about fifty managers and owners of brothels statewide. But, as Flint maintains, most of these individuals had been in the business at least twenty years and previously had never met each other. Most of the brothel owners are geographically isolated from one another and in infrequent contact. The result is a system in which the day-to-day functioning of the NBA is at the behest of Flint, whose public statements give the impression that the industry is more unified than is true for its diverse and individualistic members. The NBA offers a service to the brothel industry despite the tensions over specific issues and occasional regional and personality clashes.

One rural brothel owner put it this way: "We don't participate much. George works for the big brothels most of the time, but we know it's out there and looking out for our interests. If something comes up, we'll participate then."

As the man at the helm, Flint is skilled at public relations and brokers media interest in the brothels by strategically participating in documentaries and news reports as an informed advocate of the brothels. According to most of the legislators and lobbyists we spoke with, Flint is a seasoned and respected lobbyist in the Nevada legislature. His passionate, experienced, and politically skilled voice gives legitimacy to the organization.

The Nevada Brothel Association has been successful in maintaining the brothel industry's current legal status. This is no small feat in a climate where few legislators feel comfortable advocating any other kind of a sex-positive poli-cies. At this time there is little threat to the brothel industry from the state. Currently, the brothels have a strong supporter in a powerful rural senator who has managed to kill every bill threatening to outlaw brothels. While a state ban on brothel prostitution is remote, that possibility remains a concern of the industry.

The NBA mostly works to prevent brothels' demise; it has not attempted to push for legislation to expand the rights of brothels. The laws regulating the location and number of licenses could conceivably be overturned as unfair restraint of trade, and prohibitions on recruiting prostitutes with help-wanted ads and restrictions on brothel advertising could be challenged as unconstitu-tional. These policies remain largely unchallenged.

Why this reluctance to fight for more favorable legislation? For one thing, owners recognize that the state poses little threat to the general legal status of brothels, so most politics is still local. Most of the individual brothel owners can influence politicians and civic leaders individually, without the help of the NBA. As long as they remain good corporate citizens vis-à-vis local govern-ments, and continue to bring revenue into the local economy, most owners feel little threat to their livelihood. They would prefer to accept traditional restric-tions than raise controversy in their communities or across the state. And lit-tle economic incentive to change the system exists because licensing restrictions limit competition. As a result, considerable profit can be made even at a small brothel with only two or three women. In large brothels, the profit margin is extraordinary.

In its attempt to simply preserve the existing brothel system rather than initiating changes more favorable to owners, workers, and the industry, the association continues to reproduce the status quo of the Old West. The NBA believes that keeping quiet is strategically best. Customers can have their sexual needs met safely and efficiently, as long as it remains a largely hidden exchange.

At the same time, the brothel industry is divided between "traditionalists" and "squares." "Traditionalists" are old-timers who have worked as either prostitutes, madams, or managers, or people who were directly trained by these individuals. The "squares" are the newer, modern owners. They are more likely to be businessmen who see the brothel as a business operating just like any other industry. The former are in the brothel business based on tradition, a commitment to the legal availability of sex, and a strong sense that brothels are a unique business enterprise; the latter are in the brothel business for sheer economic reasons—selling sex legally is a promising business investment with potential for huge profit.

Before legalization, many of the traditionalists were women, as it was considered inappropriate for anyone other than a woman to run the business. The new breed are more likely to be men, and even today there remains a general mistrust of men in the business, expressed either as a mistrust of men who have not been trained about sexuality by a sex worker, or a fear that workers have to have sexual relations with the owner to get a job. In addition, many of the trusted traditionalists were descendants of or trained under Joe Conforte and Sally Burgess. While many of the true traditionalists have died or sold out, much of that culture remains; among the remnants is an old-timer mentality that sees the industry as endangered by outsiders coming into the business just to "make a buck." These corporate business "squares" are replacing the traditional women-run, women-organized brothel culture with a more corporate and bureaucratic model of selling sex.

In short, some in the industry—including George Flint—have a strong sense that newcomers pose the largest threat to the continued existence of brothels. Several owners we spoke with claimed that their greatest fear was outside businessmen who see brothels as an investment. Flint referred to one newcomer who had previously been a condominium developer:

> He scared me to death because he wanted to operate it like a regular business. Conforte says these new people don't know the business.... In some ways, when you see a business run by a square, it puts us on edge. The delicateness, the sensitiveness, the tenuousness of it. Aggressive marketing frightens us all.... They jeopardize their ability to survive and make legislators very nervous.[23]

Increasingly, newer owners talk of the business as if it is not significantly different than any other small business, except for being more delicate and a little more precarious in its legal standing. These owners are pushing for a more bureaucratized workplace. One owner of a very small brothel reported that his biggest labor complaint is that the women "don't take a business approach to their work. They get absorbed in the party and don't work the bar as well as they could. There is a tendency for them to make only the dates they are comfortable making and not really hustle." According to both the working women and some owners, many owners do not treat the working women with much respect.

The NBA's charismatic leadership by George Flint, its inability to mobilize all brothels, its deference to local needs rather than long-term collective needs, and a prevailing attitude of quiet compliance to conserve the status quo all attest to an Old West attitude. At the same time, the organization faces some challenges that reflect the clash between a cowboy culture and a more metropolitan culture.

CONCLUSIONS: A COWBOY'S MIRAGE
OR A VISION FOR THE FUTURE?

We draw four major conclusions from our study. First, it is clear that the legal brothels of Nevada are situated between traditions of the Old West and innovations of the New West. Remnants of the "Wild West" history of brothels are still evident today. That many regulations differ among counties attests to the power of local tradition and the influence of charismatic community leaders. The persistence of restrictions on brothel owners and workers that would be rejected as unfair and unconstitutional for other legal businesses exemplifies the Old West pattern of local norms governing business enterprises. In sum, the structure of the brothel industry is still characterized by the culture of the Old West.

This is the anachronism: Brothels exist in Nevada today because they have a rich history that has been ensconced in the rural and frontier economies and culture of the Old West. This tradition has normalized brothel prostitution, allowing it to persist even in the changing context of the postindustrial economy, the growing metropolitan sensibility and tourist market, and the modernizing culture of the New West. The brothel system, as currently constituted and structured, is an historical abnormality premised upon values and norms that fit more comfortably in the Old West than the New West. And yet changes such as the emergence of the Nevada Brothel Association, the influx of outside business interests into the brothel industry, and the increase in state oversight through Health Department regulations have all contributed to the apparent adaptation of brothels to the contemporary economic and cultural climate in Nevada.

Second, the brothel industry is not integrated into the larger service economy or with other components of the legal sex industry. Brothels are largely invisible and remain localized exceptions to the rule of criminalizing other forms of prostitution. The brothel industry is quite separate from other types of sex businesses for several reasons. Other adult businesses, such as gentlemen's clubs, adult book/video stores, and phone/cyber sex operations, often defend their status as legal businesses on the basis that they do not sell actual sexual contact. This means that building alliances with brothels, even though they are legal in Nevada, may tarnish the image of adult businesses operating in regions where prostitution is illegal and stigmatized. Adult businesses also compete with brothels, and the competition would increase were brothel prostitution legalized in Reno and Las Vegas. Although some brothel owners indicated a desire to cross-fertilize their business with other legal adult businesses (for example strip clubs, Internet sex sites, and adult film production), these connections are difficult to establish in the business climate surrounding prostitution in Nevada. They would be viewed as a controversial and provocative move toward expanding legal prostitution or mainstreaming the brothel industry. Finally, the simple geographic distance between brothels and urban centers where other parts of the sex industry flourish makes interindustry alliances difficult to organize.

Third, it is clear that this marginalization of legal prostitution is a response to the conventional sexual norms and values that permeate American society in general. The brothel industry recognizes the tensions and risks inherent in selling sex. To survive, brothels must present themselves in quiet, innocuous, and traditional ways, as opposed to rationalizing the business and making decisions that are driven by pure profit making.

There is also widespread resistance to establishing any non-traditional brothels. For example, a few years ago an entrepreneur interested in opening an all-male gay brothel in Pahrump was discouraged as it was seen as too politically controversial. Likewise, nearly every brothel owner scoffed at the idea of staffing male prostitutes to service heterosexual women. While a few county ordinances explicitly prohibit hiring male prostitutes in brothels, in many parts of Nevada the absence of male brothel prostitutes is more a product of tradition and gender role stereotypes (men cannot perform on demand; women do not have the money or desire for sex, or they can get it for free).

Finally, we argue that the Nevada brothel industry is at a critical juncture. Rooted in the Old West but facing the challenges of the New West, the brothel system is at a crossroads, and the status quo may be increasingly untenable. Owners, especially in frontier and rural regions, need to be able to advertise for workers and potential customers in order to remain economically viable; gaming interests remain almost unanimously opposed to legal prostitution and are likely to continue to push for legislative efforts to criminalize; the NBA continues to experience some divisiveness, and its future is uncertain if George Flint leaves his position.

The integration of brothels into their communities, a tradition that permits the sale of sexual services, the profitability of the brothels for savvy owners, and the demand for safe, legal, and lucrative employment options for women who choose to prostitute are powerful forces for the continued existence of legal prostitution. But to survive, brothels will eventually need to adapt to the imperatives of the postindustrial landscape, and begin acting as if they are businesses deserving the same opportunities and regulations as any other business. This is likely to improve work conditions and employment options for working women.

APPENDIX 1
CITY OF CARLIN REGULATIONS FOR PROSTITUTES

1. All new prostitutes, prior to applying for a work card, shall obtain a vaginal culture and blood test. Proof of these tests must be shown at the time of application for the work card.
2. A fee of $30.00 will be imposed for original work cards with a $20.00 annual renewal rate. A $5.00 fee will be charged for replacement of a lost work card. Work cards are good for one year. A prostitute's work card will automatically expire if a leave of absence exceeds thirty (30) days, unless good cause is shown, i.e. family illness, or emergencies.
3. Prostitutes are required to have weekly vaginal cultures and monthly blood tests administered. Doctor slips will be checked once each week and those for vaginal cultures shall be no more than seven (7) days old.
4. Applicants for work cards must furnish proof of age, Social Security number, a photo identification card, complete work history, and addresses must be filled out completely.
5. Falsifications or omissions on applications may be grounds for not issuing or revoking a work card. While true names must be used on applications, prostitutes may use nicknames or other fictitious names with customers. Such nicknames or fictitious names are required to be listed on the application, past or present.
6. Nude or semi-nude sunbathing in public view is not permitted.
7. Prostitutes are permitted to dine in restaurants and to conduct personal business and shopping in Carlin between the hours of 7:00 A.M. to 7:00 P.M. Prostitutes will be appropriately attired so as to not invite speculation of their occupation. Under no circumstances will a prostitute approach or allow herself to be approached by a potential customer when out of the house under the above-stated circumstances. Prostitutes shall not be absent from their place of employment between 7:00 P.M. and 7:00 A.M. Prostitutes will not be allowed to loiter in or around any business or public functions while in the employ of the brothel. This shall include, but not be limited to, public dances, ball games, etc.
8. Prostitutes will refrain from exhibiting themselves to passing motorists in attempts to entice such persons into the house.
9. Prostitutes on vacation are not permitted to loiter about Carlin, and if traveling to another destination, must use the most expeditious transport out of Carlin.
10. Prostitutes will be permitted to tend bar on condition of their work card being properly endorsed for such activity by the Carlin Chief of Police.
11. No license shall employ any male person, except for the position of bartender.
12. Individuals and firms offering repair, maintenance and similar services to the general public need not obtain a work card to perform that same service to a house.

13. Customers between the ages of 18 and 21 years of age shall use only the designated entrance to enter and leave the establishment. No customer under the age of 21 shall be provided nor consume alcohol at any time while on the premises. Management should ask for photo identification to avoid illegality.

APPENDIX 2
BROTHEL RULES: THE RANCH

1. Ladies are self-employed and are therefore independent contractors. Ladies are liable for all taxes (local, state, federal, etc.).
2. Ladies must obtain doctor clearance and sheriff cards before "working."
3. Room and board is $20.00 per day. If a lady books over $800.00 Sunday, Monday, Tuesday, Wednesday or Thursday no room and board fee will be charged. If a lady books over $1,000.00 on Friday or Saturday no room and board will be charged.
4. The bookings will be split 50% / 50% between the house and the lady.
5. Ladies are responsible for their money and valuables. Be smart ... be safe ... lock up! The RANCH will not be responsible for items lost, misplaced or otherwise.
6. Clean up after yourself ... in the kitchen, the TV area, the bathroom and your own room. The RANCH is not a hotel and you are not on vacation.
7. Ladies are not allowed behind the bar.
8. At approximately 1:30 P.M. each and every day there is a hot meal served; ladies are welcome to help themselves to the eats in the refrigerator and cabinets.
9. Absolutely no drugs are to be brought into the RANCH.
10. Husbands, boyfriends, pimps, etc. are not allowed in the RANCH.
11. If it is necessary for a lady to leave the house (supplies, post office, etc.) advise bartender as follows: let bartender know nature of errand, when you are going out and approximate time when you will return. Whatever the errand, however, the lady must be back and ready for the floor by 4:00 P.M.
12. Advise any person that will be calling ... call before 8:00 P.M ... on the pay phone.
13. Remember ... be polite and treat each other and staff with respect and common courtesy.
14. If a lady has a problem with another lady or staff member, see management promptly.
15. Ladies ... if a lady asks another lady to borrow money, think once, think twice, then think again. A lady may obtain a "draw" from the house; it is not necessary to borrow money from one another.
16. BOOKING $$$ ... Please be advised as follows: A lady and the gentleman she is negotiating with come to an agreement ... for example ... $150.00 for 1/2 hour of her time ... that lady must book the $150.00. By not book-

ing the entire $150.00 the lady would be committing a crime ... it's called stealing. Any lady caught stealing will be terminated immediately. NO EXCEPTIONS!!!

17. Definition of a TIP ... A lady and her customer have a GREAT party. She gets dressed, he gets dressed and on the way out the door that very happy customer hands the lovely lady money ... this is a TIP!!! And it belongs to YOU!!!

18. An amount of $15.00 per week will be deducted from your amount to be paid; this $15.00 goes directly to the person cleaning your room. If you are leaving on vacation the amount deducted will be $20.00 for cleaning the room and this amount goes directly to the person cleaning the room.

APPENDIX 3 BROTHEL MENU: CALICO CLUB

Welcome... to the Calico Club! We are a legal brothel here to serve your needs. If this is your first visit, let us explain that you are under no obligation to party with a lady or to "do something," so just relax and have a good time!

In a few minutes (if he or she hasn't already) the bartender will introduce the ladies to you. Then you may choose one of them to sit with you and answer any questions you may have. Even after you choose a lady, you are under no obligation to go any further. But we know you'll be glad if you do!

If you just can't decide, because they're all so beautiful, they'll sort of decide for you and come around one by one and introduce themselves while you enjoy your coffee or drink. If you see a lady you would like to talk to at any time, ask the bartender to introduce you to her. It is perfectly all right to just talk—you still are not obligated to "do something," though it is a nice gesture to buy the lady a drink, as she gets half of the $5 charge. It is a way you can say thank you for the time she spends with you.

All discussions about price and the sort of party you want are done in the lady's room, not in the bar. Again, you are under no obligation if you go back to the lady's room to talk, but there is a 10-minute limit on negotiating time. If you can't "make a deal" with one lady, or if you change your mind about who you want to be with, don't hesitate to ask to be introduced to someone else—the lady you are with will be happy to help you!

We hope you enjoy your visit!

Appetizers...

1. Massage
2. Breast Massage
3. X-rated Movies
4. Hot Tub Party
5. Champagne Bath
6. Bubble Bath
7. Lingerie Show
8. Body Painting
9. Swedish Sauna

Entrees...

1. Straight Party
2. Half & Half
3. 69 Party
4. 69 Party Lay
5. Double Party Show
6. Double French
7. Double Party Lay
8. Salt & Pepper
9. Drag Party
10. Dominatrix
11. Vibrator Party
12. Friends & Lovers
13. All Night Date
14. Out Date

Desserts...

1. Hot & Cold French
2. Whipped Cream Party
3. Flavored Pussy Party
4. Flavored French

If you don't see your personal preference listed, please do not hesitate to ask!

POLICE AND PROSTITUTION: VICE SQUADS IN BRITAIN

Catherine Benson and Roger Matthews

There has been almost no research on the attitudes of police officers and their activities regarding the control of prostitution. The following study provides new insight into this subject.

The regulation of prostitution is seen by many police officers as a low-status activity and not "proper" police work. In Britain, the need to caution a woman twice before she can be arrested makes the policing of street prostitution a time-consuming, drawn-out process. If a woman is seen soliciting on a third occasion she can be arrested, charged, and tried. In the vast majority of cases the women who appear in court charged with "soliciting for the purposes of prostitution" are found guilty and are given a fine and subsequently return to the street to earn the money to pay off the fine. This form of "turnstile justice" is seen by many uniformed police officers as tedious and pointless. Police powers over men who drive around the streets looking for prostitutes to hire—called "curb crawlers" in Britain—are even more circumscribed. Under the existing law, the police lack the power of arrest for curb crawlers and can take action only where there is evidence of "persistence," although the legal definition of "persistence" remains unclear.[1]

Police vice squads have been established around the country to deal with prostitution. These squads are responsible for the regulation of both the street and the off-street trade. The number of police officers in each of these squads varies according to the extent of prostitution in different areas and the resources available, but the majority of vice squads outside of London tend to have

CATHERINE BENSON AND ROGER MATTHEWS

between four and eight officers. The low status of this work and the dangers of fraternization with prostitutes has led many forces to rotate their vice officers on a regular basis. Many officers are attached to these specialist squads for a year or less.

In order to gain a better understanding of the practices and attitudes of vice squads, we mailed semistructured questionnaires to the thirty-nine squads in Britain. Three forces—West Mercia, North Wales, and Cheshire—responded by stating that incidents of prostitution were minimal in their area, and they declined to participate in the survey. Questionnaires were returned by twenty-three squads. Seven of the remaining vice units were approached and asked if they would participate in face-to-face interviews. All seven agreed, and more detailed interviews were carried out with representatives from Coventry Plain Clothes Department, Digbeth Commercial Vice Unit, Leicester Vice Squad, Mosley Plain Clothes Department, Nottingham Anti-Vice Squad, Stoke-on-Trent Special Enquiries Department, and Wolverhampton Vice Squad. Thus, the total number of vice squads in the sample was thirty, although not all respondents answered all questions, and in some tables below figures had to be adjusted accordingly. In the majority of cases, information was provided by the most senior officer available in the unit. The research was carried out between January and March 1994.

AIMS AND ACTIVITIES OF VICE SQUADS

The two most frequently stated aims of the vice squads in relation to prostitution were the reduction of the number and visibility of street prostitutes and curb crawlers. Six vice squads stated that they sought to actively reduce off-street prostitution. Four squads felt that the "elimination" of prostitution was their main aim, but the majority reported that they believed prostitution was inevitable and saw their main role as minimizing the harm and nuisance experienced by members of the public as a consequence of prostitution. The view expressed by a number of vice squads was that they could do little more than "keep the lid on it." Indicative of their feelings about the policing role was the fact that half of the squads stated that their main aims were to react to public complaints rather than operate proactively. One officer reflected the widespread pessimism among vice squads about their potential impact on prostitution when he remarked:

> It's the oldest profession in the book. You'll never get rid of it. Sometimes we feel like we're getting it under control a bit, but you can guarantee as soon

as you turn your back it's back again. It's a never-ending problem. That's why personally I think they ought to legalize it and give them somewhere they can work.

The majority of respondents (80 percent) said they had specific methods of measuring their performance in controlling prostitution. Nineteen of the squads indicated that they use arrest rates. Eighteen more indicated that they use "the number of prostitutes working in the area" as a performance measure. "The number of public complaints" was used by twelve squads, while "the number of curb crawlers in the area" was used by eleven squads. Six squads had no means of measuring performance, while seven others reported that they used all four measures.

The questionnaire asked for details about the nature of complaints received from the public over the previous month. The complaints included problems of noise, litter, and the disturbance associated with street prostitution. In some areas, concerns were expressed about prostitutes openly selling sex, particularly near schools and parks. Complaints were also directed toward the activities of curb crawlers, particularly in relation to the harassment of local female residents (see Table 14.1).

Complaints mentioned by only one squad included prostitutes standing outside religious premises, brothels in residential areas, clients ringing the wrong doorbells, increased traffic in the area, drug addicts leaving needles around, and the discouragement of investment in the area. Many vice squads stated that compared to other problems and crimes in these areas, street prostitution was the principal issue that residents wanted the police to deal with.

Public complaints regarding street prostitution and curb crawling tended to encourage a number of responses from the police. Primarily, they resulted

TABLE 14.1 COMPLAINTS TO THE POLICE REGARDING STREET PROSTITUTION

PUBLIC'S MAIN COMPLAINTS	NUMBER OF SQUADS
Prostitutes openly working in residential areas	16
Noise from vehicles and prostitutes/clients	9
Harassment of nonprostitute women by curb crawlers and clients in general	7
Litter left by prostitutes/clients (e.g., condoms, tissues)	5
Prostitution conducted outside business premises	2
The presence of curb crawlers in a residential area	2

in a greater police presence and visibility in the area, at least for a limited time. This frequently also resulted in an increased number of arrests. A number of vice squads stated that they operated with a combination of strategies, normally including heightened visibility and "cracking down" on the prostitutes. These strategies were deemed necessary by some respondents to placate local residents. As one officer explained, "You've got to be seen to be doing something, even if they [the prostitutes] do just go straight back out there. If we didn't, we'd be overrun with girls and complaints about them." The main focus of vice squad activity was to keep the level of street prostitution within manageable limits and to do enough to satisfy the demands of local residents, although many officers clearly had serious misgivings about the measures that they used to deal with prostitution. In interviews, a number of respondents expressed disillusionment with the sanctions available to respond to complaints.

STREET PROSTITUTION

Street prostitution was reported to be present in both residential and industrial districts. In the majority of cases (79 percent), street prostitution was concentrated within a mile radius and tended to be most prevalent at night, though in some areas it was a twenty-four-hour-a-day problem.

Vice squads were asked to indicate the number of women currently engaged in street prostitution in their area. Only one squad (Blackpool) reported that it had no street prostitution at all, but only off-street prostitution. The majority reported having between ten and forty women actively engaged in prostitution on a regular basis.

Respondents were asked to indicate whether the number of women on the street in their area had increased or decreased over the previous twelve months. Out of twenty-seven respondents, four stated that the numbers had increased, fourteen replied that the numbers had remained fairly stable, while nine said that there had been a decrease. Significantly, in those areas where increases were reported (Bristol, Leeds, Sheffield, and Wolverhampton) the numbers were relatively few.

Officers described a fairly rigid hierarchy among women involved in different forms of prostitution, and consequently women rarely moved from the streets to indoor work. But there was considerable geographical movement reported among the women on the streets. As one officer explained:

They [prostitutes] come from all over the country.... What tends to happen is that they will come and try different areas—given a reputation by word of mouth. Sometimes they'll move to an area because the police are hitting them hard in their own area. It's a problem of national displacement—that's why we arrest any new girls we see; we don't want them telling others its easy down here. Other areas do the same.

The most frequently mentioned areas in which "new recruits" were reported to have come from were the West Midlands, West Yorkshire, Leicester, Birmingham, and Nottingham. The number of new "recruits" drawn to particular areas can be seen as a guide to the availability of clients and the level of police activity there.

Respondents were asked about their arrests of female prostitutes over the previous twelve months. Variation among the squads in the number of arrests was considerable, as was variation in the rate of arrests (per number of prostitutes working in the area), ranging from 0.2 arrests per working woman in Cambridge to twenty-five in Bradford (see Table 14.2). Some vice squads indicated that they were selective in making arrests, depending on whether the women cooperate with police, while other squads indicated that their decision to arrest was conditioned by the location where working women solicit. For instance, one officer interviewed in Wolverhampton stated that the women who work in the more industrial areas are arrested far less frequently than those who choose to stand in residential areas. As one vice squad officer stated:

> It's not that we don't arrest them, exactly, it's just that we target the girls who are causing the most problems, and they happen to be those who work in the residential areas. If they all worked in the industrial areas then we'd concentrate our efforts there, but at the moment we're happier if they're away from the residents.

In contrast, vice squads in Balsall Heath and Mosley arrest prostitutes wherever they are working. There was a feeling in the Mosley vice squad that it was important to keep police pressure on in all areas. One woman had been arrested sixty-eight times during one year. It was not uncommon for some squads to arrest a woman two or three times in one night.

There was also some discrepancy in the use of cautioning, or formal warnings by the police. The cautioning procedure was used, but not for "new girls" in most areas, whom police preferred to arrest as a "short sharp shock" in the hopes of deterring future activity.

Vice squads were also asked if they did anything to encourage women to leave prostitution. Out of twenty-eight respondents who answered this question, twenty-three stated that they did make some efforts to encourage women

TABLE 14.2 PROSTITUTES IN THE VICE AREAS AND ARREST RATES, TWELVE-MONTH PERIOD

VICE AREA	ARRESTS	AVERAGE NUMBER OF ACTIVE WOMEN	WOMEN: ARREST RATES
Bradford	250	10	1:25
Manchester	900	40	1:22.5
British Transport	523	30	1:17
Mosley, Birmingham	689	40	1:17
Stoke-on-Trent	310	20	1:15.5
North Staffordshire	266	20	1:13
Norwich	271	30	1:9
Bristol	161	20	1:8
Cardiff	150	20	1:7.5
Northampton	120	20	1:6
Doncaster	150	30	1:5
Middlesborough	140	30	1:5
Hull	140	40	1:3.5
Bournemouth	48	20	1:2
Leeds	80	40	1:2
Derby	20	20	1:1
Leicester	40	40	1:1
Essex	4	10	1:0.4
Plymouth	12	40	1:0.3
Cambridge	2	10	1:0.2

to leave prostitution. The type of assistance offered by the various squads ranged from referring women to the relevant agencies to providing general advice and support. Only one squad (Mosley) indicated that it provided long-term assistance, which included periodic visits, and claimed, "We'd rather get one girl off the game than arrest fifty for prostitution." Other respondents said that they helped women to leave prostitution by locking up their pimps, while other squads claimed that they deterred prostitutes by frequently arresting them. Most squads, however, offer prostitutes either advice or referral to other agencies or both. The task of actively encouraging prostitutes to leave prostitution was considered by most of the officers to be beyond their purview. Most vice squads found social services and the local health authority to be the most helpful agencies, and their attempts to work with other agencies were not always productive: "We find that the 'caring' agencies are not so caring when it comes to prostitutes. They still see it as a police matter and keep out."

Vice squads were asked to state their views regarding the existing laws on street prostitution. Out of twenty-five respondents, eleven expressed the view that arrest and fines did not provide an effective deterrent to prostitutes. One officer described the inadequacy and contradictory nature of arrest:

> The main problem is that there is no real deterrent. The system just basically regurgitates them. It's a vicious circle. They work because they've no money, they get arrested and fined, then to pay the fine they go back onto the streets, and round and round they go. It doesn't bother them. It's just a blip in their earning capacity for that evening, or a form of taxation.

Five squads mentioned problems with bail. Prostitutes' nonappearance at court is a particular problem for the police, especially when the women use aliases or are not working in their local areas. Measures to restrict bail are already being experimented with by some forces by imposing conditional bail on prostitutes who have been charged. This involves a ban from the vice area, or the provision of sureties before granting bail to those women who do not live in the locality.

The sex bias in the law on soliciting and loitering was mentioned by three squads, and four squads also mentioned the lack of power to arrest clients. One officer remarked:

> It seems foolish to me that a woman stands on the street corner loitering or whatever and straight away we can arrest her, but if a man does it [solicits/curb crawls], there's no power of arrest.... If you can eliminate the customers, they [Parliament] say, you can eliminate the problem; then they don't give us the power to do it!

Respondents were asked what changes to the current legislation they thought would be most advantageous in helping to provide a more effective response to the issue. Most respondents indicated that any changes that might be introduced would have to be directed toward both the "demand" and the "supply" side of the equation. Consequently, the majority of respondents called for the power of arrest to be made applicable to curb crawlers as well as to female prostitutes. Some squads, however, felt that the time had come for experimentation with alternatives such as legalization (three squads) or community service sanctions for both curb crawlers and prostitutes (one squad). Some other respondents felt that the public had unrealistic expectations regarding the ability of the police to significantly reduce the problem and felt

251

that police intervention only displaced prostitution into other areas. The predominant response, however, involved a call for increased powers of arrest and more punitive measures including higher fines, bail restrictions, and custodial sentences. As one officer stated, "The law's too soft on prostitutes and too strict on us."

The vice squads therefore varied in their perceptions of street prostitution and curb crawling. Although a number of respondents expressed considerable frustration with existing practices—particularly those of periodically "cracking down" on the prostitutes—they felt that they had to continue such action to provide a response to public complaints. In some forces, however, more constructive and imaginative responses, including collaboration with other agencies, were being developed. In relation to the current legal situation, most respondents expressed dissatisfaction with the status quo. Although a number of squads argued that they needed an extension of police powers, there was little overall agreement about the ways the law should be changed. There was a growing preference for enforcement against curb crawlers in many areas, but the police felt constrained by the wording and complexity of the law on curb crawling.

OFF-STREET PROSTITUTION

When asked how many women work from off-street locations in their area, two vice squads simply stated "loads" or "too many to count." Seven squads indicated that they did not record these figures. Estimated numbers of indoor workers were provided by twenty squads, ranging from three in Liverpool to 400 in Bristol. Where the location was stated, it was usually in private residences. Other locations included massage parlors, saunas, home visiting services, brothels, and strip bars. One officer cynically remarked:

> Invariably these places have managed to get planning permission to run a legitimate business, but they soon become an illegitimate business, because the legitimate side doesn't make any money.

The amount of time that different squads spent on regulating off-street prostitution varied considerably. The variation depended to some extent on the organization of prostitution in each particular locality. However, the fact that no area spent more than 25 percent of its time checking premises and that 90 percent of squads reported that they spent less than 10 percent of their time on this work seems to suggest that either off-street prostitution is not defined as much of a problem in these areas or that vice squads are reluctant to spend time regulating the off-street trade.

Half of the squads did not proactively police off-street prostitution and only intervened in response to public complaints. These squads displayed a degree of informal tolerance often stating that their main priority was to "clean up the streets ... not to police sex," as one senior officer put it. Other areas, such as Blackpool, Doncaster, and Leicester, provided monthly or "regular" visits to off-street establishments, while Bournemouth, Cardiff, Derby, Leeds, Sheffield, and Portsmouth reported that they actively policed these establishments through regular observations, surveillance, and occasional raids.

Eight squads saw no major problems with the law on off-street prostitution. The rest felt that the law was too limited, especially in relation to the Sexual Offenses Act (1956). Respondents mentioned practical problems such as the expense of operations as well as a general lack of police powers. They also referred to specific problems arising from the law. Table 14.3 summarizes these responses.

Eleven squads reported problems with gathering evidence and identifying offenders under this law. Indeed, they explained that large and lengthy surveillance operations were frequently necessary in order to establish what was going on in the premises, who was working there, and who owned and managed them. They explained that until the owner or manager was identified, there was little point in trying to prosecute the women working on the premises who they felt could easily be replaced. The fast turnover of women in some establishments led some officers to conclude that in general the police had insufficient powers to control off-street prostitution, and five squads specifically noted that the lack of power of arrest ensured that these prostitutes were beyond the control of the police. Three squads thought that

TABLE 14.3 MAIN PROBLEMS WITH THE LAW ON OFF-STREET PROSTITUTION

MAIN PROBLEMS	NUMBER OF SQUADS
Evidence and identification problems	11
Lack of power to arrest women	5
Lack of any control over the women who work as staff	3
Lack of any offense to work from private property alone	2
Expensive and lengthy surveillance needed for conviction	2
Insufficient powers in general to control off-street prostitution	1

TABLE 14.4 LEGAL CHANGES ADVOCATED REGARDING OFF-STREET PROSTITUTION

MAIN CHANGES	NUMBER OF SQUADS
Power of arrest and entry	10
Legalization	7
Power to arrest staff and clients	3
Burden of proof to be on the defense in immoral earnings cases	3
Simplify and update legislation	2
Power of closure for such establishments	2

lack of any identifiable offense for individuals who worked in these premises was an obstacle to intervention, while two squads mentioned the lack of any offense for a single woman working from private premises (whereas two women working from a single premise is deemed to be a brothel).

The vice squads favored several legal changes with regard to off-street prostitution (Table 14.4). Despite a general feeling that off-street prostitution is less undesirable than street prostitution, the vice squads felt strongly that the law does not allow for the effective regulation of off-street prostitution. The majority of vice squads called for an extension of punitive and controlling measures, extending to all parties involved and including extra powers of arrest, entry, and closure, as well as changes in the evidential rules that could shift the burden of proof onto the defense in cases in which individuals are charged with "living off immoral earnings." However, a quarter of the squads favored some form of legalization. (In some cities like Edinburgh and Birmingham, de facto legalization arguably exists today with many forms of commercial prostitution being licensed under entertainment or sauna regulations.) At the same time, other vice squads continue to prosecute these premises for their unlawful activities. These local and in some cases ad-hoc arrangements appear less than satisfactory. In many areas, police actions seem to be based on local considerations rather than being a product of a national, publicly endorsed policy.

CUSTOMERS

Police forces in many areas have turned their attention increasingly toward the control of the male curb crawler. Prosecutions are normally carried out in relation to the Sexual Offenses Act (1985), but three squads stated that they were experimenting with other laws. Nottingham has prosecuted curb crawlers for traffic offenses, with limited effect. A few squads (Bristol, Nottingham, and Bournemouth) have also experimented with a strategy of "binding over" curb crawlers (where the offender agrees to refrain from curb crawling) under the Justice of the Peace Act (1361).

Table 14.5 shows the number of formal cautions and prosecutions of curb crawlers over a twelve-month period. In the relatively few cases in which curb crawlers were prosecuted, sanctions were criticized by respondents as provid-

TABLE 14.5 CAUTIONS AND PROSECUTIONS OF CURB CRAWLERS

SQUAD	NUMBER OF CAUTIONS	NUMBER OF PROSECUTIONS
Charing Cross Vice Unit	325	161
Blackpool Plain Clothes Department	0	0
Bournemouth Vice Squad	43	37
Bradford Vice Squad	49	*
Bristol Community Action Team	12	*
British Transport Force Intelligence	*	2
Cambridge Force Intelligence Unit	0	0
Cardiff Priority Policing Team	0	25
Derby Proactive Unit	13	*
Doncaster Plain Clothes Department	40	60
Hull Criminal Intelligence Unit	84	0
North Staffordshire Vice Squad	6	43
Leeds Vice Squad	10	2
Leicester Vice Squad	14	6
Liverpool Criminal Intelligence Unit	12	5
Middlesborough Licensing Unit	*	164
Mosley Plain Clothes Department	0	113
Northampton Special Crimes Unit	0	0
Norwich Vice Squad	4	74
Plymouth Special Ops. Unit	0	12
Portsmouth (East) Vice Squad	0	0
Southampton Plain Clothes Department	29	53
Stoke-on-Trent Special Enquiries Department	4	5
Wolverhampton Vice Unit	0	100

* not available

ing little deterrent. Fourteen squads indicated the average level of fines for curb crawlers in their area was in the region of £50 to £100, but there was substantial variation in the fines actually imposed—ranging from £25 to £300. These variations led some officers to suggest that the system of fines is "something of a lottery" and that, given the considerable amount of time involved in gathering and processing the evidence, efforts to prosecute curb crawlers were not very cost-effective. As one chief inspector stated, "Prosecution is an aggravation, a lot of work; piles of evidence, bureaucracy, and inevitable not-guilty pleas from most curb crawlers.... Not surprisingly, most police forces are looking at other ways of attacking curb crawlers."

Verbal and Written Warnings

One alternative to prosecution that has been tried in a number of forces is the use of verbal warnings or letters sent to the curb crawler's home. Informal warnings, or cautions, were used by a quarter of the squads, some of which noted that they were particularly useful for "cruisers," those curb crawlers who persistently circle vice areas but rarely, if ever, actually solicit women. The letters usually take the form of a warning to the person concerned, explaining that the police are targeting curb crawlers in certain areas and that their car had been seen in the vicinity. In some areas, these methods are used in conjunction with arrests, while in other areas they are a substitute for arrests.

High-Profile Policing

A high-profile police presence in a prostitution area was a widely used alternative to arrest of curb crawlers. The main aim of this strategy is to deter and prevent curb crawlers in particular areas. It has proved reasonably successful, at least for a limited time, in reducing the visibility of prostitution in Nottingham, Greater Manchester, Sheffield, Bristol, Derby, Middlesborough, Plymouth, and Northampton. It also deters new women from moving into these areas and makes residents feel safer. However, the considerable amount of resources that high-profile policing requires limits the duration of these operations, and as police action decreases, street prostitution and curb crawling reappear.

Liaison with the News Media

Many squads reported that they work with the media to disseminate the names of curb crawlers. Publicity is seen as an effective deterrent for a curb crawler who may be married with a family. As Golding has argued, it may be that such initiatives are just as effective as arrest and prosecution, given that curb crawlers are probably equally if not more effectively deterred by public exposure and stigmatization.[2]

Liaison with Residents

A number of police forces regularly meet with residents' committees. Some officers described these meetings as purely "talking shops" and an inefficient use of police time. However, others found that by securing residents' cooperation, there were fewer complaints concerning prostitution and curb crawlers in the area, because the residents were kept informed about current police action and initiatives. In some areas such as Southampton, residents have joined together to help police, keeping records of the license plates of cars of suspected curb crawlers, and actively patrolling the area themselves. However, in other areas such practices have been discouraged by the police because of the potential friction that may occur between innocent drivers and residents.

CCTV and Videotaping

Some forces have introduced closed-circuit TV cameras. These include Doncaster, Middlesborough, and Plymouth. Norwich has videotaped curb crawlers, and other squads are considering such initiatives, which they see as having the additional advantage of simultaneously monitoring a range of other crimes that may occur in the area. However, these schemes are expensive, and the problem of displacing prostitution into another locale was often mentioned as a likely consequence of this type of action.

Traffic Management Schemes

A number of forces have experimented with traffic management, which has met with varying degrees of success. Much appears to depend upon the design of the scheme and how sustained the efforts of police officers are.[3] For example, in Bristol a road traffic scheme a few years ago closed off a few minor roads in the red-light area in order to break the curb crawler circuit onto the main road. However, the resulting closures made police access difficult, and the area subsequently attracted other crimes; the experiment was abandoned. Similarly, problems have continued to be reported in Cheddar Road, in Balsall Heath, despite the implementation of a road closure scheme. Although the vice squad officers acknowledge a general decrease in traffic in the area, the creation of a cul-de-sac has not deterred many curb crawlers from using the road.

The methods used to police curb crawlers are more diverse and generally less punitive than those used against female prostitutes, despite the fact that a number of squads see the curb crawler as a greater nuisance and often the more "vulnerable" to policing strategies than the prostitutes. The total number of curb crawlers prosecuted over the period was 862 compared to over 9,000 female prostitutes. This disparity becomes even more pronounced when we bear in mind that there are considerably more curb crawlers than prostitutes.

Respondents were asked what they thought were the main problems in implementing the laws on curb crawling. Three respondents did not answer this question, and two others stated that they felt no changes should be made in the present law. The main limitations of the current legislation were identified as the lack of power of arrest for curb crawlers, which reduced the possibility of taking immediate and effective action. The stringent standards of proof that must be satisfied for the Crown Prosecution Service to proceed with a case under the law were also felt to be a major problem. Gathering evidence was made more difficult, according to respondents, by the fact that definitions of key phrases within the law such as "persistent" and "in the vicinity of a motor vehicle" were variously interpreted by representatives of the local Crown Prosecution Service (CPS). A summary of the responses to this question is given in Table 14.6.

Six more vice squads specifically mentioned the wording of the legislation, particularly the emphasis on "persistence" and "nuisance." The Home Office (Circular 52/1985) states that "persistence" requires "the solicitation of at least two women on the same occasion, or the same woman at least twice." In a recent review of the legislation the Metropolitan Police Service stated:

TABLE 14.6 PROBLEMS IN ENFORCING THE CURB CRAWLING LAWS

PROBLEM	NUMBER OF SQUADS
Evidential problems stemming from law	9
Lack of power of arrest for curb crawlers	9
Limitations of "persistence" and "nuisance" in law	6
Lack of manpower and resources to carry out operations	4
Lack of power to control cruisers or clients on foot	2
Lack of support from courts, CPS	1
Continued presence of prostitutes	1

This does not in any way reflect the nature of the encounter between the prostitute and the curb crawler. The law and advice contained within the Home Office circular that accompanied the Act exhibit a flawed understanding of how curb crawlers interact with prostitutes. In the overwhelming majority of cases, the man will only solicit one prostitute to make his sought-for contact.[4]

The unenforceability of the "persistence" aspect of the legislation has forced many squads to rely on the second element of this legislation, which relates to "the likelihood of nuisance to other persons in the neighborhood." Since the word "likelihood" was used in the law, actual evidence of nuisance is not required by the courts (*Paul v. DPP*, 1989). Rather, local magistrates can rely on their knowledge of an area where residents are likely to be affected. While this has made prosecutions easier, squads who police prostitution in nonresidential or sparsely populated areas report that they still find themselves severely constrained by the present legislation.

Similarly, the 1985 law does not apply to those clients who solicit women on foot or those who "cruise" around the area. Three squads emphasized that the problems of nuisance, noise, and solicitation of nonprostitute women can be compounded by these two groups of clients, against whom the police feel relatively powerless.

Evidential burdens make operations lengthy and costly in terms of police time and resources. Lack of officers and resources to carry out curb crawler operations were mentioned by four squads, which may be one reason squads are keen to examine alternatives. Respondents were asked to identify the changes which they would favor to allow more effective control of curb crawlers. As Table 14.7 illustrates, the main changes advocated by half the

TABLE 14.7 CHANGES ADVOCATED REGARDING CURB CRAWLING LAWS

MAIN CHANGES	NUMBER OF SQUADS
Removal of "persistence," "nuisance" wording	12
Power to arrest curb crawlers	9
Inclusion of "cruisers" and clients on foot into legislation	2
Shifting burden of proof to the curb crawler	2
Introduction of video evidence into court cases	1
Introduction of larger and more uniform fines for curb crawlers	1

respondents was removal from the law of the words "persistence" and "nuisance." Nine squads suggested that the legislation should include the power of arrest for curb crawlers, while two squads argued for the inclusion of the "cruiser" and client on foot into the legislation. Two more squads felt that the burden of proof should fall on the curb crawler to explain why he was continually driving around a particular area.

In short, most squads were frustrated by the law on curb crawling, the Sexual Offences Act (1985). One officer stated:

> It's a nonsense act of Parliament. They said they were going to give us the powers to be able to do something about curb crawlers, but they've framed it [the legislation] in such a way that we've ended up essentially powerless, and it's us that have borne the brunt of criticism that nothing's being done about the curb crawlers.

The limited effectiveness of the law has led to a greater reliance on verbal and written warnings, liaison with the news media and residents' groups, the use of closed-circuit TV cameras, and traffic management schemes. These are localized initiatives, however, and as a result there is lack of consistency in the response to curb crawlers across the country.

PIMPING

The survey included questions about the role of pimps and the police response to pimps. The respondents were left to define "pimps" themselves, although the majority stated that they took the meaning of "pimp" to be the legal definition in the Street Offences Act (1959): "a man who exercises control, direction, or influence over a prostitute's movements in a way which shows he is aiding, abetting, or compelling her prostitution with others." Some squads noted that there is a gray area between nonexploitative partners, who may have a commercial interest in the prostitutes' earnings, and those pimps who were exploitative and exercised a degree of coercion over the women. The law does not clearly distinguish between the two types of men and thus potentially treats both groups alike.

One chief inspector said that he found the legislation "out of step" with the current practices of pimps and argued that it frequently allowed some pimps to remain outside the control of the law. He explained that the legal definition was built upon a belief that pimps directly control the women's lives, forcing them onto the streets and taking most of their earnings. One officer pointed out:

> These days many "pimps" don't live with these women, they tend to live in separate areas, although they may set the woman up in a flat and drive her to a specific area. Money is often not directly passed to the men; sometimes it is handed over via a courier and sometimes in the form of drugs. There is frequently little visible association to be able to gather evidence for a case, and in many cases the job is visibly little more than a transportation and accommodation job.

A total of eighty-two pimps were arrested over a twelve-month period. The number varied by squad between zero and fourteen, with an average of three arrests per squad per year. Half the squads reported that they had had no successful prosecutions for pimping over the previous twelve months, while only two squads reported that all their prosecutions had been successful. Not surprisingly, there is disillusionment over the current situation. One officer stated:

> They're [pimps] nasty pieces of work, and many women wouldn't be out there now if it wasn't for them. But we're fighting a losing battle because often the women are reluctant to do anything about them, especially the young ones.... It's always been difficult to get a pimp, and it does frustrate us, but at the end of the day we keep trying because successfully prosecuting a bad pimp is the feather in the cap; the raison d'être for vice squads.

Out of twenty-six respondents, only four indicated that they thought there were no real problems with the present legislation related to pimping. Seventeen squads stated that the main difficulty they encountered in implementing the law on pimping involved evidential difficulties in proving that someone was "living off immoral earnings" (Table 14.8). Testimony from the prostitute is crucial: "Pimps [are] not that easy to initially identify or arrest without the prostitutes' confirmation." However, a case cannot proceed solely on the uncorroborated word of a prostitute, or on police evidence alone. Instead, it is necessary to provide evidence of association, employment, and financial dealings.

Seven respondents mentioned the lack of resources available to carry out lengthy and demanding operations, which were seen as necessary to gather sufficient evidence against pimps. They added that their operations were further frustrated by changes in evidential requirements, which some officers described

TABLE 14.8 PROBLEMS WITH THE LAWS ON PIMPING

MAIN PROBLEMS	NUMBER OF SQUADS
Evidential problems of proving "living off immoral earnings"	17
Lack of resources and manpower needed to conduct lengthy operations	7
Sanctions imposed by the courts are inadequate and are no deterrent	5
Witnesses are unprotected by court system	2
Witnesses are fearful of short sentences	1
Inconsistent approach to "pimping" by prosecutors	1

as a process of continually "moving the goalposts." Five other officers expressed the frustration they felt when successful operations resulted in what they considered to be minimal financial penalties. As one officer emphasized:

> Even when you've sat out in the cold for nights, done all your homework, and eventually got a conviction, the fines are so minimal.... And then, even a couple of years in prison to these people is a calculated risk against earnings up to £1,000 a night.

Some officers argued that the uncertainty of successful prosecutions and the modest fines imposed by the courts made it difficult to encourage prostitutes to come forward out of fear of retribution from pimps. Officers felt that they were unable to offer any long-term protection to witnesses, and consequently many cases were dropped without reaching court.

The officers suggested a number of changes in the law. In general, they advocated harsher penalties for those convicted of pimping. Of the twenty-six squads who answered this question, six favored harsher and maximum sentences for all pimps. Two other squads wanted to see conviction for "living off immoral earnings" carry a mandatory prison sentence. The removal of bail was advocated by two squads as a way of improving the protection of witnesses. Financial disincentives were also suggested, such as confiscation of assets, for those convicted of "living off immoral earnings." Six squads suggested that cases should be able to proceed to court on the word of a prostitute, as in other criminal cases, and four other squads stated that once the prima facie case had been made, the burden of proof should be on the accused to explain where his or her income had come from.

INTERAGENCY COOPERATION

In recent years the police have come to realize that their ability to effectively control street prostitution is limited.[5] For this reason they have increasingly worked with other agencies to address the issue.[6] Significantly, three out of four respondents stated that they were involved in some cooperation with other agencies.

The agencies included social services departments, local government authorities, prostitute support groups, and outreach projects. Other agencies mentioned were immigration and customs, Barnardos, Women's Aid, the Salvation Army, YWCA, churches, residents' groups, rape crisis centers, and victim support services. Police also referred to specific projects, such as the SAFE outreach project in Birmingham, Street Health Project in Manchester, Southampton University Hospital project, and the Genesis Leeds project.

Few vice squads, however, stated that this kind of liaison was regular. Interagency cooperation was mainly a mixture of voluntary and short-term projects aimed at promoting the health and increasing the protection of the women involved in prostitution. As Golding found, the majority of vice squads were not involved in regular liaison with any other agencies on issues relating to street prostitution.[7] Some forces, however, emphasized that a strong informal network of cooperation is available when required.

CONCLUSION

Despite the widespread skepticism regarding the cost-effectiveness of arresting and rearresting female prostitutes who work on the streets, this remains the main control strategy used by the majority of vice squads. This is largely a function of the powers of arrest for soliciting and loitering available to police officers and the need to be seen to be doing something to appease residents. Arrests also provide a tangible measure of vice squad activity, and over the last few years they have become an important indicator of vice squad "success," despite the strong belief of many officers that arrests, by themselves, are unlikely to substantially reduce street prostitution.

Action to control customers, however, although generally less punitive, is viewed as being potentially more effective. Despite the legal constraints on the police (in both the wording of the Sexual Offences Act [1985] and the lack of specific powers of arrest), vice squads have increasingly come to recognize the importance of the "demand" side of the prostitute-client relationship. Indeed, there has been a growing realization that the curb crawler may be vulnerable to police intervention and formal sanctions.[8]

The majority of squads use the 1985 Sexual Offences Act, although they have increasingly resorted to a number of alternative strategies for addressing the problems caused by curb crawlers. These strategies include verbal and written warnings, high-profile policing, CCTV, liaison with residents and news media, and traffic management schemes. Thus, male curb crawlers continue to be dealt with in a more informal manner than prostitutes, although the number of curb crawlers prosecuted has increased slightly.

High-profile policing of street prostitution is not only very expensive in terms of labor and resources, but can lead prostitutes to simply move to other locales. Since it is impossible to maintain high-profile policing over a protracted period, it offers a strategy which is essentially short-term and is arguably short-sighted. The development of more sustained and potentially more effective strategies requires the involvement of other agencies. Interagency cooperation involves more diverse strategies that can address the issue in a more comprehensive manner. Although police are participating in interagency work more than in the past, the extent of such collaboration remains limited.

At present, the police response to off-street prostitution tends to be very localized and dictated by senior police officers. Given the constraints of the existing laws which necessitate long and expensive operations in order to gather sufficient evidence for a conviction, more forces will likely move toward the informal toleration of these off-street establishments. A number of officers interviewed appear to embrace the fallacy that the growth of the off-street trade will substantially reduce street prostitution. As recent research has shown, prostitutes' mobility between the streets and off-street locations is limited.[9]

Gaining convictions for pimping also places a considerable evidential burden on the police. Even when they have gathered sufficient evidence for a conviction, a number of vice squads felt that the penalties were too mild. Officers wanted more punitive sanctions for those convicted of procuring or forcing women—particularly young women—into prostitution. This, they felt, could help to reduce recruitment into prostitution.

In sum, a number of problems were identified in enforcing the prostitution laws. Vice squad officers perceived the law on curb crawling to be cumbersome, and they felt that the laws relating to prostitution required an urgent and comprehensive review. This, they said, would allow vice squads to more effectively respond to public demands to "clean up the streets" and to reduce the problems associated with prostitution.

NOTES

CHAPTER 1

I am grateful to Kathleen Guidroz for her comments on this chapter.

1. Eric Schlosser. 1997. "The Business of Pornography." *U.S. News and World Report,* February 10: 42-50.
2. Schlosser, "The Business of Pornography"; 1998 figure reported in *New York Times,* March 21, 1999.
3. Luke Harding. 1997. "Media: Dirty War on the Top Shelf." *The Guardian,* January 13.
4. James Davis and Tom Smith. 1994. *General Social Survey: Cumulative Codebook.* Chicago: NORC.
5. Gallup Organization. 1991. *Gallup Poll Monthly,* no. 313, October.
6. *Time* magazine poll, conducted by Yankelovich/Clancy/Schulman, July 7-9, 1986, N=1,017.
7. Schlosser, "The Business of Pornography."
8. CBS News poll, February 2, 1999, N=1,782.
9. Davis and Smith, *General Social Survey.*
10. Edward Laumann, John Gagnon, Robert Michael, and Stuart Michaels. 1994. *The Social Organization of Sexuality: Sexual Practices in the United States.* Chicago: University of Chicago Press.
11. ITV poll, reported in *Agence France Presse,* November 16, 1998, N=2,000.
12. 1988 Gallup poll, cited in *Toronto Star,* March 9, 1992.
13. *Time* poll, 1986.
14. 1994 poll, Davis and Smith, *General Social Survey.*
15. *Newsweek*/Princeton Survey Research Associates poll, July 27-28, 1995, N=752.
16. NBC News/ *Wall Street Journal* poll, June 10-14, 1994, N=1,502.
17. Penn, Shoen, and Berland poll, sponsored by Democratic Leadership Council, July 23-27, 1997, N=1,009 registered voters.
18. *Time* magazine poll, conducted by Yankelovich/Skelly/White, July 26-31, 1977, N=1,044 registered voters.
19. Gallup poll, May 28-29, 1996, N=1,019.
20. Gallup poll, 1991.

21. *USA Today* poll, conducted by Gordon Black, August 4-8, 1988, N=1,283 registered voters.
22. Frederique Delacoste and Priscilla Alexander. (Eds.). 1987. *Sex Work: Writings by Women in the Sex Industry.* Pittsburgh: Cleis; Kathleen Barry. 1979. *Female Sexual Slavery.* Englewood Cliffs, NJ: Prentice Hall; Andrea Dworkin. 1981. *Pornography: Men Possessing Women.* New York: Putnam; Laurie Bell. (Ed.). 1987. *Good Girls/Bad Girls: Feminists and Sex Trade Workers Face to Face.* Seattle: Seal Press; Lisa Duggan and Nan Hunter. (Eds.). *Sex Wars.* New York: Routledge, 1995; Annette Jolin. 1994. "On the Backs of Working Prostitutes: Feminist Theory and Prostitution Policy." *Crime and Delinquency* 40: 69-83.
23. Though it is impossible to arrive at precise figures on the number of workers in this hidden domain, a rough estimate is that street prostitution accounts for 10-20 percent of all prostitution in the United States (Priscilla Alexander. 1987. "Prostitutes Are Being Scapegoated for Heterosexual AIDS." In *Sex Work*, ed. Delacoste and Alexander). A recent study of London estimated that 12 percent of the city's prostitutes worked on the street (Roger Matthews. 1997. *Prostitution in London: An Audit.* Middlesex, UK: Middlesex University).
24. Though call girls are generally stigmatized by virtue of being prostitutes, they experience less direct censure. Bryan writes that "the call girl rarely experiences moral condemnation through interpersonal relations" (James Bryan. 1966. "Occupational Ideologies and Individual Attitudes of Call Girls." *Social Problems* 13: 441-450, at p. 450).
25. Barbara Heyl. 1977. "The Madam as Teacher: The Training of House Prostitutes," *Social Problems* 24: 545-555.
26. See also Barbara Heyl. 1979. "Prostitution: An Extreme Case of Sex Stratification." In *The Criminology of Deviant Women,* ed. F. Adler and R. Simon. Boston: Houghton Mifflin.
27. Most victimization studies in the sex work field can be faulted for the absence of comparison groups (i.e., nonprostitutes), and for a reliance on unrepresentative convenience samples, such as street prostitutes who had contacted service agencies, prostitutes who were simply approached on the street and interviewed, or prostitutes who were interviewed in jail (examples include Jennifer James and Jane Meyerding. 1977. "Early Sexual Experience and Prostitution." *American Journal of Psychiatry* 134: 1381-1385; Neil McKeganey and Marina Barnard. 1996. *Sex Work on the Streets: Prostitutes and Their Clients.* Buckingham: Open University Press; Mimi Silbert and Ayala Pines. 1982. "Victimization of Street Prostitutes." *Victimology* 7: 122-133; Melissa Farley and Howard Barkan. 1998. "Prostitution, Violence, and Posttraumatic Stress Disorder." *Women and Health* 27: 37-49). The high victimization rates reported may be influenced by self-selection bias, that is, prostitutes with the most experience of victimization and, hence, the most desperate segment of the population may be most likely to approach service providers or agree to street interviews. Still, there is no question that street prostitutes experience significant rates of violence in the course of their work: Virtually all street

prostitutes are the targets of violence at some point, even if only a minority of total encounters involve violence.

28. Few studies of indoor workers mention violence as a problem, and those that do mention violence find that it is rare (e.g., Roberta Perkins and Garry Bennett. 1985. *Being a Prostitute.* London: George Allen and Unwin, pp. 239, 300; Roberta Perkins. 1991. *Working Girls.* Canberra: Australian Institute of Criminology, p. 290). One survey of forty-one indoor workers, who were members of COYOTE, a prostitutes' rights group—not a representative sample of indoor workers—found that 95 percent said they had not been coerced into sex work, and 71 percent had never experienced any violence related to their work (Wendy McElroy. 1995. *XXX: A Woman's Right to Pornography.* New York: St. Martin's).

29. HIV infection rates are highest among street prostitutes who inject drugs and lowest among call girls. One study of seventy-eight call girls found that only one tested positive for HIV, and she had injected drugs in the past (Mindell Seidlin. 1988. "Prevalence of HIV Infection in New York Call Girls." *Journal of AIDS* 1: 150-154). None of the women working in Nevada's legal brothels has tested positive for HIV (*Las Vegas Review Journal,* March 7, 1998).

30. John Exner, Joyce Wylie, Antonnia Leura, and Tracey Parrill. 1977. "Some Psychological Characteristics of Prostitutes." *Journal of Personality Assessment* 41: 474-485, at p. 483.

31. Frank Farley and Sandy Davis. 1978. "Masseuses, Men, and Massage Parlors." *Journal of Sex and Marital Therapy* 4: 219-225; Tanice Foltz. 1979. "Escort Services: An Emerging Middle Class Sex-for-Money Scene." *California Sociologist* 2: 105-133. See also Bryan, "Occupational Ideologies"; and Albert Verlarde and Mark Warlick. 1973. "Massage Parlors: The Sensuality Business." *Society* 2: 63-74.

32. William E. Thompson and Jackie L. Harred. 1992. "Topless Dancers: Managing Stigma in a Deviant Occupation." *Deviant Behavior* 13: 291-31; Marilyn Salutin. 1971. "Stripper Morality." *Transaction* 8: 12-22.

33. Foltz, "Escort Services"; Jacqueline Boles and Kirk Elifson. 1994. "The Social Organization of Transvestite Prostitution and AIDS." *Social Science and Medicine* 39: 85-93; Amy Flowers. 1998. *The Fantasy Factory: An Insider's View of the Phone Sex Industry.* Philadelphia: University of Pennsylvania Press; Robert Prus and S. Irini. 1980. *Hookers, Rounders, and Desk Clerks: The Social Organization of the Hotel Community.* Salem, WI: Sheffield.

34. Edward Donnerstein, Daniel Linz, and Steven Penrod. 1987. *The Question of Pornography: Research Findings and Policy Implications.* New York: Free Press.

35. Cecilie Hoigard and Liv Finstad. 1992. *Backstreets: Prostitution, Money, and Love.* University Park: Pennsylvania State University Press, pp. 76, 183.

36. Robert Jensen. 1997. "Introduction" in Gail Dines, Robert Jensen, and Ann Russo. *Pornography.* New York: Routledge, p. 5.

37. Shannon Bell. 1995. *Whore Carnival.* New York: Autonomedia, p. 16.

38. McElroy, *XXX,* p. 148.

39. Nadine Strossen. 1995. *Defending Pornography.* New York: Anchor, p. 166.
40. Laura Kipnis. 1996. *Bound and Gagged: Pornography and the Politics of Fantasy in America.* New York: Grove; Alan Soble. 1986. *Pornography: Marxism, Feminism, and the Future of Sexuality.* New Haven: Yale University Press; Alan Soble. 1996. *Sexual Investigations.* New York: New York University Press; Linda Williams. 1989. *Hard Core: Power, Pleasure, and the "Frenzy of the Visible".* Berkeley: University of California Press.
41. McElroy, *XXX,* p. 148.
42. Perkins, *Working Girls,* p. 348.
43. Arlene Carmen and Howard Moody. 1985. *Working Women: The Subterranean World of Street Prostitution.* New York: Harper and Row, p. 88.
44. See Holly Bell, Lacey Sloan, and Chris Strickling. 1998. "Exploiter or Exploited: Topless Dancers Reflect on Their Experiences." *Affilia* 13: 352-368.
45. Perkins, *Working Girls,* p. 292.
46. Donnerstein, Linz, and Penrod, *The Question of Pornography.*
47. Jan Browne and Victor Minichiello. 1996. "Research Directions in Male Sex Work." *Journal of Homosexuality* 31: 29-56; Paula Dressel and David Peterson. 1982. "Becoming a Male Stripper." *Work and Occupations* 9: 387-406; David Pittman. 1971. "The Male House of Prostitution." *Transaction* 8: 21-27; David Luckenbill. 1986. "Deviant Career Mobility: The Case of Male Prostitutes." *Social Problems* 31: 283-296; Edna Salamon. 1989. "The Homosexual Escort Agency." *British Journal of Sociology* 40: 1-21; Carol Ronai and Rebecca Cross. 1998. "Dancing with Identity: Narrative Resistance Strategies of Male and Female Strippers." *Deviant Behavior* 19: 99-119; Sari van der Poel. 1992. "Professional Male Prostitution: A Neglected Phenomenon." *Crime, Law, and Social Change* 18: 259-275.
48. David Duncan. 1989. "Trends in Gay Pornographic Magazines: 1960 through 1984." *Social Science Research* 73: 95-98; Carl F. Stychin. 1992. "Exploring the Limits: Feminism and the Legal Regulation of Gay Male Pornography." *Vermont Law Review* 16: 857-900.
49. No poll is exclusive to the heterosexual population, but since heterosexuals constitute the vast majority of the population, the poll results can be taken as a rough barometer of straight opinion.
50. Christina Milner and Richard Milner. 1972. *Black Players.* Boston: Little Brown; Jennifer James. 1973. "Prostitute-Pimp Relationships." *Medical Aspects of Human Sexuality* 7: 147-160.
51. American Law Institute. 1980. *Model Penal Code and Commentaries, Part II, Sections 240.0 to 251.4.* Philadelphia: American Law Institute, p. 468.
52. Quoted in *New York Times,* November 14, 1984.
53. Interview by Julie Pearl; transcript on file with author and at *Hastings Law Journal.*
54. Richard A. Posner and Katherine B. Silbaugh. 1996. *A Guide to America's Sex Laws.* Chicago: University of Chicago Press, p. 156.

55. Frances Bernat. 1985. "New York State's Prostitution Statute: Case Study of the Discriminatory Application of a Gender Neutral Law." In *Criminal Justice Politics and Women*, ed. C. Schweber and C. Feinman. New York: Haworth; John Lowman. 1990. "Notions of Formal Equality Before the Law: The Experience of Street Prostitutes and Their Customers." *Journal of Human Justice* 1: 55-76.
56. Seattle Women's Commission. 1995. *Project to Address the Legal, Political, and Service Barriers Facing Women in the Sex Industry.* Report to the Major and City Council, Seattle.
57. Lowman, "Notions of Formal Equality."
58. Julie Pearl. 1987. "The Highest Paying Customer: America's Cities and the Costs of Prostitution Control." *Hastings Law Journal* 38: 769-800.
59. Ronald Weitzer. 1991. "Prostitutes' Rights in the United States: The Failure of a Movement." *Sociological Quarterly* 32: 23-41; Valerie Jenness. 1993. *Making it Work: The Prostitutes' Rights Movement in Perspective.* New York: Aldine de Gruyter.
60. Eileen McLeod. 1981. "Man-made Laws for Men? The Street Prostitutes' Campaign against Control." In *Controlling Women: The Normal and the Deviant*, ed. B. Hutter and G. Williams. London: Croom Helm; Barbara Sullivan. 1997. *The Politics of Sex: Prostitution and Pornography in Australia Since 1945.* Cambridge: Cambridge University Press; Kemala Kempadoo and Jo Doezema. (Ed.). 1998. *Global Sex Workers: Rights, Resistance, and Redefinition.* New York: Routledge.
61. See also Ronald Weitzer. 1994. "Community Groups vs. Prostitutes." *Gauntlet* no. 7: 121-124.
62. Duggan and Hunter, *Sex Wars;* Louis Zurcher and R. George Kirkpatrick. 1976. *Citizens for Decency: Antipornography Crusades as Status Defense.* Austin: University of Texas Press.
63. Gordon Hawkins and Franklin Zimring. 1988. *Pornography in Free Society.* New York: Cambridge University Press; Carole Vance. 1986. "The Meese Commission on the Road." *The Nation*, August 2-9: 76-82; Michael Kanter. 1985. "Prohibit or Regulate?" *Osgoode Hall Law Journal* 23: 171-194; A.W.B. Simpson. 1983. *Pornography and Politics: A Look Back at the Williams Committee.* London: Waterloo.
64. Hawkins and Zimring, *Pornography in a Free Society.*
65. Daniel Linz, Edward Donnerstein, and Steven Penrod. 1987. "The Findings and Recommendations of the Attorney General's Commission on Pornography." *American Psychologist* 42: 946-953.
66. Vance, "The Meese Commission"; Larry Baron. 1987. "Immoral, Inviolate, or Inconclusive?" *Society* 24: July-August: 6-12.
67. U.S. Department of Justice. 1988. *Beyond the Pornography Commission: The Federal Response.* Washington, D.C.: GPO.
68. U.S. Department of Justice. *Beyond the Pornography Commission*, p. 31.
69. Jim McGee and Brian Duffy. 1996. *Main Justice.* New York: Simon and Schuster, pp. 282, 293.

70. Ted Gest. 1989. "The Drive to Make America Porn-Free." *U.S. News and World Report,* February 6: 26-27.
71. Jim McGee. 1993. "U.S. Crusade Against Pornography Tests the Limits of Fairness." *Washington Post,* January 11.
72. Interview with official in Child Exploitation and Obscenity Unit, February 24, 1999.
73. Boles and Elifson, "The Social Organization of Transvestite Prostitution."
74. Foltz, "Escort Services"; Salamon, "The Homosexual Escort Agency."

CHAPTER 2

1. Luis T. Garcia, Kathleen Brennan, Monica DeCalo, Rachel McGlennon, and Sandra Tait. 1984. "Sex Differences in Sexual Arousal to Different Erotic Stories." *Journal of Sex Research* 20: 391–402; Gunter Schmidt, Volkmar Sigusch, and Siegrid Schafer. 1973. "Responses to Reading Erotic Stories: Male-Female Differences." *Archives of Sexual Behavior 2:* 181–199.
2. Scot B. Boeringer 1994. "Pornography and Sex Aggression: Associations of Violent and Nonviolent Depictions with Rape and Rape Proclivity." *Deviant Behavior* 15: 289–304; Edward Donnerstein and Daniel Linz. 1986. "Mass Media Sexual Violence and Male Viewers: Current Theory and Research." *American Behavioral Science* 29: 601–618.
3. Larry Baron. 1990. "Pornography and Gender Equality: An Empirical Analysis." *Journal of Sex Research* 27: 363–380.
4. Gail Dines, Robert Jensen, and Ann Russo. 1998. *Pornography: The Production and Consumption of Inequality.* New York: Routledge; Lisa Duggan and Nan Hunter. 1995. *Sex Wars: Sexual Dissent and Political Culture.* New York: Routledge; Diana Russell. 1993. *Making Violence Sexy: Feminist Views on Pornography.* New York: Teachers College Press.
5. Catharine MacKinnon and Andrea Dworkin. 1997. *In Harm's Way: The Pornography Civil Rights Hearings.* Cambridge, MA: Harvard University Press; Nadine Strossen. 1995. *Defending Pornography: Free Speech, Sex, and the Fight for Women's Rights.* New York: Scribner; Tamara Packard and Melissa Schraibman. 1994. "Lesbian Pornography: Escaping the Bonds of Sexual Stereotyping and Strengthening Our Ties to One Another." *UCLA Women's Law Journal* 4: 299-328.
6. Within the industry, actors and actresses are often referred to, and refer to themselves as, "talent." This term is used to differentiate their role from those who act in the "straight" (non-X-rated) industry, while providing a sense of legitimacy and normality to their occupations.
7. Patrick Biernacki and Dan Waldorf. 1981. "Snowball Sampling." *Sociological Methods and Research* 10: 141–163.
8. Sharon A. Abbott. Forthcoming. "Careers of Actors and Actresses in the Pornography Industry." Ph.D. dissertation, Department of Sociology, Indiana University, Bloomington.

9. Similar figures were reported in Chris Heath. 1996. "A Hard Man Is Good to Find." *Details* September: 96–291.
10. Double Penetrations or "DPs" refer to either two organs (usually penes) in a single orifice, such as an anus or vagina, or two organs in a single individual (for example, one male penetrating a woman's anus, and another her vagina). The latter is more common.
11. Because they are typically freelance employees, they are not offered health insurance by the companies they work for. Even the handful of talent on contract are not offered health benefits. Protecting Adult Welfare, an industry action group, is attempting to organize a low-cost health insurance package for the industry.
12. Similar findings were reported in Susan Faludi. 1995. "The Money Shot." *New Yorker*, October 30: 64–87.
13. Phasing in and out of the industry is fairly common, particularly for actresses. The most common pattern reported by trade magazines is for actresses to become romantically involved with someone outside of the industry, and to drop out for the duration of the relationship.
14. Interestingly, *Adult Video News*, the industry's premier trade publication, reports that pro-amateur features have a higher sales and rental rate than professional features.
15. A handful of the largest companies offer exclusive contracts to a few talent each year. The contracts assure actresses and actors a number of features each year, as well as public appearances and modeling engagements. While the contracts offer some stability, they also limit talent's exposure to other companies, and thus are often regarded with ambivalence.
16. Emanuel Levy. 1990. "Social Attributes of American Movie Stars." *Media, Culture, and Society* 12: 247–267.
17. Carol Rambo Ronai and Carolyn Ellis. 1989. "Turn-Ons for Money: Interactional Strategies of the Table Dancer." *Journal of Contemporary Ethnography* 18: 271–298.
18. D. Allen. 1980. "Young Male Prostitutes: A Psychosocial Study." *Archives of Sexual Behavior* 9: 399–426.
19. Interestingly, the likelihood of "being under contract" is not linked to years experience, as it might be with other industries. The reasons for this are twofold. First, actresses' status typically decreases with years in the industry, becoming less profitable and thus less desirable with time. Secondly, many experienced talent reported that contracts are often too restrictive and are not advantageous to a "successful" career.
20. Talent in the heterosexual porn industry are tested for HIV antibodies every thirty days, and must have their test results available on production sets.
21. Emanuel Levy, "Social Attributes of American Movie Stars."
22. Female talent also claimed that girl-girl scenes were easier and faster, since they did not require "waiting for wood" (erections).
23. Professional companies usually make both a hard-core and a soft-core version of each video produced in order to reach multiple outlets, including cable, home

video, international, and hotel markets. Soft-core versions show no actual penetration and are restricted in allowable language.

24. Nearly two-thirds of the female respondents self-identified as bisexual, although only half of them had had sex with women prior to entering the industry.

25. Laura Leets, Gavin de Becker, and Howard Giles. 1995. "Fans: Exploring Expressed Motivations for Contacting Celebrities." *Journal of Language and Social Psychology* 14: 102-123.

26. Several awards are also offered for the "Best New Face" of the year, although, ironically, the end of the first year often marks the halfway point in an actress's career.

27. Most respondents reported that they watch videos they appear in only for the "acting" (dialogue), not the sex. Interestingly, producers interviewed suggested that the audience fast-forwarded through the dialogue to get to the sex scenes.

28. Currently, two large agencies in Los Angeles represent nearly all of the working talent, the World Modeling Agency and the offices of Reb Sawitz.

29. Actresses are usually asked who they would like to work with on a particular production and are given the opportunity to reject possible actors. Actors reported that they were far less likely to be solicited for this information, although it did happen occasionally.

30. While being involved in the subculture is beneficial to actresses and actors, it does have its negative aspects. For example, there is a great deal of gossip in the porn subculture, which can damage a career. Several male respondents reported that at some point in their career, another actor had accused them of being gay or of appearing in gay pornography. While homosexuality is generally used to insult someone's masculinity, in the porn world this gossip carries additional weight. Actors reported that female coworkers would often refuse to work with male talent "accused" of homosexuality out of fear of HIV infection.

31. Each of these insults carries implications about women's sexuality. In one regard, they may suggest that the woman in question was "too interested" in sex. Since sex is less commonly a primary motivation for female talent, it may suggest a double standard within the industry. However, these insults may also linked to a more general phenomenon of insulting women by referring to their sexuality or genitalia. For a more detailed discussion of gender insults, see Kathleen Preston and Kimberley Stanley. 1987. "'What's the Worst Thing...?': Gender-Directed Insults." *Sex Roles* 17: 209–219.

32. Patricia A. Adler and Peter Adler. 1983. "Shifts and Oscillations in Deviant Careers: The Case of Upper-Level Drug Dealers and Smugglers." *Social Problems* 32: 195–207.

33. David F. Luckenbill, 1985. "Entering Male Prostitution." *Urban Life* 14: 131–153; William E. Thompson and Jackie L. Harred. 1992. "Topless Dancers: Managing Stigma in a Deviant Occupation." *Deviant Behavior* 13: 291–311.

34. James Bryan. 1965. "Occupational Ideologies and Individual Attitudes of Call Girls." *Social Problems* 13 (1): 441–450; Tanice G. Foltz. 1979. "Escort Services: An Emerging Middle Class Sex-for-Money Scene." *California Sociologist* 2:

105–133; Paul J. Goldstein. 1983. "Occupational Mobility in the World of Prostitution: Becoming a Madam." *Deviant Behavior* 4: 267–279.

35. David F. Luckenbill. 1986. "Deviant Career Mobility: The Case of Male Prostitutes." *Social Problems* 33: 283–296.

36. Thompson and Harred, "Topless Dancers."

37. Paula A. Dressel and David M. Petersen. 1982. "Becoming a Male Stripper: Recruitment, Socialization, and Ideological Development." *Work and Occupations* 9: 387–406; Paula A. Dressel and David M. Petersen. 1982. "Gender Roles, Sexuality, and the Male Strip Show: The Structuring of Sexual Opportunity." *Sociological Focus* 15: 151–162.

38. Martin S. Weinberg, Frances M. Shaver, and Colin J. Williams. 1997. "Gender and Sex Work: Prostitution in the San Francisco Tenderloin." Paper presented at the 1997 International Conference on Prostitution, Los Angeles, California.

CHAPTER 3

1. "Heavy Breathing," 1994. *The Economist.* 332: 64.

2. Amy Flowers. 1998. *The Fantasy Factory: An Insider's View of the Phone Sex Industry.* Philadelphia: University of Pennsylvania Press; Kathleen Guidroz. 1998. "Breaking Into the Bedroom: The Female World of Women in Telephone Sex." Paper presented at the National Women's Studies Association annual meeting, June, Oswego, New York; Grant Rich. 1998. "Phone Jams: Improvisation and Peak Experience in Phone Sex Workers." *Anthropology of Consciousness* 9: 83–84.

3. Nicholson Baker. 1992. *Vox.* New York: Random House; Grant Rich. 1998. "The Phantasically Phallic Phone: Erotic Exaggeration in Truth, Fiction, and The Starr Report." Unpublished paper.

4. Flowers, *The Fantasy Factory*; U.S. Congress. 1991. *Telephone 900 Services: Hearing Before the Subcommittee on Commerce, House of Representatives,* 102nd Congress, First Session. Washington, D.C. U.S. Government Printing Office.

5. Erving Goffman. 1963. *Stigma: Notes on the Management of Spoiled Identity.* New York: Simon & Schuster; Edwin M. Schur. 1983. *Labeling Women Deviant: Gender, Stigma, and Social Control.* Philadelphia: Temple University Press.

6. See also "Barbara." 1993. "It's a Pleasure Doing Business with You." *Social Text* 37: 11–22; Rachel James. 1993. "Heart to Heart With a Phone Sex Fantasy Girl." *Gray Areas* 2: 46–51; Mimi Freed. 1993. "Nobody's Victim." *10 Percent* 1: 48–53.

7. Howard Becker. 1963. *Outsiders: Studies in the Sociology of Deviance.* New York: Free Press.

8. Goffman, *Stigma.*

9. Christena E. Nippert-Eng, 1996. *Home and Work: Negotiating Boundaries through Everyday Life.* Chicago: University of Chicago Press.

10. All respondents' names are pseudonyms

11. The agency name is a pseudonym.
12. Gary Anthony, Rocky Bennett, and John Money. 1998. *Dirty Talk: Diary of a Phone Sex Mistress.* Buffalo, NY: Prometheus; Flowers, *The Fantasy Factory.*
13. Flowers, *The Fantasy Factory.*
14. Flowers, *The Fantasy Factory.*
15. Flowers, *The Fantasy Factory,* p. 29.
16. See also Flowers, *The Fantasy Factory.*
17. Flowers, *The Fantasy Factory;* Guidroz, "Breaking into the Bedroom."
18. Flowers, *The Fantasy Factory.*
19. Flowers, *The Fantasy Factory.*
20. Kathleen Guidroz. Forthcoming. "Breaking Into the Bedroom: Women's Employment in Escort and Telephone Sex Work." Ph.D. dissertation. George Washington University, Washington, D.C.
21. Cf. Flowers, *The Fantasy Factory.*
22. Flowers, *The Fantasy Factory,* p. 122.
23. Flowers, *The Fantasy Factory.*

CHAPTER 4

Portions of this chapter were presented at the annual meeting of the Popular Culture Association in Las Vegas in 1996 and at the World Pornography Conference in Los Angeles in 1998. Thanks to Bruce Kelton for keeping me up to date on the latest videos.

1. Mickey Skee. 1997. "Tricks of the Trade." *Frontiers* 16 (August 22): 43.
2. Richard Dyer. 1985. "Male Gay Porn: Coming to Terms." *Jump Cut* 30: 28.
3. One study showed that 57 percent of gay porn magazines in the 1980s consisted of scenes from videos. David Duncan, 1989. "Trends in Gay Pornographic Magazines: 1960 Through 1984." *Social Science Research* 73: 97.
4. Al Di Lauro and Gerald Rabkin. 1976. *Dirty Movies: An Illustrated History of the Stag Film, 1915–1970.* New York: Chelsea House, p. 97.
5. Thomas Waugh. 1992. "Homoerotic Representation in the Stag Film, 1920–1940: Imagining an Audience." *Wide Angle* 14 (April): 4–19.
6. Di Lauro and Rabkin, *Dirty Movies,* pp. 96–97.
7. Thomas Waugh. 1996. *Hard to Imagine: Gay Male Eroticism in Photography and Film from Their Beginnings to Stonewall.* New York: Columbia University Press, p. 359.
8. Richard Dyer. 1990. *Now You See It: Studies on Lesbian and Gay Film.* London and New York: Routledge, p. 171.
9. John D'Emilio and Estelle B. Freedman. 1988. *Intimate Matters: A History of Sexuality in America.* New York: Harper and Row, p. 287.
10. George Csicsery. (Ed.). 1973. *The Sex Industry.* New York: New American Library, p. 197.

11. Waugh, *Hard to Imagine*, pp. 359–361.
12. John R. Burger. 1995. *One-Handed Histories: The Eroto-Politics of Gay Male Video Pornography.* New York: Harrington Park Press, p. 14.
13. Kenneth Turan and Stephen F. Zito. 1974. *Sinema: American Pornographic Films and the People Who Make Them.* New York: Praeger, pp. ix, 141–143.
14. Turan and Zito, *Sinema,* p. 191.
15. Dennis Altman. 1982. *The Homosexualization of America.* Boston: Beacon Press, p. 88.
16. Duncan, "Trends in Gay Pornographic Magazines," p. 96.
17. Burger, *One-Handed Histories,* p. 25.
18. Jamoo. 1997. *The Films of Kristen Bjorn.* Laguna Hills, CA: Companion Press, pp. 22, 37; Dave Kinnick. 1993. *Sorry I Asked: Intimate Interviews with Gay Porn's Rank and File.* New York: Masquerade Books, p. 58.
19. Jamoo, *The Films of Kristen Bjorn,* pp. 17–19.
20. Mickey Skee. 1998. *Bad Boys on Video: Interviews with Gay Adult Stars.* Laguna Hills, CA: Companion Press, pp. 206–216.
21. Burger, *One-Handed Histories,* p. 25.
22. Burger, *One Handed Histories,* pp. 27–28.
23. Camille Paglia. 1991. *Sexual Personae: Art and Decadence from Nefertiti to Emily Dickinson.* New York: Vintage.
24. Susie Bright. 1992. *Susie Bright's Sexual Reality: A Virtual Sex World Reader.* Pittsburgh: Cleis Press; Susie Bright. 1995. *Susie Bright's Sexwise.* Pittsburgh: Cleis Press; Susie Bright. 1997. *Susie Bright's Sexual State of the Union.* New York: Simon and Schuster.
25. Pat Califia. 1991. *The Advocate Adviser.* Boston: Alyson Publications.
26. Douglas Sadownick. 1996. *Sex Between Men: An Intimate History of the Sex Lives of Gay Men Postwar to Present.* San Francisco: HarperSanFrancisco, p. 190.
27. Steven Minuk. 1997. "Sex, Guys, and Videotapes." *Icon* (July): 22.
28. Skee, *Bad Boys on Video,* pp. 173, 181, 193.
29. Chi Chi LaRue [Larry Paciotti] with John Erich. 1997. *Making It Big: Sex Stars, Porn Films, and Me.* Los Angeles: Alyson Books.
30. Hal Rubenstein. 1998. "Bye-Bye Barbie: Ken Ryker Comes Out (And We Don't Mean to Play)." *Genre* (October): 38–41, 74–75.
31. David Groff. 1998. "Letter From New York: Fallen Idol." *Out* (June): 43–50; Eric Gutierrez. 1997. "Porn Again: Life After Skin Flicks." *Out* (July): 64–68, 105; Dan Levy. 1996. "Falcon Rising." *Out* (July): 73–75, 106–107.
32. Kinnick, *Sorry I Asked.*
33. Skee, "Tricks of the Trade," p.43.
34. Some documentary evidence does support this assertion, in addition to the anecdotal evidence. For instance, in the free Texas gay weekly *This Week in Texas,* the issue of October 15–21, 1982, featured sixty-one bar ads, none of which mentioned male dancers. In the issue of July 24–30, 1998, almost half mentioned male dancers, although the total number of bar ads had diminished to twenty.

35. In Ronnie Larsen's 1997 documentary film *Shooting Porn,* a number of performers explained that video rarely paid the bills, but rather established a reputation for them to build on as escorts and dancers.
36. Gary Indiana. 1993. "Making X: A Day in the Life of Hollywood's Sex Factory." *Village Voice* 38 (August 24): 30; Minuk, "Sex, Guys, and Videotapes," p. 20; Skee, "Tricks of the Trade," p. 43.
37. "Working Stiffs." 1998. *Unzipped.* 13 (October): 13–27.
38. Scott Seomin. 1997. "Infomercial for a Hustler." *Icon* (July): 14–16; Indiana, "Making X," p. 30.
39. Seomin, "Infomercial," p. 15. Blake echoed this sentiment in Ronnie Larsen's film *Making Porn.*
40. ATKOL Forums: www.atkol.com/forums.htm
41. Nina Hartley's comments were made at a panel discussion at the annual meetings of the Society for the Scientific Study of Sexuality, Lost Angeles, November 13, 1998.
42. James Spada. 1979. *The Spada Report: The Newest Survey of Gay Male Sexuality.* New York: New American Library, p. 135.
43. Austin Foxxe. 1997. "That Type of Guy." *Frontiers* 16 (August 22): 65–68.
44. Michael Bronski. 1984. *Culture Clash: The Making of Gay Sensibility.* Boston: South End Press, pp. 165–166.
45. Richard Dyer. 1989. "A Conversation About Pornography." In *Coming on Strong: Gay Politics and Culture.* London: Unwin Hyman, p. 210.
46. Charles Isherwood. 1996. *Wonder Bread and Ecstasy: The Life and Death of Joey Stefano.* Los Angeles: Alyson Publications, p. 62.
47. Bradley Moseley-Williams. 1997. "The Porn Boy Next Door." *Icon* (July): 27.
48. Robert Hofler. 1998. "The Men of Koo Koo Roo." *Buzz* 9 (January): 65.
49. Richard Dyer. 1994. "Idol Thoughts: Orgasm and Self-Reflexivity in Gay Porn." *Critical Quarterly* 36 (1): 54. Dyer gives an extensive list of films about making porn films, as well as an extensive analysis of this trend.
50. Daniel Harris. 1997. *The Rise and Fall of Gay Culture.* New York: Hyperion, pp. 124-128; Michelangelo Signorile. 1997. *Life Outside—The Signorile Report on Gay Men: Sex, Drugs, Muscles, and the Passages of Life.* New York: HarperCollins, pp. 145–146. Harris excoriates contemporary porn and compares it unfavorably with pornography from the seventies. Signorile points out the elevated status of porn stars and their ideal physiques and connects it to gay men's use (abuse in Signorile's mind) of steroids and plastic surgery. They echo their condemnation in Hofler, "The Men of Koo Koo Roo," p. 78.
51. John Stoltenberg. 1991. "Gays and the Propornography Movement: Having the Hots for Sex Discrimination." In *Men Confront Pornography,* ed. Michael Kimmel. New York: Meridian Books; Christopher N. Kendall. 1993. "Real Dominant, Real Fun: Gay Male Pornography and the Pursuit of Masculinity." *Saskatchewan Law Review* 57: 21–58.

52. Thomas Waugh. 1995. "Men's Pornography: Gay vs. Straight." In *Out in Culture: Gay, Lesbian, and Queer Essays on Popular Culture,* ed. Corey Creekmur and Alexander Doty. Durham, N.C., and London: Duke University Press.
53. Scott Tucker. 1991. "Radical Feminism and Gay Male Porn." In *Men Confront Pornography.*
54. Carl F. Stychin. 1992. "Exploring the Limits: Feminism and the Legal Regulation of Gay Male Pornography." *Vermont Law Review* 16: 857–900, at 899–900.
55. Marc Mann. 1998. "The 'Daddy' Genre in Gay Porn." Paper presented at the World Pornography Conference, Los Angeles. Marc Mann is both a performer in "daddy" niche market videos and the proprietor of Video Horizons in Laguna Beach, California. He reports that the products featuring young eastern European men are his best sellers and renters.
56. James Williams. 1998. "Gay Porn for a Specific Audience: Mature and Uncut Men." Paper presented at the World Pornography Conference, Los Angeles. Williams is the owner of Altomar Productions.

CHAPTER 5

Research for this chapter was supported by a grant from the National Institute of Justice (Grant 97-IJ-CX-0033). I thank Norma Hotaling, director of San Francisco's First Offenders Prostitution Program, for data on the men attending her program. I also thank Steve Garcia and Holly Pierce for their excellent research assistance.

1. Arlene Carmen and Harold Moody. 1985. *Working Women: The Subterranean World of Street Prostitution.* New York: Harper and Row; Nannette Davis. 1993. *Prostitution: An International Handbook on Trends, Problems, and Policies.* London: Greenwood Press; Barbara Sullivan. 1992. "Feminist Approaches to the Sex Industry." In *Sex Industry and Public Policy,* ed. Sally-Anne Gerull and Boronia Halstead. Canberra, Australia: Australian Institute of Criminology.
2. Eleanor Miller, Kim Romenesko, and Lisa Wondolkowski. 1993. "The United States." In Davis, *Prostitution;* Sullivan, "Feminist Approaches to the Sex Industry."
3. Priscilla Alexander. 1987. "Prostitution: A Difficult Issue for Feminists." In *Sex Work: Writings by Women in the Sex industry,* ed. F. Delacoste and P. Alexander. Pittsburgh: Cleis Press; Miller, Romenesko, and Wondolkowski, "The United States."
4. Alexander, "Prostitution."
5. Miller, Romenesko, and Wondolkowski, "The United States."
6. Davis, *Prostitution.*

7. Neil McKeganey and Marina Barnard. 1994. *Sex Work on the Streets: Prostitutes and Their Clients.* Philadelphia: Open University Press; Special Committee in Prostitution and Pornography. 1985. *Pornography and Prostitution in Canada.* Ottawa, Canada: Canadian Government Publishing Centre.

8. Edward G. Armstrong. 1978. "Massage Parlors and Their Customers." *Archives of Sexual Behavior* 7: 117–125; Harold R. Holzman and Sharon Pines. 1982. "Buying Sex: The Phenomenology of Being a John." *Deviant Behavior* 4: 89–116.

9. George L. Stewart. 1972. "On First Being a John." *Urban Life and Culture* 3: 255–274; Louis Diana. 1985. *The Prostitute and Her Clients: Her Business Is Your Pleasure.* Springfield, IL: Charles Thomas.

10. Carmen and Moody, *Working Women;* Sheron Boyle. 1995. *Working Girls and Their Men: Male Sexual Desires and Fantasies Revealed by the Women Paid to Satisfy Them.* London: Smith Gryphon.

11. Holzman and Pines, "Buying Sex"; Jan Jordan. 1997. "User Buys: Why Men Buy Sex." *Australian and New Zealand Journal of Criminology* 30: 55–71.

12. Robert T. Michael, John H. Gagnon, Edward O. Laumann, and Gina Kolata. 1994. *Sex in America: A Definitive Survey.* Boston: Little, Brown and Company.

13. Alfred C. Kinsey, Wendell B. Pomeroy, and Clyde E. Martin. 1948. *Sexual Behavior in the Human Male.* Philadelphia: W.B. Saunders.

14 Harold Benjamin and R.E.L. Masters. 1964. *Prostitution and Morality.* New York: Julian Press.

15. Michael et al., *Sex in America.*

16. Martin A. Monto. 1998. "Holding Men Accountable for Prostitution: The Unique Approach of the Sexual Exploitation Education Project (SEEP)." *Violence Against Women* 4: 505–517.

17. Max Millard. 1996. "First Offender Program Offers Creative Solution to an Age Old Problem." *Bay Area Reporter* 52 (15): 1.

18. Martin A. Monto. 1999. "A Comparison of the Clients of Street Prostitutes with a Nationally Representative Sample." Unpublished paper.

19. Matthew Freund, Nancy Lee, and Terri Leonard. 1991. "Sexual Behavior of Clients with Street Prostitutes in Camden, N.J." *Journal of Sex Research* 28: 579–591.

20. Freund et al., "Sexual Behavior of Clients."

21. Mimi H. Silbert. 1981. "Occupational Hazards of Street Prostitutes." *Criminal Justice and Behavior* 8: 395–399; Davis, *Prostitution*; Hoigard and Finstad, *Back Streets.*

22. Silbert, "Occupational Hazards"; McKeganey and Barnard, *Sex Work on the Streets.*

23. Martha R. Burt. 1980. "Cultural Myths and Supports for Rape." *Journal of Personality and Social Psychology.* 38: 217–230.

24. Martin A. Monto and Norma Hotaling. 1998. "Rape Myth Acceptance Among the Male Clients of Female Street Prostitutes." Presented at the annual meetings of the Pacific Sociological Association, San Francisco.

25. Kinsey et al., *Sexual Behavior in the Human Male.*
26. Michael et al., *Sex in America.*
27. McKeganey and Barnard, *Sex Work on the Streets;* Holzman and Pines, "Buying Sex"; Jordan, "User Buys."
28. Holzman and Pines, "Buying Sex."
29. Keith Blanchard. 1994. "Young Johns." *Mademoiselle* 100(5):130–133, 183.
30. Neil McKeganey. 1994. "Why Do Men Buy Sex and What Are Their Assessments of the HIV-Related Risks When They Do." *AIDS Care* 6: 289–301.
31. McKeganey and Barnard, *Sex Work on the Streets.*
32. Jordan, "User Buys."

CHAPTER 6

This chapter is based on the Los Angeles Women's Health Risk Study, a RAND project supported by Grant R01 HD24897 from the National Institute of Child Health and Human Development. The authors are grateful to David E. Kanouse and Sandra H. Berry for their generosity in sharing their data, and to Sally Carson for her technical assistance.

1. Alfred C. Kinsey, Wendell B. Pomeroy, and Clyde E. Martin. 1948. *Sexual Behavior in the Human Male.* Philadelphia: W.B. Saunders; Charles Winick. 1962. "Prostitutes' Clients' Perceptions of the Prostitutes and of Themselves." *International Journal of Social Psychiatry* 8: 289–297.
2. Arlie Russell Hochschild. 1983. *The Managed Heart: Commercialization of Human Feeling.* Berkeley: University of California Press.
3. An "escort" is anyone who can be reached by calling escort or outcall massage services or certain dating and modeling services that advertise in sex tabloids, phone directories, and newspaper or magazine personal columns. The "call girl" can only be reached via a referral system, most typically through a "madame," another call girl, or a call girl's other clients.
4. Christine Overall. 1992. "What's Wrong with Prostitution? Evaluating Sex Work." *Signs* 17: 705–724.
5. Hochschild, *The Managed Heart,* p. 46.
6. Paul Cressey's classic book *The Taxi-Dance Hall* (Chicago: University of Chicago Press, 1932) describes the role of the "dime-a-dance" ballrooms for the lonely immigrant men pouring into Chicago during the Depression. Taxi-dance halls mostly disappeared, then reappeared in the 1970s with the contemporary wave of immigration; there are still a few in New York, Honolulu, and Oakland, but nowhere in the United States are they thriving as they do in Los Angeles, where there are eleven establishments with permits for "hostess dancing" within a mile of the downtown convention center.

7. Stephen Braun. 1989. "For Asians, a Ritual Sip of Home." *Los Angeles Times* (February 16): A-1, 3, 25.

8. Marilyn S. Paguirigan. 1992. *A Hostess' Script: An Ethnographic Study of the Dramaturgical Work of a Hostess.* Master's thesis, Department of Sociology, University of California at Los Angeles; Anne Allison. 1994. *Nightwork: Sexuality, Pleasure, and Corporate Masculinity in a Tokyo Hostess Club.* Chicago: University of Chicago Press.

9. For sampling methodology, see David Kanouse, Sandra Berry, Naihua Duan, Janet Lever, Sally Carson, Judith Perlman, and Barbara Levitan. 1999. "Drawing a Probability Sample of Female Street Prostitutes in Los Angeles County." *Journal of Sex Research* 36: 45-51.

10. Janet Lever and David E. Kanouse. 1998. "Using Qualitative Methods to Study the Hidden World of Offstreet Prostitution in Los Angeles County." In *Prostitution,* ed. J. Elias. Amherst, N.Y.: Prometheus.

11. Stephen R. Marks. 1994. "Intimacy in the Public Realm: The Case of Coworkers." *Social Forces* 72: 843-858.

12. For more detail on condom use, see Sandra Berry. 1992. "Risky and Non-Risky Sexual Transactions." Poster presented at the International Conference on AIDS, Amsterdam.

13. Kinsey et al., *Sexual Behavior.*

14. Winick, "Prostitutes' Clients' Perceptions."

15. Matthew Freund, Nancy Lee, and Terri Leonard. 1991. "Sexual Behavior of Clients with Street Prostitutes in Camden, N.J." *Journal of Sex Research* 28: 579–591.

16. Edward O. Laumann, John H. Gagnon, Robert T. Michael, and Stuart Michaels. 1994. *The Social Organization of Sexuality: Sexual Practices in the United States.* Chicago: University of Chicago Press, p. 98.

17. Lillian Breslow Rubin. 1984. *Intimate Strangers: Men and Women Together.* New York: Harper Perennial Library; Catherine Riessman. 1990. *Divorce Talk: Women and Men Make Sense of Personal Relationships.* New Brunswick, NJ: Rutgers Press.

18. *Washington Post*/Kaiser Family Foundation/Harvard University Survey of Americans on Gender. March 1998, Kaiser Family Foundation, Menlo Park, CA.

19. Riessman, *Divorce Talk.*

20. Veronica F. Nieva and Barbara A. Gutek. 1981. *Women and Work: A Psychological Perspective.* New York: Praeger.

21. Donald J. West. 1993. *Male Prostitution.* New York: Harrington Park Press.

22. West, *Male Prostitution,* p. 247.

23. S. E. Caukins and M. A. Coombs. 1976. ""The Psychodynamics of Male Prostitution." *American Journal of Psychotherapy* 30: 441–451.

24. Amy S. Wharton and Rebecca J. Erickson. 1993. "Managing Emotions on the Job at Home: The Consequences of Multiple Emotional Roles." *Academy of Management Review* 18: 457–486.

CHAPTER 7

The authors would like to express their gratitude to Rebeca Barragan, Jose Alvarez, and the staff of Congreso de Latinos Unidos for their encouragement and sponsorship, Robert Washington and Arthur Paris for their helpful suggestions, and the sex workers with whom we worked for their willingness to confide their concerns.

1. Heather G. Miller, Charles F. Turner, and Lincoln E. Moses. 1990. *AIDS: The Second Decade.* Washington, D.C.: National Academy Press.
2. Barbara O. de Zalduondo. 1991. "Prostitution Viewed Cross-Culturally: Toward Recontextualizing Sex Work in AIDS Intervention Research." *Journal of Sex Research* 28: 233–248.
3. Judith Cohen, Priscilla Alexander, and Constance Wofsy. 1988. "Prostitutes and AIDS: Public Policy Issues." *AIDS and Public Policy* 3: 16–22.
4. Priscilla Alexander. n.d. *Patterns of Prostitution in North America and Europe.* Oakland: California Prostitutes' Education Project.
5. Michael Zausner. 1986. *The Streets: A Factual Portrait of Six Prostitutes as Told in Their Own Words.* New York: St. Martin's Press; Arlene Carmen and Howard Moody. 1985. *Working Women: The Subterranean World of Street Prostitution.* New York: Harper and Row; Bernard Cohen. 1980. *Deviant Street Networks: Prostitution in New York City.* Lexington, MA: D.C. Heath and Co.; Paul J. Goldstein. 1979. *Prostitution and Drugs.* Lexington, MA: D.C. Heath and Co.
6. Mitchell S. Ratner. (Ed.). 1993. *Crack Pipe as Pimp: An Ethnographic Investigation of Sex for Crack Exchanges.* New York: Lexington Books; James A. Inciardi, Dorothy Lockwood, and Ann E. Pottgieter. 1993. *Women and Crack Cocaine.* New York: Macmillan; Terry Williams. 1992. *Crackhouse.* Reading, MA: Addison-Wesley; Mindy T. Fullilove, Elizabeth A. Lown, and Robert E. Fullilove. 1992. "Crack 'Hos and Skeezers: Traumatic Experiences of Women Crack Users." *Journal of Sex Research* 29: 275–287; Katherine Edin. 1991. "Surviving the Welfare System: How AFDC Recipients Make Ends Meet in Chicago." *Social Problems* 38: 462–473; Miller et al., *AIDS.*
7. Miller et al., *AIDS.*
8. Neil McKeganey and Marina Barnard. 1996. *Sex Work on the Streets: Prostitutes and Their Clients.* Philadelphia: Open University Press.
9. Joyce L. Wallace, Allen Steinberg, and Adele Weiner. 1992. "Patterns of Condom Use, Crack Use, and Fellatio as Risk Behaviors for HIV Infection among Prostitutes." Paper presented at the annual conference of the American Association of Public Health, Washington, D.C.; Carol A. Campbell. 1991. "Prostitution, AIDS, and Preventive Health Behavior." *Social Science and Medicine* 32: 1367-1378.
10. McKeganey and Barnard, *Sex Work*; Miller et al., *AIDS.*
11. Wallace et al., "Patterns of Condom Use."
12. John Davidson. 1986. *The Stroll: Inner City Subcultures.* Toronto: New Canada Press; Zausner, *The Streets*; Cohen, *Deviant Street Networks.*

13. Ratner, *Crack Pipe as Pimp*; Michelle G. Shedlin. 1990. "An Ethnographic Approach to Understanding HIV High Risk Behaviors: Prostitution and Drug Abuse." In *AIDS and Injection Drug Use: Future Directions for Community-Based Prevention Research,* ed. Carl G. Leukefeld, Robert J. Battjes, and Zili Amsel. Washington, D.C.: National Institute of Drug Abuse, NIDA Research Monograph 93.

14. Ratner, *Crack Pipe as Pimp.*

15. Davidson, *The Stroll*; Zausner, *The Streets.*

16. Inciardi et al., *Women and Crack Cocaine*; Shedlin, "An Ethnographic Approach."

17. Ratner, *Crack Pipe as Pimp;* Inciardi et al., *Women and Crack Cocaine* ; Fullilove et al., "Crack 'Hos and Skeezers."

18. Inciardi et al., *Women and Crack Cocaine*; Ratner, *Crack Pipe as Pimp*; Inciardi et al., *Women and Crack Cocaine;* Wallace et al., "Patterns of Condom Use."

19. Joyce Wallace, Judith Porter, Adele Weiner, Allen Steinberg. 1997. "Oral Sex, Crack Smoking, and HIV Infection among Female Sex Workers Who Do Not Inject Drugs." *American Journal of Public Health* 87: 470.

20. Sherry Deren, W. Reese Davis, Michael C. Clatts, Salvador Balcorta, Mark M. Beardsley, Jesus Sanchez, and Don des Jarlais. 1997. "Dominican, Mexican, and Puerto Rican Prostitutes: Drug Use and Sexual Behavior." *Hispanic Journal of Behavioral Science* 19: 202-213.

21. McKeganey and Barnard, *Sex Work.*

22. Department of Public Health. 1992. *Vital Statistics Report.* Philadelphia: Department of Public Health.

23. McKeganey and Barnard, *Sex Work.*

24. Cindy Thomas, Nina Mulia, and Jon Liebman. 1992. "HIV Seropositivity among Injection Drug Users Recruited from Street Settings in North Philadelphia." Philadelphia Health Management Corporation (unpublished).

25. Adele Weiner. 1996. "Understanding the Social Needs of Streetwalking Prostitutes." *Social Work* 4: 97–105.

26. Fullilove et al., "Crack 'Hos and Skeezers"; Shedlin, "An Ethnographic Approach."

27. Weiner, "Understanding the Social Needs."

28. Shedlin, "An Ethnographic Approach."

29. John L. Gwaltney. 1980. *Drylongso.* New York: Random House; Charles A. Valentine. 1970. *Culture and Poverty.* Chicago: University of Chicago Press; Carol B. Stack. 1974. *All Our Kin.* New York: Harper and Row.

30. Weiner, "Understanding the Social Needs."

CHAPTER 8

This research was supported by the Integrated Action Program of the British Council and the Spanish Ministry of Education, which gives seed money to conduct comparative research in England and Spain. The authors thank the British Council, the

Spanish Ministry of Education, APRAMP Director Rocío Nieto, Cristina Rechea Alberola, Raquel Bartolomé, María Dolores Romero, María Teresa Cano Ibáñez, Rita Soria Sahuquillo, Victoria Escribano Piqueras, María Dalia Lima Fernández Jesús, Emilia Miguel Martínez, Sue Johnson, Mo McDonald, Dave Dawson, Sue Mulroy, and the women interviewed for this project.

1. Rosemary Barbaret. 1995. *Victimologia y Prostitucion: Informe de Resultados.* Final report submitted to the Spanish Women's Institute, Madrid.
2. Aside from generic social services, no specific agency worked with prostitutes in the rural area of Albacete in Spain.
3. Maggie O'Neill. 1997. "Prostitute Women Now." In *Rethinking Prostitution,* ed. G. Scambler and A. Scambler. London: Routledge; Judith Green, Susan Mulroy, and Maggie O'Neill. 1997. "Young People and Prostitution from a Youth Service Approach." In *Child Prostitution,* ed. D. Barrett. London: The Children's Society.
4. *Anuario El País.* 1997. Madrid: Ediciones El País, pp. 159–160.
5. Mark Lee and Rachel O'Brien. 1995. *The Game's Up: Redefining Child Prostitution.* London: The Children's Society.
6. Maggie O'Neill, Nicola Goode, and Kristan Hopkins. 1995. "Juvenile Prostitution—The Experiences of Young Women in Residential Care." *Childright* 113.
7. Barbaret, *Victimologia y Prostitucion.*
8. Susan Edwards. 1990. "Violence Against Women: Feminism and the Law." In *Feminist Perspectives in Criminology,* ed. L. Gelsthorpe and A. Morris. Philadelphia: Open University Press, p. 89.
9. Maggie O'Neill. 1991. *Prostitution in Nottingham: Towards a Multi-Agency Approach.* Pilot Study for Nottingham Safer Cities. Nottingham: Nottingham Polytechnic.

CHAPTER 9

1. Ideological positions are reviewed in Annette Jolin. 1994. "On the Backs of Working Prostitutes: Feminist Theory and Prostitution Policy." *Crime and Delinquency* 40: 69–83; and Ann Ferguson. 1989. "Sex War: The Debate Between Radical and Libertarian Feminists." *Signs* 10:106–112.
2. Kathleen Barry. 1984. *Female Sexual Slavery.* New York: New York University Press; Kathleen Barry. 1995. *The Prostitution of Sexuality: The Global Exploitation of Women.* New York: New York University Press.
3. R. Sawyer. 1988. *Children Enslaved.* London: Routledge.
4. Suzanne E. Hatty. 1989. "Violence Against Prostitute Women: Social and Legal Dilemmas." *Australian Journal of Social Issues* 24: 235–248; Evelina Kane. 1987. *Support for Women Leaving Prostitution: Project Summary and Recommendations Final Report.* Minneapolis: Minnesota Coalition for Battered Women; Melissa Farley. 1995. "Research Shows Harm That Prostitution Does to Emotional

Health." *Minneapolis Star Tribune,* June 12; Mimi H. Silbert. 1981. "Occupational Hazards of Street Prostitutes." *Criminal Justice and Behavior* 8: 395–399.

5. Barbara Heyl. 1979. "Prostitution: An Extreme Case of Sexual Stratification." In *The Criminology of Deviant Women,* ed. F. Adler and R. J. Simon. Boston: Houghton Mifflin; Nanette J. Davis and Clarice Stasz. 1990. *Social Control of Deviance: A Critical Perspective.* New York: McGraw-Hill.

6. Nanette J. Davis. 1993. "Introduction: International Perspectives on Female Prostitution." In *Prostitution: An International Handbook on Trends, Problems, and Policies,* ed. N. Davis. Westport, CT: Praeger.

7. Valerie Jenness. 1990. "From Sex as Sin to Sex as Work: COYOTE and the Reorganization of Prostitution as a Social Problem." *Social Problems* 37: 403–420; Ronald Weitzer. 1991. "Prostitutes' Rights in the United States." *Sociological Quarterly* 32: 23–41.

8. Nanette J. Davis, Susan Kay Hunter, and Vicky Neland. 1990. "Alternatives to Prostitution: Reflections on the Victimization and Devictimization Process." Paper presented at the annual meetings of the Pacific Sociological Association.

9. Joe Parker. 1998. "How Prostitution Works." Portland, OR: CPA.

10. Sheila Redman. 1990. *Council for Prostitution Alternatives Report,* Portland, OR: CPA, amended by Nanette J. Davis, 1998.

11. Vicki Neland. 1998. *CPA Handbook.* Portland, OR: CPA, p. 3.

12. Interview with Susan Kay Hunter, March 1990.

13. Neland, *CPA Handbook,* p. 4

14. Interview with social work staff, February 1990.

15. Ron Weitzer. 1994. "Community Groups vs. Prostitutes." *Gauntlet* no. 7: 121–124.

16. Interview with Susan Kay Hunter, February 1991.

17. Neland, *CPA Handbook,* p. 4.

18. Neland, *CPA Handbook,* p. 8.

19. Neland, *CPA Handbook,* p. 9.

20. WHISPER, *Progress Report,* 1988.

21. Debra Boyer. (Ed.). 1988. *In and Out of Street Life: A Reader on Interventions with Street Youth.* Portland, OR: Tri-County Youth Services Consortium; Debra Boyer and Jennifer James. 1982. "Easy Money: Adolescent Involvement in Prostitution." In *Justice for Young Women,* ed. Sue Davidson. Tucson, Arizona: New Directions for Young Women.

22. Parker, "How Prostitution Works," pp. 1–2.

23. Nanette J. Davis. 1999. *Youth Crisis: Growing Up in the High Risk Society.* Westport, CT.: Praeger.

24. Neland, "Dedication," *CPA Handbook.*

25. Neland, *CPA Handbook,* p. 6.

26. David Matza. 1964. *Delinquency and Drift.* New York: John Wiley.

27. Nanette J. Davis. 1978. "Prostitution: Identity, Career, and Legal Economic Enterprise." In *The Sociology of Sex,* ed. J. M. Henslin and E. Sagarin. New York: McGraw-Hill.

28. Mimi Silbert and A.M. Pines. 1983. "Early Sexual Exploitation as an Influence in Prostitution." *Social Work* 28: 285–289; and Davis, "Prostitution."
29. Neland, *CPA Handbook*, p. 5.
30. Neland, *CPA Handbook*, p. 7.
31. Neland, *CPA Handbook*, pp. 7–8.
32. Neland, *CPA Handbook*, p. 8.
33. Neland, *CPA Handbook*, p. 10.
34. Neland, *CPA Handbook*, p. 16.
35. Neland, *CPA Handbook*, p. 28.
36. Neland, *CPA Handbook*, p. 27.
37. Neland, *CPA Handbook*, p. 26.
38. Molly Greenman. 1990. "Survivors of Prostitution Find PRIDE." *Families in Society: The Journal of Contemporary Human Services.* 71: 110–113.
39. Vern Bullough and Bonnie Bullough. 1987. *Women and Prostitution: A Social History.* Buffalo, NY: Prometheus.
40. Judith Walkowitz. 1980. *Prostitution and Victorian Society: Women, Class and the State.* Cambridge, UK: Cambridge University Press.

CHAPTER 10

1. Bureau of Justice Statistics. *Sourcebook of Criminal Justice Statistics.* Washington, D.C.: U.S. Government Printing Office, annual.
2. Julie Pearl. 1987. "The Highest Paying Customer: America's Cities and the Costs of Prostitution Control." *Hastings Law Journal* 38: 769–800. More recently, San Francisco spent $7.6 million on prostitution control in 1994 (San Francisco Task Force on Prostitution. 1996. *Final Report.* San Francisco Board of Supervisors).
3. Federal Bureau of Investigation. *Uniform Crime Reports.* Washington, D.C.: U.S. Department of Justice, annual.
4. Bernard Cohen. 1980. *Deviant Street Networks: Prostitution in New York City.* Lexington, MA: Lexington Books.
5. Jerome Skolnick and John Dombrink. 1978. "The Legalization of Deviance." *Criminology* 16: 193–208, at p. 201.
6. *San Francisco Examiner,* December 6, 1995.
7. "The Task Force therefore recommends that the City stop enforcing and prosecuting prostitution crimes" (San Francisco Task Force, *Final Report,* p. 6).
8. Interview, April 29, 1997.
9. M. Anne Jennings. 1976. "The Victim as Criminal: A Consideration of California's Prostitution Law." *California Law Review* 64: 1235–1284; Raymond Parnas. 1981. "Legislative Reform of Prostitution Laws." *Santa Clara Law Review* 21: 669–696.
10. Interview with Julia Harrison, June 7, 1993.

11. Cohen, *Deviant Street Networks.*
12. *Time*/Yankelovich, Skelly, and White poll. July 26–31, 1977, N=1,044 registered voters.
13. See the poll data in Ronald Weitzer. 1991. "Prostitutes Rights in the United States: The Failure of a Movement." *Sociological Quarterly* 32: 23–41.
14. Charles McCaghy and Stephen Cernkovich. 1991. "Changing Public Opinion toward Prostitution Laws," paper presented at the World Congress of Sexology, Amsterdam.
15. Peat Marwick and Partners. 1984. *A National Population Study of Prostitution and Pornography.* Report no. 6. Ottawa, Canada: Department of Justice.
16. ITV poll, reported in *Agence France Presse,* November 16, 1998, N=2,000.
17. Sun Media Newspapers/Compas poll, reported in *Edmonton Sun,* October 31, 1998, N=1,479.
18. "Poll: French Want Brothels Legalized," *Boston Globe,* January 22, 1995.
19. Ronald Weitzer. 1994. "Community Groups vs. Prostitutes," *Gauntlet* no. 7: 121–124.
20. Interview, July 16, 1993.
21. Quoted in Ralph Jimenez. 1993. "Manchester Plans New Push on Johns'". *Boston Globe,* January 3: NH1.
22. Quoted in Linda Jones. 1989. "Festival Marks Community's Effort to Drive out Drug Dealers, Prostitutes." *Detroit News,* September 15: B1.
23. Quoted in Valarie Busheda and David Grant. 1992. "Prostitution: A Problem That Endures." *Detroit News,* February 19: B4.
24. Quoted in Stephanie Gadlin. 1989. "Hookers Get Out." *Chicago Defender,* September 6: 26.
25. Quoted in Judy MacLean. 1976. "Prostitution and the Community." *In These Times,* December 20: 12–13.
26. Helen Reynolds. 1986. *The Economics of Prostitution.* Springfield, IL: Charles C. Thomas.
27. Quoted in MacLean, "Prostitution and the Community," p. 13.
28. Quoted in Greg Mills. 1992. "Buckeye Neighborhood Coalition Attacks Crime, Grime." *Call and Post* (Cleveland), August 20: A3.
29. Quoted in Scott Winokur. 1993. "Prostitution Crackdown Nets 160," *San Francisco Examiner,* January 20: A3.
30. Quoted in Linda Wheeler. 1987. "Prostitute Disrupts D.C. Hearing," *Washington Post,* May 7: D7.
31. Interview, July 26, 1993.
32. George Kelling and Catherine Coles. 1996. *Fixing Broken Windows.* New York: Free Press.
33. This is certainly the case in the two cities I studied closely, San Francisco and Washington, D.C., based on addresses of arrested customers.
34. Interview, July 9, 1993.

35. Quoted in George Judson. 1992. "Price of a Prostitute: The Client's Car." *New York Times,* December 4: B1.
36. Interview, July 9, 1993.
37. Quoted in Katti Gray. 1991. "Prostitution Opponents Aim to Seize Johns' Cars," *Newsday,* December 5: 25.
38. Art Hubacher. 1998. "Every Picture Tells a Story: Is Kansas City's 'John TV' Constitutional?" *Kansas Law Review* 46: 551–591.
39. Courtney Persons. 1996. "Sex in the Sunlight: The Effectiveness, Efficiency, Constitutionality, and Advisability of Publishing Names and Pictures of Prostitutes' Patrons." *Vanderbilt Law Review* 49: 1525–1575.
40. "Curbing Prostitution on Demand Side," *New York Times,* April 20: B8.
41. Louis Harris poll. November 30–December 10, 1978, N=1,513.
42. *Newsweek* poll. January 26–27, 1995, N=753.
43. *Edmonton Sun,* November 8, 1998.
44. The Portland program, Sexual Exploitation Education Project (SEEP), operated from 1995 to 1997 and, unlike in San Francisco where men who attend the school and do not recidivate avoid an arrest record, men who attended SEEP were convicted of soliciting a prostitute. SEEP was an independent organization, whereas San Francisco's johns' school is under the auspices of the criminal justice system.
45. John Braithwaite. 1989. *Crime, Shame, and Reintegration.* Cambridge, UK: Cambridge University Press.
46. Personal communication from Staff Sgt. Doug Mottram, Metropolitan Toronto Police, August 7, 1997.
47. Molly Greenman. 1990. "Survivors of Prostitution Find PRIDE." *Families in Society* 71: 110–113; Evelina Kane. 1987. "Support for Women Leaving Prostitution: Project Summary and Recommendations," Minneapolis, MN: WHISPER.
48. WHISPER. 1985–1986. *WHISPER Newsletter,* no. 1, p. 1.
49. International Committee for Prostitutes' Rights. 1985. *World Charter for Prostitutes' Rights.* Amsterdam.
50. Part of the following discussion is based on Weitzer, "Prostitutes' Rights in the United States."
51. COYOTE proposes that existing business codes be used to confine prostitution businesses to commercial or mixed residential/commercial areas (Priscilla Alexander. 1979. "National Decriminalization a Must as Hypocritical, Sexist Vigilante Groups Spring into Action across the U.S." *NTFP News* 1: September–October).
52. COYOTE. 1974. "COYOTE Background." *COYOTE Howls* 1 (2).
53. One study found that call girls and brothel and massage parlor workers were well-adjusted: "capable of handling themselves well, manifesting good emotional controls, being well aware of conventionality, and doing well in the occu-

pation of their choice" (John E. Exner, Joyce Wylie, Antonia Leura, and Tracey Parrill. 1977. "Some Psychological Characteristics of Prostitutes." *Journal of Personality Assessment* 41: 474–485). Studies of escorts and massage parlor workers confirm this (see Chapter 1).

54. COYOTE, quoted in Jim Stingley. 1976. "Issues Raised by Decriminalization." *Los Angeles Times,* February 9.
55. Stingley, "Issues Raised."
56. COYOTE. 1974. "Fiction versus Fact." *COYOTE Howls* 1 (2).
57. Interview with Priscilla Alexander, San Francisco, March 16, 1987.
58. Margo St. James. 1989. "Preface." In *A Vindication of the Rights of Whores,* ed. G. Pheterson. Seattle: Seal Press, p. xix.
59. Interview with Margo St. James, September 12, 1980.
60. Some local branches of NOW, such as San Francisco's, have been more actively involved with COYOTE.
61. Erving Goffman. 1963. *Stigma.* Englewood Cliffs, N.J.: Prentice-Hall.
62. National Task Force on Prostitution. 1987. *About the NTFP.* San Francisco, p. 2.
63. Interview with Samantha Miller, June 16, 1993.
64. Ronald de Graaf. 1995. *Prostitutes and Their Clients.* The Hague: Gegenens Koninkijke, p. 15. It should be noted that a significant proportion of customers are foreign tourists and businessmen.
65. October 1997 poll, cited in Chrisje Brants. 1998. "The Fine Art of Pragmatic Tolerance: Prostitution in Amsterdam." Unpublished paper, University of Utrecht.
66. Edgar Danter. 1999. "Green Light at Last for Dutch Red Light Districts," *Deutsche Presse-Agentur,* February 6, N=2,600.
67. Interview with Sietske Altink, Red Thread, Amsterdam, March 24, 1997.
68. Interview with Klein Beekman, chairman of the Brothel Owners Association, Amsterdam, March 24, 1997.
69. Ministry of Justice figures, cited in *AP Worldstream,* January 27, 1999.
70. Interview with secretary of Window Owners Association, Amsterdam, May 28, 1998.
71. Window Owners Association, quoted in *The Guardian,* January 31, 1999.
72. Interview with the director of the Foundation of Men and Prostitution, The Hague, May 29, 1998.

CHAPTER 11

1. For more discussion on this misperception, see Gail Pheterson. 1996. *The Prostitution Prism.* Amsterdam: Amsterdam University Press.
2. My initial interviews were secured through sex worker self-advocacy organizations COYOTE (San Francisco), US PROS (San Francisco), the Red Thread (Amsterdam), and the Foundation Against Trafficking in Women (Utrecht).

That sample was expanded through a snowball method by asking those subjects to suggest others whom I might also interview. I also sought out populations otherwise underrepresented, including street prostitutes, migrant prostitutes, teen prostitutes, and older workers. Each of my interviews, most of which were tape-recorded, lasted at least one hour. Interviews with Dutch sex workers were typically conducted in Dutch and later translated.

3. Interviews included peep show workers, exotic dancers, call girls, street prostitutes, window prostitutes, pornography models/actors, escort workers, professional dominants, brothel workers, phone sex workers, and professional sex surrogates. The study is limited to women sex workers.

4. See Wendy. Chapkis. 1997. *Live Sex Acts: Women Performing Erotic Labor.* New York: Routledge.

5. For another attempt to disaggregate sex work into its various types and to explore the distinct challenges facing these workers, see Barbara Heyl. 1979. "Prostitution: An Extreme Case of Sex Stratification." In *The Criminology of Deviant Women,* ed. F. Adler and R. Simon. Boston: Houghton Mifflin.

6. Interview with Terry, San Francisco, 1993.

7. Interview with Rita, San Francisco, 1992.

8. Interview with Rita, San Francisco, 1992.

9. Carol Leigh. 1994. "Prostitution in the United States: The Statistics." *Gauntlet* no. 7: 17–18.

10. In Amsterdam, for example, one police officer in the vice squad estimated that 70 to 80 percent of women working in window prostitution are foreign, and 80 percent of those are working without proper papers (interview with Ron Beekmeijer, Amsterdam, 1994).

11. Interview with Licia Brussa, Amsterdam, 1994.

12. De Graaf Foundation. 1997. "Prostitution in the Netherlands." *Between the Lines: The Newsletter of the Dutch Institute for Prostitution Issues,* March, p. 1.

13. De Graaf Foundation, "Prostitution in the Netherlands," p. 2.

14. De Graaf Foundation, "Prostitution in the Netherlands," p. 2.

15. Interview with Teri, San Francisco, 1992.

16. Interview with Luna, San Francisco, 1992.

17. Interview with Susie, San Francisco, 1992.

18. Interview with Teri, San Francisco, 1992.

19. Interview with Susie, San Francisco, 1992.

20. Interview with Susie, San Francisco, 1992.

21. Interview with Jane, San Francisco, 1992.

22. Interview with Joan, San Francisco, 1992.

23. Interview with Jane, San Francisco, 1992.

24. Interview with Karen, Santa Cruz, 1994.

25. Interview with Karen, Santa Cruz, 1994.

26. Interview with Terez, Santa Cruz, 1992.

27. Interview with Barbara, Santa Cruz, 1987.

28. Interview with Gloria Lockett, San Francisco, 1993.
29. Interview with Jo, Amsterdam, 1993.
30. Interview with Jo, Amsterdam, 1993.
31. Interview with Julia, New York, 1994.
32. Interview with Terry, San Francisco, 1993.
33. Interview Teri, San Francisco, 1992.
34. Interview with Jane, San Francisco, 1992.
35. Interview with Teri, San Francisco, 1992.
36. Interview with Margot, Amsterdam, 1994.
37. Interview with Dawn, San Francisco, 1995.
38. Interview with Luna, San Francisco, 1992.
39. Interview with Jo, Amsterdam, 1993.
40. Interview with Terry, San Francisco, 1993.
41. Interview with Teri, San Francisco, 1992.
42. Interview with Karen, Santa Cruz, 1994.
43. A "sacred prostitute" is a sex worker who understands her services to have a spiritual and therapeutic dimension, and who locates her professional identity in the tradition of ancient temple prostitutes.
44. Interview with Vision, Amsterdam, 1993.
45. Interview with Carol, San Francisco, 1992.
46. Interview with Susie, San Francisco, 1992.
47. Interview with Candye Kane, Santa Cruz, 1995.
48. Interview with Teri, San Francisco, 1992.
49. Interview with Sandy, San Francisco, 1993.
50. Interview with Barbara, Santa Cruz, 1987.
51. Interview with Samantha, San Francisco, 1992.
52. Interview with Licia Brussa, Amsterdam, 1994.
53. Interview with Jo, Amsterdam, 1993.
54. Interview with Samantha, San Francisco, 1992.
55. Interview with Licia Brussa, Amsterdam, 1994.
56. Interview with Terry, San Francisco, 1993.
57. Interview with Samantha, San Francisco, 1992.
58. Ronald Weitzer. 1991. "Prostitutes' Rights in the United States." *Sociological Quarterly* 32: 23–41.
59. Yvette in The Red Thread. 1995. *Vluggertjes* 1: 18.
60. Interview with Terry, an Francisco, 1995.
61. David Steinberg. 1998. "Some Room of Their Own." *Spectator Magazine,* July 30–August 6: 5–7.
62. Interview with Susie, San Francisco, 1992.
63. Interview with Teri, San Francisco, 1992.
64. Steinberg, "Some Room of Their Own," pp. 5–7.
65. Terry Goodson. 1994. Unpublished letter to the California NOW Board Delegates, August 19; Dennis Pfaff. 1994. "Exotic Dancers Claim Theater Sidesteps Wage and Labor Laws." *San Francisco Daily Journal,* May 7; Susan

Seward. 1994. "Lap Dancers Battle for Respect: Women Fighting to Force Theaters To Pay Hourly Wages." *San Francisco Chronicle,* May 7: A17.
66. Steinberg, "Some Room of Their Own," pp. 5–7.
67. Kerwin Brook, 1998. "Peep Show Pimps." *San Francisco Bay Guardian,* February 4–10: 18.
68. Brook, "Peep Show Pimps."
69. Carla, quoted in Brook, "Peep Show Pimps."
70. According to Brook, the current California labor commissioner, Jose Millan, has concluded that the commission system appears to be legal (Brook, "Peep Show Pimps").
71. National Committee on Pay Equity. 1998. "The Wage Gap: Myths and Facts." In *Race, Class, and Gender in the United States,* ed. P. Rothenberg. New York: St. Martin's Press, p. 234.
72. National Committee on Pay Equity, "The Wage Gap."
73. Interview with Carol Queen, San Francisco, 1992.

CHAPTER 12

This project was funded with a grant from the National Health Research Development Program, Health Canada. I thank my co-investigator, Eleanor Maticka-Tyndale, for her work on the project and her feedback on this manuscript. I also thank my research assistants, Jocalyn Clark and June Oakes, and Jennifer Zubick, the project coordinator, whose legal expertise proved invaluable for this paper. My appreciation is also extended to all the women who took time away from their lives to speak with me.

1. For descriptions of exotic danceing see Graves E. Enck and James D. Preston. 1988. "Counterfeit Intimacy: A Dramaturgical Analysis of an Erotic Performance." *Deviant Behavior* 9: 369–381; Craig J. Forsyth and Tina H. Deshotels. 1997. "The Occupational Milieu of the Nude Dancer." *Deviant Behavior* 18: 125–142; Jacqueline Lewis. 1998. "Lap Dancing: Personal and Legal Implications." In *Prostitution: On Whores, Hustlers, and Johns,* ed. J. E. Elias, V. L. Bullough, V. Elias, and G. Brewer, Amherst, MA: Prometheus Press; Carol Rambo Ronai and Carolyn Ellis. 1989. "Turn-ons for Money: Interactional Strategies of the Table Dancer." *Journal of Contemporary Ethnography* 118: 271–298; and Carol Rambo Ronai. 1992. "The Reflexive Self Through Narrative: A Night in the Life of an Erotic Dancer/Researcher." In *Investigating Subjectivity: Research on Lived Experience,* ed. C. Ellis and M.G. Flaherty, Newbury Park, CA: Sage.
2. Lewis, "Lap Dancing."
3. Brenda Cossman. 1997. "Feminist Fashion or Morality in Drag? The Sexual Subtext of the *Butler* Decision." In *Bad Attitude/s on Trial: Pornography, Feminism,*

and the Butler Decision, ed. B. Cossman, S. Bell, L. Gotell, and B. Ross, Toronto: University of Toronto Press; and Lise Gotell. 1997. "Shaping *Butler: The New Politics of Anti-Pornography.*" In *Bad Attitude/s.*

4. The term "exotic dancer" is used by dancers to describe themselves.

5. See Cossman, "Feminist Fashion."

6. Jacqueline Boles and Albeno P. Garbin. 1974. "The Choice of Stripping for a Living: An Empirical and Theoretical Explanation." *Sociology of Work and Occupations* 1: 110-123; Sandra Harley Carey, Robert A. Peterson, and Louis K. Sharpe. 1974. "A Study of Recruitment and Socialization into Two Deviant Female Occupations." *Sociological Symposium* 8: 11–24; Jacqueline Lewis. 1998. "Learning to Strip: The Socialization Experiences of Exotic Dancers." *Canadian Journal of Human Sexuality* 7: 51–66; Robert C Prus and Styllianoss Irini. 1980. *Hookers, Rounders, and Desk Clerks: The Social Organization of the Hotel Community.* Toronto: Gage Publishing; Marilyn Salutin. 1971. "Stripper Morality." *Transaction* 8: 12–22; James K Skipper and Charles H. McCaghy. 1971. "Stripteasing: A Sex-Oriented Occupation." In *Studies in the Sociology of Sex,* ed. by J. M. Henslin. New York: Appleton-Century-Crofts.

7. Jacqueline Boles and Albeno P. Garbin. 1974. "Stripping for a Living: An Occupational Study of the Night Club Stripper." In *Deviant Behavior: Occupational and Organizational Bases,* ed. C. D. Bryant, Chicago: Rand McNally; Lewis, "Learning to Strip"; Charles H. McCaghy and James K. Skipper. 1972. "Stripping: Anatomy of a Deviant Life Style." In *Life Styles: Diversity in American Society,* ed. S. D. Feldman and G. W. Thielbar, Boston: Little, Brown; Salutin, "Stripper Morality"; William E. Thompson, and Jackie L. Harred. 1992. "Topless Dancers: Managing Stigma in a Deviant Occupation. " *Deviant Behavior* 13: 291–311.

8. Jacqueline Boles and Albeno P. Garbin. 1974. "The Strip Club and Stripper-Customer Patterns of Interaction." *Sociology and Social Research* 58: 136–144; Enck and Preston, "Counterfeit Intimacy"; Forsyth and Deshotels, "The Occupational Milieu"; Ronai and Ellis, "Turn-ons for Money."

9. Boles and Garbin, "The Strip Club"; Boles and Garbin, "Stripping for a Living"; Enck and Preston, "Counterfeit Intimacy"; Forsyth and Deshotels, "The Occupational Milieu"; Ronai and Ellis, "Turn-ons for Money"; Ronai, "The Reflexive Self"; Thompson and Harred, "Topless Dancers."

10. Enck and Preston, "Counterfeit Intimacy"; Forsyth and Deshotels, "The Occupational Milieu"; Thompson and Harred, "Topless Dancers."

11. Boles and Garbin, "Stripping for a Living"; Ronai and Ellis, "Turn-ons for Money."

12. Thompson and Harred, "Topless Dancers."

13. Boles and Garbin, "The Strip Club"; Boles and Garbin, "Stripping for a Living"; Enck and Preston, "Counterfeit Intimacy"; Forsyth and Deshotels, "The Occupational Milieu"; Ronai and Ellis, "Turn-ons for Money"; Ronai, "The Reflexive Self"; Thompson and Harred, "Topless Dancers."

14. Boles and Garbin, "Stripping for a Living"; Prus and Irini, *Hookers, Rounders.*
15. Boles and Garbin, "Stripping for a Living," p. 328.
16. Ronai and Ellis, "Turn-ons for Money"; Ronai, "The Reflexive Self."
17. Ronai, "The Reflexive Self," p. 117.
18. Ronai and Ellis, "Turn-ons for Money," p. 291.
19. Ronai and Ellis, "Turn-ons for Money"; Ronai, "The Reflexive Self."
20. Ronai and Ellis, "Turn-ons for Money," p. 292.
21. Key informants in this study included several university students who had experience working in strip clubs (e.g., shooter girl, bartender, doorman), and a dancer acquaintance who was paid to recruit other participants for the study.
22. Observational data to support dancers' accounts were unavailable because lap dancing was banned shortly after this research project began, and such dances subsequently occurred in the more private areas of the clubs that we did not have access to.
23. *R. v. Mara* (1994), O.J. No. 264 (QL).
24. Section 167(1) of the *Criminal Code of Canada*, R.S.C., 1985, c. C-46 states: "Every one commits an offence who, being the lessee, manager, agent or person in charge of a theatre, presents or gives or allows to be presented or given therein an immoral, indecent or obscene performance, entertainment or representation."
25. *Mara* (1994).
26. As established in *R. v. Butler* (1992) 1 S.C.R. 452, the community standards test is based on what the community would tolerate in terms of the harm that would flow from exposure.
27. In making his ruling, Hachborn referred to two cases: *R. v. Tremblay* (1993) and *R. v. Hawkins* (1993). According to Hachborn the conduct in *Mara* was not indecent because:

> The conduct complained of in this present case is innocuous by comparison to the conduct dealt with by the Supreme Court of Canada [*Tremblay*] and the Court of Appeal of Ontario [*Hawkins*]. If it had not been for these cases there would have been little difficulty in finding the table dancers' conduct to be indecent (*R. v. Mara* [1994]).

The Ontario Court of Appeal, however, ruled that Hachborn had erred in the application/interpretation of *Tremblay* (1993) and *Hawkins* (1993) to *Mara* (1994; 1996). According to the Ontario Court of Appeal, these cases are clearly distinguishable. Although *Tremblay* (1993) involved erotic performances during which clients were invited to remove their clothes and masturbate, in the acts in question there was no physical contact, the acts occurred in a "private" place, and there was no risk of harm. *Hawkins* (1993), on the other hand, involved the distribution of videotapes, not live sex acts, and was therefore ruled by the Ontario Court of Appeal to be distinguishable from the current case.

NOTES

28. Mike Funston. 1995. "Mississauga Bans Lap Dancing—But Clubs, Dancers Protest." *Toronto Star,* September 14, p. A6.
29. For details see City of Mississauga, Bylaw No. 351-95, *A by-law to amend By-law* 572-79 (1995); Municipality of Metropolitan Toronto, Bylaw No. 123-96, *A by-law to amend Schedule 36 to By-law No. 20-85* (1996); Municipality of Metropolitan Toronto, By-law No. 129-95, *A by-law to amend Schedule 36 to By-law No. 20-85* (1995).
30. Dale Brazao. 1995. "Lap Dancing Crosses Line from Striptease to Sleaze." *Toronto Star,* August 5, p. A16; Dale Brazao. 1995. "Lap Dancers Charged Under No-touching Law." *Toronto Star,* September 13, p. A7; Funston, "Mississauga Bans," A6; Lisa Queen. 1995. "York Outlaws Dirty Dancing." *The Liberal,* September 17, p. 3; Peter Small and Gail Swainson. 1995. "City Attacks Lap Dance Sleaze." *Toronto Star,* August 16, p. A3.
31. *R. v. Mara* (1997), 115 C.C.C. (3d) 539.
32. In *Butler* (1992), 1 S.C.R. 452, the Supreme Court of Canada ruled that the test of obscenity/indecency rests on whether it involves the "undue exploitation of sex":

    1. Explicit sex with violence: this almost always constitutes undue exploitation of sex.
    2. Explicit sex without violence that is degrading and dehumanizing: this may be undue exploitation of sex if the risk of harm is substantial.
    3. Explicit sex without violence that is not degrading or dehumanizing: this generally will not qualify as undue exploitation of sex unless it employs children.

    In *Mara* (1997), it was decided that lap dancing fell under the second category.
33. *Mara* (1997).
34. *Mara* (1997).
35. John I. Kitsuse and Martin Spector. 1973. "Toward a Sociology of Social Problems: Social Conditions, Value-Judgments, and Social Problems." *Social Problems* 20: 407–419.
36. Kitsuse and Spector, "Toward a Sociology," p. 415; Joel Best. 1989. *Images of Issues: Typifying Contemporary Social Problems.* New York: Aldine De Gruyter, pp. 1–3, 75–76.
37. Funston, "Mississauga Bans," p. A6; Small and Swainson, "City Attacks," p. A3; Gail Swainson. 1995. "Metro Bans Lap Dancing." *Toronto Star,* August 18, p. A16; James Wallace. 1995. "Ontario to Probe Lap-dance Beefs." *Toronto Sun,* August 14, p. 7. Toronto was the first municipality to institute a lap dancing law. The authority of the city to create such a law was challenged and upheld in *Ontario Adult Entertainment Bar Association v. Metropolitan Toronto (Municipality),* (1997), 118 C.C.C. (3d) 481.

38. Ian Harvey. 1995. "Teetotallers Tear Into Lap Dancing." *Toronto Sun,* July 5, p. 20.
39. Funston, "Mississauga Bans," p. A6.
40. Gail Swainson. August 1, 1995. "Metro May Ban Lap Dancing." *Toronto Star,* p. A16; Brazao, "Lap Dancing Crosses," p. A16.
41, The Association for Burlesque Entertainers was formed primarily in response to the Hachborn decision. According to an association press release (May 11, 1995) banning lap dancing from strip clubs was a top priority.
42. Association of Burlesque Entertainers. 1995. *Information Pack: Why Lap Dancing Is a Health Danger and Must Be Banned —Exotic Dancers (and Others) Speaking Out.* Toronto: Association of Burlesque Entertainers.
43. Eleanor Maticka-Tyndale, Jacqueline Lewis, Jocalyn P. Clark, Jennifer Zubick, Shelley Young. 1999. "Social and Cultural Vulnerability to Sexually Transmitted Infection: The Work of Exotic Dancers." *Canadian Journal of Public Health* 90: 19–22.
44. See Lewis, "Lap Dancing," for a detailed discussion of the impact.
45. See Boles and Garbin, "The Strip Club"; Ronai and Ellis, "Turn-ons for Money"; Skipper and McCaghy, "Stripteasing"; and Thompson and Harred, "Topless Dancers."
46. Similar to the findings of Thompson and Harred, few of the women in this study admitted to engaging in prostitution, but all indicated that they knew of other dancers who did so. Due to the stigma associated with prostitution the validity of the self-reports on this issue may be questionable.
47. McCaghy and Skipper, "Stripping: Anatomy."
48. Boles and Garbin, "The Strip Club," p. 139/
49. Although only a few of the women who participated in this study were not supportive of the lap dancing ban, some newspaper reports printed between 1995 and 1998 suggest that this point of view was much more widespread.
50. Rosie DiManno. 1995. "How the Media Made Table Dancers Paragons of Virtue." *Toronto Star,* August 21, p. A7.
51. Funston, "Mississauga Bans," p. A6.
52. Swainson, "Metro May Ban," p. A16.
53. Don Wanagas. 1995. "Lap Dancing 'Valid Trade': Councilor." *Toronto Sun,* August 16, p. 16.
54. Wanagas, "Lap Dancing 'Valid Trade,'" p. 16.
55. DiManno, "How the Media," p. A7.
56. Colin Leslie. 1996. "Lap Dancing Crisis Overblown?" *Xtra,* January 18, p. 10.
57. Timothy Appleby and Sara Jean Green. 1998. "Arrests Total 115 in Prostitution-Related Raids." *The Globe and Mail,* September 12, p. A12; Michael Hanlon. 1998. "Lap Dancing Still Hot Issue." *Toronto Star,* August 10, p. B5; Brad Honywill. 1997. "Lap Dancers Throw in the Towel." *Toronto Sun,* August 23, p. 32.

58. See Dale Brazao. 1995. "Lap Dancing Ban Kills Cash Flow," *Toronto Star,* September 18, p. A6; and Honywill, "Lap Dancers Throw," p. 32.
59. See Brazao, "Lap Dancing Crosses," p. A16.
60. See Lenore Manderson. 1992. "Public Sex Performances in Patpong and Explorations of the Edges of Imagination." *Journal of Sex Research* 29: 451–475; and Thanh-Dam Truong. 1990. S*ex, Money and Morality: Prostitution and Tourism in South-East Asia.* London: Zed Books.
61. Appleby and Green, "Arrests Total 115," p. A12; Hanlon, "Still Hot Issue," p. B5.
62. This situation could change in the future if other court cases address the issue of defining what constitutes a public versus a private space.
63. Section 210 of the *Criminal Code of Canada,* R.S.C., 1985, c. C-46, makes it illegal to keep, be an inmate of, or be found in a common bawdy house.
64. Gotell, "Shaping *Butler*", p. 70.
65. See Cossman, "Feminist Fashion"; and Gotell, "Shaping *Butler.*"
66. Cossman, "Feminist Fashion," p. 107.
67. Gotell, "Shaping *Butler,*" p. 70.
68. Gotell, "Shaping *Butler,*" p. 70.
69. Lewis, "Lap Dancing".
70. Numerous municipalities in Ontario have bylaws requiring all exotic dancers to be licensed.
71. See Brazao, "Lap Dancers Charged," p. A7; Lewis, "Lap Dancing."
72. *Mara* (1994); *Mara* (1997).
73. Lewis, "Lap Dancing."
74. See also Wendy Chapkis. 1997. *Live Sex Acts: Women Performing Erotic Labor.* New York: Routledge; Gotell, "Shaping *Butler*"; and Cossman and Bell, "Introduction."

CHAPTER 13

We would like to thank Ron Weitzer for his comments and Cheryl Radelof for her research assistance. This paper is dedicated to all of the workers, owners, and regulators we interviewed in the Nevada brothel industry; their wisdom, honesty, and insights taught and inspired us.

1. William Reibsame. (Ed.). 1997 *Atlas of the New West: Portrait of a Changing Region.* New York: Norton. See also Hal Rothman. 1998. *Devil's Bargains: Tourism in the Twentieth Century West.* Lawrence: University Press of Kansas.
2. Exceptions include John Galliher and John Cross. 1983. *Morals Legislation Without Morals: The Case of Nevada.* New Brunswick, NJ: Rutgers University Press; Ellen Pillard. 1983. "Legal Prostitution: Is It Just?" *Nevada Public Affairs*

Review no. 2: 43–47; Helen Reynolds. 1986. *The Economics of Prostitution*. Springfield, IL: Charles Thomas; Guy Rocha. 1975. *Brothel Prostitution in Nevada: A Unique American Cultural Phenomenon*. Master's thesis, San Diego State University.

3, Rocha, *Brothel Prostitution;* Richard Symanski. 1974. "Prostitution in Nevada." *Annals of the Association of American Geographers* 65: 357–377; Reynolds, *The Economics of Prostitution*.

4. Galliher and Cross, *Morals Legislation*.

5. Guy Rocha. 1997. "Nevada's Most Peculiar Industry: Brothel Prostitution, Its Land Use Implications and Its Relationship to the Community," unpublished paper, Nevada State Archives.

6. Rocha, "Nevada's Most Peculiar Industry."

7. Symanski, "Prostitution in Nevada," p. 355.

8. Wells Emergency Ordinance No. 24, cited in Symanski, "Prostitution in Nevada."

9. Symanski, "Prostitution in Nevada," pp. 363, 355.

10. Gabriel Vogliotti. 1975. *The Girls of Nevada*, Secaucus, N.J.: Citadel Press: Rocha, *Brothel Prostitution;* Symanski, "Prostitution in Nevada"; Doug McMillan. 1986. "Nevada's Sex-for-Sale Dilemma." *Reno Gazette-Journal*, November 9.

11. Mike Sion. 1995. "Conforte Changed the Face of Nevada Bordellos." *Reno Gazette-Journal*, January 20.

12. Sion, "Conforte"; Interview with George Flint, Reno, Nevada, December 12, 1997; Vogliotti, *Girls of Nevada*.

13. Sion, "Conforte"; Pillard, "Legal Prostitution: Is It Just?"; Ellen Pillard. 1991. "Rethinking Prostitution: A Case for Uniform Regulation." *Nevada Public Affairs Review* no. 1: 45–49.

14. Center for Business and Economic Research; University of Nevada, Las Vegas. Nevada State Demographer, 1997; U.S. Census Bureau. Estimates of the Population of Counties for July 1, 1997.

15. Interview with Flint, December 12, 1997.

16. Rich Thurlow. 1998. "Regulatory Ability Target of Likely Brothel Lawsuit." *Pahrump Valley Times,* April 10, p. B3.

17. Reibsame, *Atlas of the New West,* p. 108.

18. Reibsame, *Atlas of the New West,* p. 112.

19. Larry Henry. 1997. "Brothel Tour Off." *Las Vegas Sun,* April 17.

20. Henry, "Brothel Tour Off."

21. Male prostitution does not exist in any brothel in Nevada. Outside these three counties, however, men are sometimes employed as managers or bartenders within brothels.

22. Pillard, "Legal Prostitution," p. 45.

23. Interview with Flint, December 12, 1997.

CHAPTER 14

1. Catherine Benson and Roger Matthews. 1996. "Report of the Parliamentary Group on Prostitution." London: House of Commons.
2. Robert Golding. 1991. "Policing Prostitution." *Policing* 8: 60–72.
3. Roger Matthews. 1990. "Developing More Effective Strategies for Curbing Prostitution." *Security Journal* 1: 182-187.
4. Metropolitan Police Service. 1994. "Submission to the House of Commons All Parliamentary Group on Prostitution." TO9 (Crime and Divisional Policing Policy) Branch (Restricted), p. 4.
5. Catherine Benson. 1998. *Violence Against Female Prostitutes: Experiences of Violence, Safety Strategies, and the Role of Agencies.* Loughborough, UK: Loughborough University.
6. Roger Matthews. 1993. *Kerb Crawling, Prostitution, and Multi-Agency Policing.* Police Research Group: Crime Prevention Unit Series, Paper 43, London: Home Office.
7. Golding, "Policing Prostitution."
8. Golding, "Policing Prostitution"; M. Reading, I. Waters, and A. Maidment. 1992. "Kerb Crawlers, 'Cruisers' and the Community." London: Police Requirements Support Unit, Science and Technology Group.
9. Catherine Benson and Roger Matthews. 1995. "Street Prostitution: Ten Facts in Search of a Policy." *International Journal of the Sociology of Law* 23: 395–415.

RECOMMENDED READINGS

Bell, Laurie. (Ed.). 1987. *Good Girls/Bad Girls: Feminists and Sex Trade Workers Face to Face*. Seattle: Seal Press.

Browne, Jan, and Victor Minichiello. 1996. "Research Directions in Male Sex Work." *Journal of Homosexuality* 31: 29–56.

Carmen, Arlene, and Howard Moody. 1985. *Working Women: The Subterranean World of Street Prostitution*, New York: Harper and Row.

Chapkis, Wendy. 1997. *Live Sex Acts: Women Performing Erotic Labor*. New York: Routledge.

Cohen, Bernard. 1980. *Deviant Street Networks: Prostitution in New York City*. Lexington, MA: Lexington Books.

Davis, Nanette. (Ed.). 1993. *Prostitution: An International Handbook on Trends, Problems, and Policies*. Westport, CT: Greenwood.

Decker, John. 1979. *Prostitution: Regulation and Control*. Littleton, CO: Rothman.

Delacoste, Frederique, and Priscilla Alexander. (Eds). 1987. *Sex Work: Writings by Women in the Sex Industry*. Pittsburgh: Cleis.

Donnerstein, Edward, Daniel Linz, and Steven Penrod. 1987. *The Question of Pornography: Research Findings and Policy Implications*. New York: Free Press.

Flowers, Amy. 1998. *The Fantasy Factory: An Insider's View of the Phone Sex Industry*. Philadelphia: University of Pennsylvania Press.

Hawkins, Gordon, and Franklin Zimring. 1988. *Pornography in Free Society*. New York: Cambridge University Press.

Hobson, Barbara Meil. 1987. *Uneasy Virtue: The Politics of Prostitution and the American Reform Tradition*. New York: Basic Books.

Hoigard, Cecilie, and Liv Finstad. 1992. *Backstreets: Prostitution, Money, and Love*. University Park: Pennsylvania State University Press.

Kempadoo, Kemala, and Jo Doezema. (Eds.). 1998. *Global Sex Workers: Rights, Resistance, and Redefinition*. New York: Routledge.

McKeganey, Neil, and Marina Barnard. 1996. *Sex Work on the Streets: Prostitutes and Their Clients*. Buckingham, UK: Open University Press.

McLeod, Eileen. 1982. *Working Women: Prostitution Now*. London: Croom Helm.

Milman, Barbara. 1980. "New Rules for the Oldest Profession: Should We Change Our Prostitution Laws?" *Harvard Women's Law Journal* 3: 1–82.

Pearl, Julie. 1987. "The Highest Paying Customer: America's Cities and the Costs of Prostitution Control." *Hastings Law Journal* 38: 769–800.

Perkins, Roberta, and Garry Bennett. 1985. *Being a Prostitute*. London: George Allen and Unwin.

Pittman, David. 1971. "The Male House of Prostitution." *Transaction* 8: 21–27.

Reynolds, Helen. 1986. *The Economics of Prostitution*. Springfield, IL: Charles Thomas.

Roberts, Nickie. 1992. *Whores in History: Prostitution in Western Society*. London: HarperCollins.

Ronai, Carol, and Rebecca Cross. 1998. "Dancing with Identity: Narrative Resistance Strategies of Male and Female Strippers." *Deviant Behavior* 19: 99–119.

Rosen, Ruth. 1982. *The Lost Sisterhood: Prostitution in America. 1900–1918*. Baltimore: Johns Hopkins University Press.

Strossen, Nadine. 1995. *Defending Pornography*. New York: Anchor.

Stychin, Carl F. 1992. "Exploring the Limits: Feminism and the Legal Regulation of Gay Male Pornography." *Vermont Law Review* 16: 857–900.

Sullivan, Barbara. 1997. *The Politics of Sex: Prostitution and Pornography in Australia Since 1945*. New York: Cambridge University Press.

Vance, Carole. 1986. "The Meese Commission on the Road." *The Nation*, August 2–9: 76–82.

Weitzer, Ronald. 1991. "Prostitutes' Rights in the United States: The Failure of a Movement." *Sociological Quarterly* 32: 23–41.

Zurcher, Louis, and R. George Kirkpatrick. 1976. *Citizens for Decency: Antipornography Crusades as Status Defense*. Austin: University of Texas Press.

CONTRIBUTORS

Sharon A. Abbott is a doctoral candidate in sociology at Indiana University. She is currently completing work on her dissertation, "Careers of Actors and Actresses in the Pornography Industry," funded by a grant from the Social Science Research Council's Sexuality Research Fellowship Program. She is a visiting lecturer in sociology at Wittenberg University in Ohio.

Rosemary Barberet is a visiting professor of criminology in the Andalusian Institute of Criminology at the University Seville, Spain. She received her Ph.D. in criminal justice and criminology at the University of Maryland in 1994. Formerly, she was adjunct professor of criminology at the University of Castilla-La Mancha in Albacete, Spain. She has researched homicide rates, juvenile delinquency, commercial crime, domestic violence, and the needs of women prisoners.

Catherine Benson holds a master's degree in criminology and is completing her Ph.D. at Loughborough University in England. She currently is a research fellow at the Center for Drug Misuse Research at Glasgow University in Scotland, where she is doing research on client violence against prostitutes. She is the author of *Violence Against Female Prostitutes.*

Louis Bonilla is executive director of the Consortium for Latino Health in Philadelphia. He was the recipient of a Warren Weaver Fellowship from the Rockefeller Foundation and currently is a Kellogg Fellow. He has published articles on AIDS and injection drug use, and AIDS in Latino communities.

Barbara G. Brents is associate professor of sociology at the University of Nevada, Las Vegas. She received her Ph.D. from the University of Missouri in 1987. She has done research on the politics of the welfare state and business organizing. More recently, she cofounded the SABIR Project (Sex and Body Industry Research Project) at UNLV, which sponsors research on sex work and the adult entertainment industry. She is also president of the Nevada American Civil Liberties Union.

Wendy Chapkis is associate professor of sociology and women's studies at the University of Southern Maine. She is author of *Beauty Secrets: Women and the Politics of Appearance* and *Live Sex Acts: Women Performing Erotic Labor. Live Sex Acts* received the 1998 Outstanding Book Award from the Organization for the Study of Communication, Language, and Gender.

Nanette J. Davis is visiting professor of sociology at Western Washington University, and professor emerita at Portland State University. She received her Ph.D. in sociology from Michigan State University in 1973. In addition to a number of articles on prostitution and other topics, she is the author or coauthor of *Prostitution: An International Handbook on Trends, Problems, and Policies; From Crime to Choice: The Transformation of Abortion in America; Social Control: The Production of Deviance in the Modern State; Women and Deviance; Sociological Constructions of Deviance;* and *Youth Crisis: Growing Up in a High Risk Society.* She is also coeditor (with Gil Geis) of *Encyclopedia of Criminology and Deviant Behavior, vol. 3: Sexual Deviance,* to be published in 2000.

Deanne Dolnick received her master's degree from California State University at Northridge. She has worked for the RAND Corporation where she was an interviewer and researcher on the Los Angeles Women's Health Risk Study on Prostitution and AIDS.

Kathleen Guidroz is a doctoral candidate in sociology at George Washington University. Her major research interests include women's employment, the sex industry, and sexuality. She teaches courses on gender relations and sexuality. She received a master's degree in public administration from Louisiana State University.

Kathryn Hausbeck is assistant professor of sociology at the University of Nevada, Las Vegas. She received her Ph.D. from the State University of New York at Buffalo at 1997. A social theorist who specializes in the analysis of gender and culture, she is cofounder of the SABIR Project at UNLV. She also serves on the board of directors of the Nevada ACLU.

Janet Lever is associate professor of sociology at California State University, Los Angeles, and a consultant at the RAND Corporation. She has spent more than twenty years studying the social aspects of human sexuality. Since 1987 when she came to the RAND/UCLA Center for Health Policy Study on a postdoctoral fellowship, she has specialized in sexual health and social policy. In addition to her academic research, Lever served as senior analyst on three national magazine surveys and coauthored *Glamour* magazine's "Sex and Health" column from 1991 to 1998.

Jacqueline Lewis is assistant professor of sociology and criminology at the University of Windsor, Canada. She received her Ph.D. from the University of Toronto. She is currently conducting research on escorts and the impact of public policy on sex workers' lives.

Roger Matthews is professor of sociology at Middlesex University in England. He has carried out extensive research on prostitution in England and served as advisor to the Parliamentary Group on Prostitution. He edited (with Jock Young) *Rethinking Criminology* and *Confronting Crime*.

Martin A. Monto is associate professor of sociology at the University of Portland. He received his Ph.D. from UCLA in 1992. His areas of interest include social psychology, gender, and deviance. His research includes a study of childbirth and a comparison of adolescent sexual offenders with adolescent nonoffenders. He is currently collecting data on the men who attend the Portland, Oregon, and San Francisco, California, intervention programs for men arrested while trying to hire prostitutes.

Maggie O'Neill is a senior lecturer in sociology at Staffordshire University, Stoke-on-Trent, England. She received her Ph.D. from the University of Staffordshire in 1995. Formerly, she was senior lecturer at Nottingham Trent University in Nottingham, England. She has worked and published in the areas of feminist theory and research, prostitution, violence against women, and the sociology of culture.

Judith Porter is professor of sociology at Bryn Mawr College. Her major research interest is AIDS and injection drug use. She received a Shannon Award from the National Institute of Mental Health to study AIDS risk behavior in Latino communities and a National Institute on Drug Abuse grant to study needle exchange programs as a service provision strategy. She assists Congreso de Latinos Unidos and Prevention Point Philadelphia needle exchange as an outreach worker and AIDS educator.

Grant Jewell Rich was formerly assistant professor of psychology at Antioch College and is a Ph.D. candidate at the University of Chicago. He has done research on adolescent career development, the cognitive psychology of music, and workplace ethnography. He has written for such publications as the *Antioch Review, Keyboard, Massage, Massage Therapy Journal,* and *Psychology Today.* A licensed social worker, he has served on the boards of several social service agencies as well as on the editorial boards of several journals.

Joe A. Thomas is assistant professor and chair of the art department at Clarion University of Pennsylvania. A specialist in modern and contemporary art, he has published on topics ranging from Pop Art to Italian Renaissance portraiture. He is currently working on a book titled *Pop Sex: Eroticism, Pop Art, and American Culture,* as well as other topics dealing with sexuality and representation.

Ronald Weitzer is associate professor of sociology at George Washington University. He received his Ph.D. in 1985 from the University of California at Berkeley. He is the author of two books: *Transforming Settler States: Communal Conflict and Internal Security in Northern Ireland and Zimbabwe* and *Policing Under Fire: Ethnic Conflict and Police-Community Relations in Northern Ireland.* Current research includes prostitution policy in the United States and Holland, citizen attitudes toward the police in America, and a book on police relations with African-Americans in Washington, D.C.

INDEX

brothel rules, 240-41
health testing and, 229
history of, 220-22
Old vs. New West, 218-23, 227, 236
the state and, 228-33, 239
structure of, 223-28
Nieva, Veronica F., 99

Obscenity Enforcement Unit, 11, 12
off-street prostitution, police vice squads
and, 252-54
O'Neill, Maggie, 7, 11
The Other Side of Aspen 3 (film), 57
Out, 59

Paglia, Camille, 57
Parker, Joe, 141
peep show, 185
Perkins, Roberta, 6, 7
phone sex
agency description, 37-38
male callers and worker identity, 44-47
public opinion of, 2
stereotypes about, 35-36
phone sex workers
characteristics of, 40
identity construction and job socialization, 38-41
impression management and stigma,
41-47
self-esteem and, 43-45, 47
worker identity and male callers, 44-47
Piazza, Jerome, 9
Pillard, Ellen, 230
pimps, 8, 152, 230
in England/Spain, 124-29
park prostitutes and, 113-14
vice squad and, 260-62
Pines, Sharon, 77, 80
Playing with Fire (film), 56
police vice squads, 245
aims and activities of, 246-48
closed-circuit TV, 257
high-profile policing, 256
interagency cooperation, 263
liaison with residents, 257
male customers, 254-60
news media and, 256-57

off-street prostitution, 252-54
pimping and, 260-62
public's complaints, 247-48
street prostitution and, 248-52
traffic management schemes, 257-60
verbal/written warnings, 256
Poole, Wakefield, 52
pornography; *see also* gay pornography
acting career in, 5, 17-18
career strategies, 30-31
freedom and independence of, 22-24
maintaining industry involvement, 27-34
mobility and commitment, 31-34
money as motivator, 19-21
motivations for, 19-27, 33
opportunity and sociability of, 24-26
recognition (fame) as motivator, 21-22, 28
sexual norms and attitudes, 26-27
antipornography campaigns, 11
community standards and, 12
exhibitionists and, 26
men and, 8
morality and, 2
niche markets and, 65
star system and, 60
Supreme Court rulings, 51
violence and, 8
Porter, Judith, 4, 10
PRIDE (From Prostitution to Independence, Dignity, and Equality), 173
"Project Postporn," 11
Prostitute Outreach Workers (POW), 124,
136
prostitutes' rights movement, 174-80
prostitution; *see also* call girls; Nevada's legal
brothel industry; street prostitution
antiprostitution campaigns, 166-73
clients' motivations, 67-69, 77-82
competition and, 129
criminalization of, 159
cross-cultural study of, 123-24
customers' background characteristics,
71-73, 89-97, 169-70, 172
customers' sexual behavior, 72-75, 172
decriminalization of, 76, 160-61, 175
England's penal code, 123-25
factors in entering prostitution, 127-28,
142, 149-50